The New Telephony

Stephen M. Walters

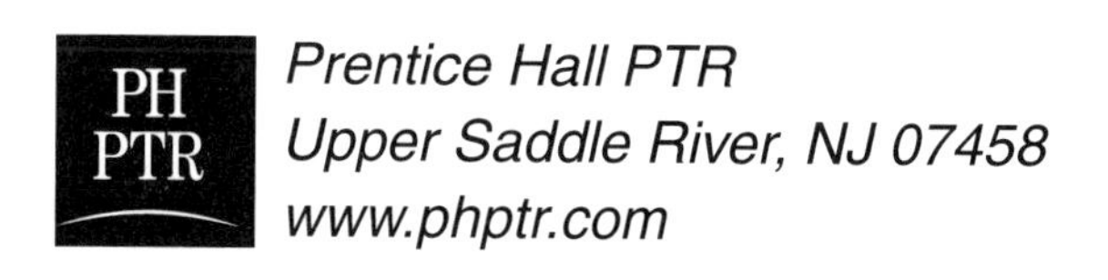

Prentice Hall PTR
Upper Saddle River, NJ 07458
www.phptr.com

A CIP catalogue record for this book can be
obtained from the Library of Congress

Editorial/Production Supervision: *Kathleen M. Caren*
Executive Editor: *Mary Franz*
Editorial Assistant: *Noreen Regina*
Marketing Manager: *Dan DePasquale*
Manufacturing Buyer: *Maura Zaldivar*
Cover Design Director: *Jerry Votta*
Cover Designer: *Nina Scuderi*

Prentice-Hall, Inc.
Upper Saddle River, NJ 07458

Prentice Hall books are widely used by corporations and government agencies for training, marketing, and resale. The publisher offers discounts on this book when ordered in bulk quantities.
For more information, contact Corporate Sales Department, Phone: 800-382-3419;
Fax: 201-236-7141; Email: corpsales@prenhall.com
Or write: Prentice Hall PTR, Corp. Sales Dept., One Lake Street, Upper Saddle River, NJ 07458

Printed in the United States of America

10 9 8 7 6 5 4 3 2 1

ISBN 0-13-035814-2

Pearson Education LTD.
Pearson Education Australia PTY, Limited
Pearson Education Singapore, Pte. Ltd.
Pearson Education North Asia Ltd.
Pearson Education Canada, Ltd.
Pearson Educación de Mexico, S.A. de C.V.
Pearson Education—Japan
Pearson Education Malaysia, Pte. Ltd.

CONTENTS

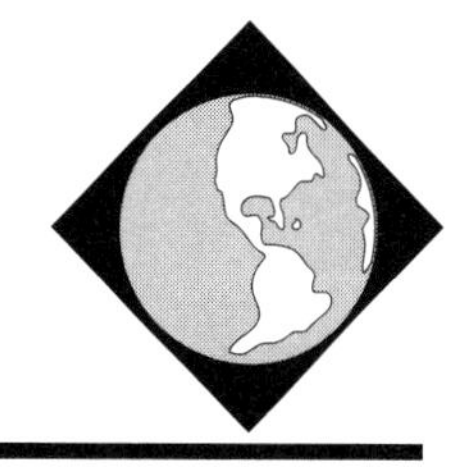

FOREWORD

When I was a boy, I had a neighbor who worked for the telephone company. One day I found a book about the telephone system in his trash. I was fascinated by the diagrams and pictures of equipment, but the thing that stuck in my mind was a drawing that showed how they were able to get three telephone circuits on only two pairs of wires, using something called a "phantom" circuit. How mysterious! I puzzled about this for a long time, but the explanation was beyond my uneducated grasp.

Much later, when I was studying engineering in college, I read that the telephone company was able to transmit six voice conversations on a pair of copper wires. I remembered that old book and the phantom circuit, and I imagined that they had phantoms upon phantoms in some devilish system to extract extra circuits on a single pair of wires. Somehow, I thought of copper wires as being confined to audio frequencies, and it didn't occur to me that they could modulate the six audio signals onto the wires just as in AM radio. But to me, that was what the phone system was all about. It was about copper wires and modulation; it was about telephones and rotary switches.

When I joined Bell Labs in the 1960s, the telephony world was an ordered place. There were encyclopedia-sized references that described every aspect of the system as it was, and the evolution of the network had been planned meticulously. The transmission system of the future was to be the millimeter waveguide, and the telephone instrument of the future was to be the Picturephone. For those of us who worked in the Bell System, the future was ours to plan and implement.

Even in those days of the ordered monopoly, however, the faint tremors of an oncoming revolution were heard from afar. In 1964 Paul Baran at Rand conceived the idea of packet communications. In 1973 Bob Metcalfe at Xerox invented Ethernet, a practical local area network that was going to sweep the world, and in 1969 Arpanet, the precursor of the Internet, began operation. Meanwhile, in the Bell System the millimeter waveguide project was abruptly ended by the emergence of the optical fiber, and the Picturephone died a hasty death in the marketplace. Soon the Justice Department would begin an antitrust action that would result in the breakup of the Bell System. The ordered world was falling apart.

Many engineers and scientists in the Bell System were aware of the Arpanet from its earliest days, and some research was directed towards packet communication. A few people even suggested at that time that the entire telephone network could be made to look like a hierarchical local area network. But the business executives were largely unaware of the rise of the Internet. Besides, it was unreliable and only for data. And look at all that investment in the existing plant!

Through several decades while voice traffic grew at 5% to 9% annually, the traffic on the Internet doubled every year. By the late 1990s, it was seen by nearly everyone as posing a real threat to the existing telephone network. Steve Walters' book has been written at the cusp of a critical time when the data traffic has now exceeded the voice traffic.

Within a few years, the data traffic will overwhelm the voice traffic, yet the great majority of the revenue comes from that vanishing sliver that represents voice. The industry needs new business models on how to derive revenue from that data traffic, and is currently mired in a deep recession.

As the Internet has grown over the last two decades, two different cultures have emerged: the Bellheads and the Netheads. The Bellheads are typically the engineers working for the telecommunications service providers and equipment vendors. The Netheads are typically the computer scientists and programmers working in the computer industry. The contrasts between these cultures are rather profound.

The first part of this book describes the technology from the point of view of the Bellheads. Their world is full of systems and the physical equipment that comprises these systems—telephones, transmission systems, switching systems, and a system for signaling and control. Somewhere in this world, maybe someone even still knows about phantom circuits.

The second part of the book is the network technology from the point of view of the Netheads. This is a world of computer science, software, and protocols. Although everyone here knows that somewhere underneath the protocol stack there is a physical layer, no one really cares much about it. The telephone people will take care of that detail. No Nethead has never heard about phantom circuits. Things like that are part of the quaint lore of old telephony, and have no place in modern computer communications.

In the world of the Bellheads, applications and services are centrally derived and administered. Intelligence in the network is centralized, because the network was designed to support the dumbest, cheapest terminal in the world—the standard telephone handset. The basic architecture of the telephone network was decided at a time when intelli-

gence was expensive. No one at that time had ever dreamed of Moore's Law—that digital circuitry would get half as expensive every 18 months—or that intelligence would one day be so cheap as to litter the world.

The Netheads argue that the network should not be intelligent at all. In fact, they go so far as to say that it should be stupid. Intelligence should be at the periphery. Applications should reside at the periphery, where innovation is open to all, not just the telephone companies. The problem with having the intelligence in the center of the network is that it is not adaptable to new applications and becomes a bottleneck to innovation. The Netheads would have as little in the center of the network as possible.

The Internet protocol stack can be viewed conceptually as an hourglass. At the narrow neck of the hourglass, representing the network core, is the Internet internetworking protocol, IP. At the wide top of the hourglass are all the applications that ride on top of IP, while at the wide bottom of the hourglass are all the physical media over which IP can run. Everything is held together by that narrow neck of IP, through which all data must flow—whatever application the data represents and whatever media is beneath. The beauty of IP is that it defines just enough to ensure internetworking compatibility and adds no unnecessary complications or functionality.

A central tenet of Bellhead philosophy is the absolute reliability of the network. Extreme measures have been taken in the design of the network to ensure that it will work 99.999% of the time—the famous "five-nines" of reliability. Of course, this level of reliability has an associated cost, and the Netheads reject this philosophy. In fact, the IP protocol does not even ensure reliable transport of packets. They can be lost, and IP doesn't really care—that is the job of the higher level protocols, such as TCP. This is a job for both ends of the system to negotiate from the periphery. It is one example of the Internet's guiding principle, which has been described as "end-to-end." In contrast, the world of the Bellheads might be described as radiating outwards from the center.

Having described the technology of the traditional telephone network and the technology of the Internet, this book turns its attention to the merger of these disparate worlds. This is the "new telephony," or what is sometimes called the Next Generation Network (NGN). In this merged system, all traffic is carried as data packets, including voice. In fact, voice is regarded as just another application. Voice does, however, require special handling to ensure its quality, and there are issues about how call control is managed. Walters describes two protocols that can be used here. These two protocols reflect the differing philosophies of the telecommunications and computer camps. One protocol is mainly oriented towards control from the periphery, while the other is a more central control.

The telecommunications people speak of this merger as "convergence." It is a popular word in that community, implying the nirvana of a single network that handles voice, data, video, and other data applications in a seamless manner. In the computer community, however, that word is heard less often. As one prominent venture capitalist put it, "When a small stream joins the Missouri river, you don't call it convergence; you call it the Missouri."

In the final portion of this book, Steve Walters looks at the telecommunications business and its future. As he points out, it is a very uncertain time in the industry. Only a year ago, all the projections for the business were optimistic, but the market recession, overbuilding of the network, withdrawal of capital, and failures of carriers have left the industry in a weakened and very conservative condition. For now, the new telephony is on hold. No one knows what business models will evolve in the near future.

By the time this is being read, conditions may be radically different in the industry. That is the unavoidable danger in writing about the business of telecommunications. Nevertheless, the technology described here will still be relevant.

Even though those phantom circuits may be long gone, the TCP/IP protocol suite has lasted for more than a quarter of a century already. While the technology may come and go, principles and protocols remain.

As I read this text, I wondered about who the ideal reader would be. It always helps to know something about a subject before you start. Just as a dictionary defines words in terms of other words, this text presumes a certain prior general knowledge of communications or computer systems. Perhaps the reader may be a Bellhead looking for more information about the Internet, or alternatively, a Nethead looking to know more about the telephone network. It is rare that these views come together in one book, but here they do, for all of us to ponder and appreciate.

—Robert W. Lucky

PREFACE

The telecommunications industry is being rocked by change fueled by the advent of the tremendous success of the Internet and its technologies. This book considers the future of telephony in that light. For quite some time, there has been competition in the telephony business. Long-distance rates have seen continuous decreases for two decades as new carriers sought to capture greater and greater market share. Local carriers have seen competition for interconnecting the networks of large corporate customers and for providing them access to long-distance services. So, competition and change are not new issues in telecommunications.

But the Internet has forced an entirely new set of changes on the phone business. There are new carriers, new business scenarios, new technologies, and new ways of thinking about end users and the services they seek. The pathos of change has escalated as Internet service providers and application providers seek to provide their new services to the end users, usually through the networks of the existing carriers. For a long time, these services were too small in service volume to attract the attention of the

major carriers, and the Internet grew without their involvement.

So now, after more than 20 years of growth, improvement, and experimentation, the Internet has become a major issue for large carriers. On the one hand, it threatens their existing business in several ways. On the other, it represents an opportunity to offer new services to their customers. In between the two, there is a goldmine of new technology that might be applied to their existing networks in novel and innovative ways. The Internet and its technologies can no longer be ignored by the telephone business. Central to resolution of this confrontation are voice services. It seems inevitable that the voice business will disappear into the Internet.

In addition, by its very nature, there is no natural "owner" of the Internet. To many, the Internet is a bewildering morass of networks and companies that exist in a state of chaos. Indeed, this is a reasonable description of the Internet, since there is no central authority, no single entity that is "The Internet." The Internet exists because of the adoption of a few simple sets of rules and protocols that enable the exchange of information. Business arrangements are unregulated, which allows a dynamic market attitude and rapid progress. Because companies involved in the Internet as a networking business can adopt any business model, it is not possible to make broad, sweeping statements about much of anything relating to Internet business issues. Overall, this is a good thing, but it makes for difficulty in understanding the Internet as a business and in having uniform metrics and values for services and charges.

It is possible that this aspect of the Internet will change in the coming years. Like any frontier, the Internet is now operating in many widely varying business models. But just as the Wild West eventually adopted a more tame posture as it matured, so will the Internet. As this occurs, it is interesting to speculate who and what may become the primary

forces in the "New Internet." Those companies who are the prime movers of the Internet today may or may not find themselves displaced as time moves forward and more uniform practices prevail. Certainly, there are many powerful companies with extensive resources who would like to become the major forces in the Internet network business. The question is, Who will be the "owners" of the Internet? Will it be those who operate it today? Or will other, more powerful companies, supercede the present businesses?

In his epic song, the great bard Bob Dylan explains the changes he foresaw during the 1960s in America. Even though he contemplated a far different set of issues than those that confront the telecommunications industry, his words are, in my view, quite appropriate to set the stage for what is to come. In each stanza, he offers advice for (respectively) public switched telephone network operators, authors, regulators, and the original creators of the Internet. As an author, I intend to follow his advice, because I am certain that "the wheel's still in spin" and it will be for some years to come. The fundamental question that is addressed by this book echoes in the final stanza.

The Times They Are A-Changin'[1]

Come gather 'round people
Wherever you roam
And admit that the waters
Around you have grown
And accept it that soon
You'll be drenched to the bone.
If your time to you
Is worth savin'
Then you better start swimmin'
Or you'll sink like a stone
For the times they are a-changin'.

1. Copyright © 1963, 1964 by Warner Bros. Inc. Copyright renewed 1991 by Special Rider Music. All rights reserved. International copyright secured. Reprinted by permission.

Come writers and critics
Who prophesize with your pen
And keep your eyes wide
The chance won't come again
And don't speak too soon
For the wheel's still in spin
And there's no tellin' who
That's namin'.
For the loser now
Will be later to win
For the times they are a-changin'.

Come senators, congressmen
Please heed the call
Don't stand in the doorway
Don't block up the hall
For he that gets hurt
Will be he who has stalled
There's a battle outside
And it is ragin'.
It'll soon shake your windows
And rattle your walls
For the times they are a-changin'.

Come mothers and fathers
Throughout the land
And don't criticize
What you can't understand
Your sons and your daughters
Are beyond your command
Your old road is
Rapidly agin'.
Please get out of the new one
If you can't lend your hand
For the times they are a-changin'.

The line it is drawn
The curse it is cast
The slow one now
Will later be fast
As the present now
Will later be past
The order is
Rapidly fadin'.
And the first one now
Will later be last
For the times they are a-changin'.

Bob Dylan, 1964

The primary purpose of this book is to place those things that are a-changin' in the telecommunications industry into a rational framework. This book explains what the telecom industry is, how the Internet and its technologies relate to voice services, and how telecom may evolve in the coming years. Knowledge of the technology and business issues will give you insight into the changes as they occur in the telecommunications industry. As Bob Dylan advises, I will resist making specific spectacular predictions. Instead, I will frame and explain various issues, pressures, and possible events that could affect the ultimate outcome. As new events and business pressures arise, I encourage you to synthesize and examine for yourself the plausible outcomes. As much as possible, the book is couched in business considerations, including assets, workforce, financing issues, investments, and profitability. Technology is also explained so that you will have a solid understanding of how the networks operate from a perspective of technology, complexity, and management needs

The book provides an overview of the confrontation that is now occurring within the industry. It then reviews human speech and requirements that a network must meet to ensure successful operation. Then, the technology and operation of the existing public switched telephone net-

work are described, after which the Internet and its key technologies are explained. Once the technical approach of carrying voice over Internet technology is explored, the structure of the "new telephony" and its control schemes are defined. Next, drivers for change in the business approach that affect competition and the rate at which change can occur are proposed, and scenarios are constructed based on the possible competitors and partners. For each scenario, the various forces at play that could influence its outcome are discussed. The concluding chapter discusses what the future might bring to the industry and some issues affecting its direction.

I hope you find this book enjoyable and informative.

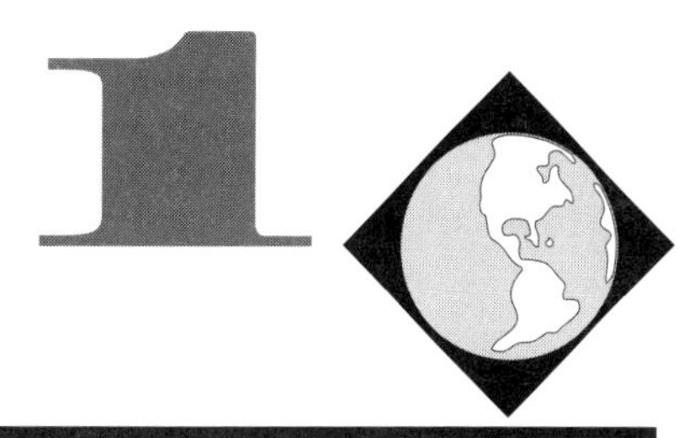

THE CONFRONTATION

The Internet and its technologies have intruded on the telecommunications scene like a dragon flying from the sky, invading a sleepy little hamlet. In the hamlet, all was well before the dragon came. Everyone understood their purpose and the village functioned well. There was enough to eat, there was order, and even though there was an occasional conflict between villagers, competition had its boundaries that were implicitly observed. The dragon changed all that. At first, the dragon lived apart from the village and there was no problem. Villagers rarely saw it, and when they did, it was easily ignored. But as the dragon's haunt encroached on the village, problems arose. Now and then one of the workers would fail to return from the fields. At times, the dragon would swoop down on the village and devour everything in sight. Peasants were unwilling to go into the fields to harvest crops, conflicts between villagers increased, and everyone wanted to kill the dragon. Wizards and sorcerers gave all manner of advice on dealing with the dragon and offered to destroy it or run it away. But all these things proved impossible: The dragon was there to stay.

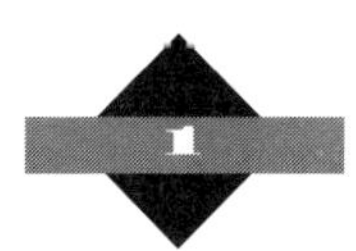

The Telephone Business

Like the villagers in the hamlet, the former Bell System understood its objectives and the engineering means for achieving them. The Bell System was never in a hurry. It chose excellence over time-to-market and reliability over low cost. The well-understood concept of Universal Service was an overriding requirement for everything done. No expense was spared to achieve the highest quality system. No stone was left unturned in the quest for high reliability. These were admirable objectives for the engineering community. And the proof is in the pudding: the U.S. network today is the best anywhere. The scope, sophistication, reliability, and performance of the U.S. network are unmatched by any network in the world.

But today, the divestiture of the Bell System, deregulation of telephone service, and the rapid success of the Internet are causing everyone to reconsider their business objectives and engineering means. And why not, the Internet is the king of telecommunications. We can go anywhere and communicate with anyone with the click of a mouse. The rise of the World Wide Web (WWW) and electronic commerce has proven the value of the Internet, and it appears to have no end in sight. And, as all telecommunications engineers know, the Internet is nothing like the telephone network.

Yet the attitudes towards quality, time-to-market, and engineering means of most carriers remain much as it was prior to 1984. And while the business model for telephony has seen some innovation, it is much the same as it always was. Most of this is due to the long-standing success of the large carriers. Their culture is steeped in decades-long traditions, regulations, union practices, and a century of financial success. In his book *The Innovator's Dilemma*, Clayton Christensen shows clearly the difficulty of maintaining market success when faced with the innovation of a disruptive technology. The most successful corporations who follow their established market needs can be overwhelmed by technical innovations in niche markets, which could suddenly be applied to their market or which can redefine the value proposition for the market. As Christensen shows, this is nearly impossible to predict and to avoid.

Besides the problems of the market, it is very hard to change a corporation's culture, even if it wants to change. Even when senior management mandates a change in corporate direction, it can prove impossible to get responses from the employees who have spent years, possibly decades, working in the way they know best. And besides, these can be enormous organizations with tens of thousands of people. Like the proverbial aircraft carrier, such large corporations cannot turn on a dime. This does not mean they are stupid organizations or that they are dinosaurs marching to extinction. It is just that making changes in an organization of 100,000 employees is far more difficult than changing the culture of an operation that has 100 people.

Because the telecommunications industry comes from a heritage of regulation, there are concepts and business practices that have been driven largely into a state of irrationality. Taken one by one, each new regulatory step seemed more or less logical. But after an eternity of incremental small changes in regulation, the current morass of price control, depreciation rules, and cross-business restrictions are surrealistic. This creates an artificial environment for competition, which in the long run cannot be maintained. Of course, regulators realize this, but it is difficult to decide what actions to take that will increase competition fairly while maintaining a service base for the public. These are not easy steps, and there is no certain way to accomplish this. For quite some time, regulators will play a key role in the outcome we are contemplating.

Because the large successful carrier has a business base with millions of customers and an investment measured in tens of billions of dollars, rapid technological change is not likely. The financing, manpower, and planning needed to change such an enormous embedded base quickly would overwhelm the financial strength of even the largest of corporations in this business. And if such investment is simply a way of retaining current market share, it will be very hard to convince management and investors to take the plunge. Even if the investments will produce new services and some growth in revenues, it may prove impossible to get the funding to "tune up" the core business.

A key facet of the technology in the Public Switched Telephone Network (PSTN) is that it is built on the "circuit" concept. This comes from the most basic origins of telephony, where a pair of wires formed a circuit from the user to the operator and the operator would complete the circuit between a pair of users based on the caller's request. Later, the operator was replaced by switching systems and the analog circuits were replaced by digital channels. But the overall operation of the network has not really changed in overall concept. Based on indications from a caller, a digital circuit is established between users that carries the bits of information they wish conveyed. The circuit is present for the duration of the call; whether or not the users want, it is continuously conveying bits between them. This concept of "circuit" permeates the engineering and operation of today's telephone network. As will be explained later, this is both the strength and the weakness of the telephone network. On the one hand, circuits are easy to engineer and maintain. On the other hand, they are not always the best choice for transporting information.

As time went on and more services were introduced, the telephone network added increased intelligence and processing to the core of the network. Services such as call forwarding were based inside the network. Users would interact with the network systems using their simple telephone and would control these functions using schemes that reused the signaling systems within the network. This allowed these services to work pretty much the same way everywhere and to be extremely reliable. Usually, these were modest incremental changes to software operating in

the switching systems. Today, these features are very tightly bound together, and making changes to the call control systems requires great expertise and careful testing to ensure that the features do not interact badly.

Those companies that provide the basis for the PSTN are the Local Exchange Carriers who provide local phone service and the Interexchange Carriers who provide long-distance services. Collectively, these are the "telcos." They currently have high revenues, but there is little if any growth likely in the telephone business. Because it has existed for a long time, the current phone business within the United States has already expanded to its maximum market size, and growth is quite limited. Most growth is in the area of wireless and second-line service for Internet access.

For all of these reasons, the PSTN and its carriers are not going to make any massive overnight change in direction. While they might begin moving in a new direction, the core business and networks of these carriers is too large, too complex, too successful, too inflexible, and too regulated to "turn on a dime."

The Internet Business

While the telephone companies of the world were busy selling service and incorporating incremental technological innovations into their networks, the Internet and its new technology was born and hardened in a very different environment. ARPANET (Advanced Research Projects Agency Network) was conceived and deployed during the 1970s through colleges, universities, and research institutions. The culture of the Internet was one of innovation and research, with the overall attitude that they were playing in the world's greatest sandbox. Some of the craziest technical ideas imaginable have been attempted on the Internet. And many, perhaps most, have been successful in one way or another. Built on the concept that "all ideas are good ideas until proven otherwise" and on open deliberation of technical concepts through the Internet Engineering Task Force (IETF), the Internet was born in a collegial and entrepreneurial incubation think tank.

Two key facets of the Internet that define its operational properties are that it has a single unit of delivery, the packet, and that it makes no guarantees whatsoever about any aspect of packet delivery. This is in stark contrast to the thinking of Bell System engineers, who sought every means possible to ensure that information would arrive in a timely and uncorrupted manner. These two fundamentally different perspectives are due to the nature of the media being transported. Voice can tolerate distortion and noise but not delay, whereas data has precisely the opposite requirements. Internet engineers believed that the lowest level systems should be as simple as possible and should not depend on the capability of lower layers. To this end, they restricted the packet-switching function primarily to the straightforward task of forwarding packets to the next appropriate location based on an address provided in the packet. This scheme, called connectionless routing, provides a single, low-cost transport mechanism with no guarantees about quality of service. Any quality mechanisms, such as guaranteed delivery of packets, must be implemented outside the network in the user's equipment or applications.

Restricting the network to such a simple least common denominator has allowed many different protocols and applications to be implemented and tested. All that was required was a common definition of the packet and its addressing. Computers could simply drop a packet addressed to another computer into the network, and the network would deliver it. Applications that simply wanted to poll some device for a piece of information could just send a message requesting the information to the desired device and start a timer. The polled device would return a message (the sender's address is also in the packet) and include the requested information. And if the network did not deliver one or the other of these messages, or if it was too slow, the application's timer would expire and the application could decide what to do. It might send a second request, or it might wait longer, or it might give up and tell the user the information cannot be retrieved.

Notice that even in this simple application, it is the application or the user that makes these choices, not the network, and no particular outcome is mandated by the network's operation. Internet engineers consider this the most appropriate way of dealing with problems. After all, it is the application that knows what is being done, not the network. If the application can take the time to retransmit the information, then do that. If it has some critical real-time need that does not allow retransmission, then it can take some other more appropriate action. This approach enables a broad host of applications to be formulated and used without placing any additional requirements on the network. This is one of the great powers of the Internet.

In order for the network to route packets to the proper destination, a series of protocols have been defined that enable the automatic discovery of the presence of systems attached to the network and their addresses. This has allowed the network's user base to rapidly expand without substantial human intervention in databases or routing procedures. Indeed, if it were necessary to manually administer the addressing and routing of the Internet, growth would be very slow. Because of the assumption that nothing can be trusted, each routing system will periodically re-examine its routing tables and will discover alternate routes to use should a primary route be unavailable due to a computer failure or should it be working slowly due to a heavy traffic burden.

As any user would say, the early Internet had very low quality standards. It was subject to frequent and lengthy outages and proved to be quite unreliable. These problems were not due to the underlying protocol for delivering packets; they were due to the low reliability of the computers doing the forwarding. The early Internet made use of normal computers in university laboratories. Many of these were used for other experiments and for studies that made them unavailable to the Internet. Also, early computer systems were not extremely reliable and had frequent hardware and software problems. Sometimes, it took days for a packet to travel from coast to coast, and often it would not arrive at all. But for applications like email, an early and continuing Internet success, these delays were not of major importance: The email application would just keep re-sending the packet and would inform the user if it eventually gave up.

So, over time, the software-based computer version of the Internet evolved to far more reliable hardware based systems. As performance increased, so did the number of users and the applications they attempted over the Internet. Because these concepts were conceived and executed by university faculty and graduate student researchers, a lot of new state-of-art concepts in networking and applications were reduced to practice. Industrial labs were involved, some from the very outset, and these brought concrete practical ideas to the implementations as well as some interest in moving to commercial systems. This blend of ARPA-funded university and industry research brought the Internet to its current state of success.

Once the World Wide Web and browser technology were defined, commercial use of the Internet began to dramatically increase and involvement by non-experts rapidly expanded. The WWW made it possible for users to "surf the Net" and for companies to exploit commercial ideas with a large base of potential customers. The Internet took off like a rocket, initially doubling in capacity every 100 days, the so-called "Internet Year," and continues to grow at a very high rate. Modern, ultra-high-speed, large-scale routing systems now dominate the backbone of the Internet, and as the user base has grown, more high-speed modern computers have been connected at each user's site. Electronic commerce has forced corporations onto the

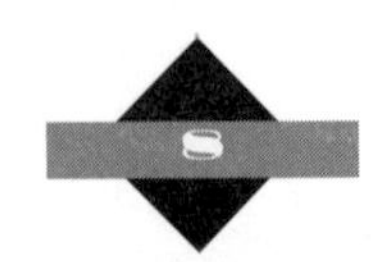

Internet, and to accomplish this, their large computing base has been forced to modernize and integrate with the online Internet systems. All in all, the thrust for online electronic commerce has required modernization of information technology at every level. The consequence has been rapid evolution of all parts of the Internet itself and of the client–host computers at its edges.

The companies now participating most completely in the Internet as operators include Internet Service Providers (ISP), Backbone Providers (BP), and Network Access Providers (NAP). The companies in these segments are to be considered apart from the normal "dotcom" companies known on various stock exchanges. These companies, the *Netcos,* are the providers of the Internet, just as the *Telcos* are the providers of the PSTN. These are the companies that enable the Internet and are the candidates for taking over the voice business, just as those companies that make up the Telco segment wish to become the new owners of the Internet. They currently have small but rapidly growing revenues, and there is enormous growth potential in their future, especially if they successfully capture the revenues of voice telephony.

Today's successful carriers in the Internet may not be the ultimate winners. The Internet has taken on a life of its own, and the open nature of the Internet makes it possible for nearly anyone to become successful. An acquisition strategy executed by a party with deep financial strength could make them a leading carrier overnight.

The Confrontation

For 20 years, the Internet has been growing, refining its technology and improving itself through the creation of new applications and the addition of new users. Now, suddenly, the Internet appears poised to usurp the telephone business. After all, voice transport is just another application. If an application is constructed properly, shouldn't it be possible to provide telephone service over the Internet?

Carriers around the world are staggered by this possibility. They imagine their base of revenues eroding overnight and the desertion of their customers to new upstart Internet entrepreneurs. No doubt this scenario invades the dreams of many CEOs and the large shareholders of the carriers.

The flip side of this is also of concern to the Internet entrepreneurs. That is, could the large telephone carriers rapidly deploy Internet technology and create an alternative that could be marketed to the carriers' existing customers? By bundling telephone service with Internet service, it might be possible for a large carrier to produce an attractive package and capture much of the Internet service market. But, because of the circuit nature of the telephone network, it is impossible for the carriers to provide Internet service without deploying a second network. And at present, regulation prevents this from being a serious threat except in a few limited cases. But these Internet CEOs probably have increasing concerns about their protected status because many large carriers are now evolving their present networks using Internet technology. This is being done in a way that the new network should be able to provide fully integrated services for voice, data, and video. If all that remains is the regulatory barrier, the entrepreneurs may find themselves with a flimsy shield from the carriers who, having the strength of Hercules, would be very formidable adversaries.

There are a good many of these evolution scenarios available to both parties in this confrontation. Chapter 7 will enumerate these and discuss the merits of each. As will be explained, neither side has a silver bullet for extinguishing the other side. The carriers' primary strengths lie in their customer base, their large scale, and their tremendous financial power. Their weaknesses are slow response, their regulatory constraints, and the key fact that their enormous network assets are poorly matched to the needs of the Internet. The Internet companies' strengths are in their ability to rapidly innovate, their deep technical understanding of the Internet and its technologies, and their freedom from regulation. Their weaknesses are their small size, their small financial power, and that their present network lacks the ability to consistently and reliably deliver speech packets.

In his book, *The Innovator's Dilemma,* Christensen examines the question of why corporations who are leaders in a market can fall prey and fail completely when faced with a major paradigm shift in their industry. He examines several industries, and comes to the conclusion that the very basis on which a company becomes successful is indeed the reason for its ultimate failure: it listens too closely to its customers. Customers invariably want stability in their product choice and prefer a well-understood purchase to a new, unknown approach. For these reasons, customers will usually tell a supplier that they are happy with things as they are and that they just wish the product was cheaper. Since the customer is already buying the product, he or she is probably reasonably happy, so this is no surprise. Likewise, customers always would like to see a cheaper product. As a result, successful companies holding the largest market share for any product focus very closely on incremental improvements that will reduce cost, thereby enabling either greater profits or lower prices. They will also seek improvements that will increase product performance with little or no increase in cost. As Christensen points out over and over, these same companies will be dabbling in new break-through technologies and are carefully watching such technologies that seem relevant to their business, but they are rarely in the forefront of the cutting edge.

According to Christensen, the demise of these companies is that they get blindsided by a new technology or industry that doesn't seem relevant when it first starts. The new technology will appear to them as a curious, interesting approach, but it will not appear to be an immediate threat or as something that could invade their marketplace. Besides, they reason, long before that could happen, they'll be on top of it. But usually, they never do get on top of it. The new technology incubates in a seemingly irrelevant or distant industry to that of the successful incumbent, and when it does invade, it is with swiftness and certainty. Customers who the incumbent thought could never use the new technology abandon in droves to adopt the new approach that has now been shown superior or cheaper than the established product. Time was on the side of the new technology, and it has been honed to a sufficiently fine edge to attack the incumbent's market. Too late, the incumbent tries to mount a response, but now there are too many variables to be mastered, and its credibility is based on the old approach, not the new one. The market leader sinks like a stone.

The telephone industry and the Internet industry are now engaged in just such a situation. For many years, while the Internet and its technologies were incubating, the world's telephone companies either ignored it or dabbled in it. The Internet used breakthrough technology; the telephone industry created incremental improvements. They are now entering a battle for their corporate lives. This is a very complex struggle between two powerful industries, and it is a struggle to the death, as depicted in Figure 1–1. It will not be over quickly either: Many years will pass as the technology base and regulatory controls shift.

FIGURE 1–1 *The Confrontation. ("Wrestlers" by Janice Weaver. ©2001. All rights reserved. Used with permission.)*

It is a struggle over money, the $227 billion per year that is projected to be spent in the United States on local and long-distance services for telephony in 2002, shown in Figure 1–2. By comparison, Internet carriers captured just $32.5 billion in revenues during 2000, of which Internet telephony was estimated to be around $3 billion and growing. Obviously, Internet carriers would like to capture the telephony market, and the technology to enable this is being deployed today. Likewise, the incumbent carriers would like to retain their existing revenues and capture those of the Internet.

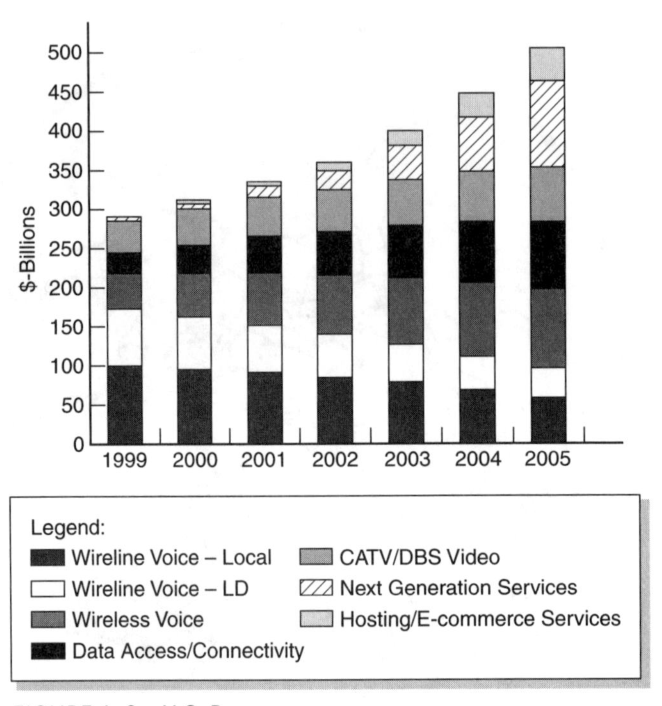

FIGURE 1–2 *U.S. Revenues*

As both sides grapple with these issues, those of us who are trying to predict the outcome should heed Bob Dylan's words in his second stanza from the Preface. Namely that it is too soon to predict the outcome of this struggle for the wheel is still turning and there is no certainty as to the winners. This will be a lengthy battle with no quick conclusion.

References

Christensen, Clayton M. *The Innovator's Dilemma,* Harvard Business School Press, 1997.

Gates, Bill. *Business @ the Speed of Thought,* Warner Books, 1999.

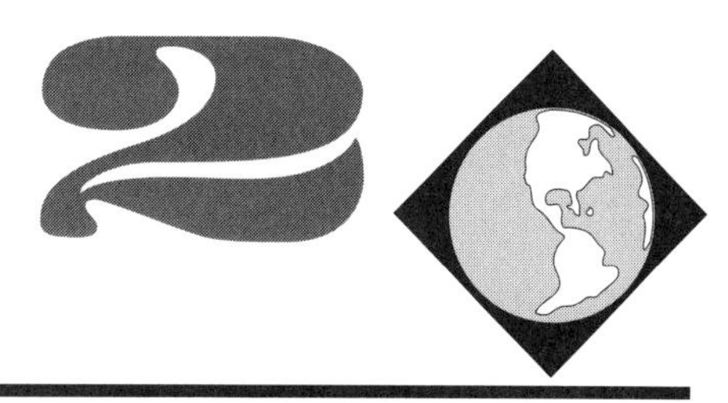

Speech and Transport

We take for granted our ability to speak, listen, and comprehend information at a distance when using the telephone network. Not only is raw information transmitted, but speech can also convey a great deal of knowledge about the speaker. This places the content of the speech in a specific context. This can allow the listener to better judge and utilize the information. For example, if my broker calls with a stock tip, her credibility is a very important input to my decision. The broker's credibility will depend on her tone of voice and other sounds, such as breathing, that are conveyed by the telephone. If my spouse calls to tell me to come home from work, I can easily tell how urgent the request is and whether or not it's going to be a good evening at home. These details of tone and subtle mannerisms of speech are important to humans, and whatever method of transport we choose, we must realize that certain impairments of the communication channel may cause the listener to misinterpret or miss altogether some of the more subtle aspects of the conversation. We may choose to formulate a service that will alter or degrade the audio and other aspects of the conversation, but we should not do this unknowingly or without carefully considering and testing whether or not the market we are attempting to address will accept this grade of service.

There are many acceptable grades of service that customers will accept in various situations but not in others. For example, few users would say that mobile telephones have the same quality as a normal telephone call, but the convenience of mobility outweighs the lower quality of the transmission. Likewise, the quality of normal telephone service is well below that of the compact audio disk, but it has proven acceptable for providing intelligible conversation at a distance. It is important to realize the impact that channel impairments will have on the customer, because if quality is below some threshold, the customer will call the network operator and complain or ask for a refund. This will require paid service representatives for dealing with complaints and making repairs, refunds, and other remedial actions. To support the service representatives, the network operator will have to have mechanisms in its operations flow that will allow a refund to be given, a process for deciding whether or not to give the refund, and a system for actually refunding the customer. If these problems recur, the customer may abandon the network operator for another one, resulting in lower revenues. So low quality comes at a price. Indeed, this can be a downward spiral, because a quality problem will increase costs and also decrease revenues. So, it is important to make a knowledgeable decision about quality.

Before we consider the technical aspects of any particular network, let's first consider the information we wish to communicate across the network—namely, the human voice and what is required to transport it. Then we can examine the different ways it may be transported—by circuits or by packets—and the various impairments each of these methods will impart to the communications. We will also consider other impairments associated with the use of the telephone, such as call completion times, dropped calls, and blocking. All these things taken together will establish the quality of the service.

Mean Opinion Scores and Quality

For determining service quality, a time-honored scheme of Mean Opinion Score (MOS) has been devised (see Table 2–1). Using this method, sample phrases of speech such as "we were away a year ago"[1] are encoded, sent through a transmission channel sometimes with impairments, decoded, and then played for a listener. These impaired speech segments represent the end-to-end quality that a conversation will experience and are conveniently generated using computers. Invariably, a "clear channel" test using unimpaired transmission is used as a baseline so that the difference in quality perceived by the listener can be compared objectively to the normal telephone network quality. Other cases will include various transmission impairments, such as the introduction of bit errors and discarding whole segments of the speech, as well as the introduction of echoes or various speech compression schemes.

1. Such sentences are known as phonetically balanced sentences because the words are chosen to include a maximum of phonemes. Other somewhat humorous examples include "Joe took Father's shoe bench out" and "In these days, a chicken leg is a rare dish."

TABLE 2-1 *Mean Opinion Score*

Mean Opinion Score (MOS)	Quality
5	Excellent
4	Good
3	Fair
2	Poor
1	Bad

Listeners are asked to classify the quality of the speech as bad, poor, fair, good, or excellent. In most tests, the critical issue is to determine if the speech quality is "good" or "better," since this would appear to be reasonable criteria for a commercial network. By averaging the scores of listeners who hear many different impaired and reference speech segments, it is possible to obtain a statistically significant measure of quality. This can help the network operator determine if there might be a significant problem with the service, which could lead to complaints and expenses. ISDN, an end-to-end digital service with excellent speech quality, is rated around 4.2. The toll quality service that is experienced by most long-distance users is in the range of 3.5 to 4.0. Analog cellular phone service quality lies between 3.3 and 3.5, while digital mobile service quality falls between 3.6 and 3.8. These scores represent the quality the user will experience when everything is working well in the network. As we all know, especially cellular users, there are bad moments when the quality is considerably degraded.

Frequency Spectrum of Speech

Sounds made by humans involve lungs, the respiratory system, the brain, and the larynx. Under control of the brain, an air stream is generated by the lungs and passes between the vocal cords that are part of the larynx. These two small muscular folds can restrict the passageway in such a manner as to vibrate and create sounds. Depending on the air pressure and the tension in the muscles, the loudness and frequency of the vibrations can be controlled by the brain.

Above the vocal cords are chambers that can be adjusted in volume so as to create a resonance. These chambers include the mouth, the nasal tract, and the region of the windpipe above the vocal cords. Depending on the frequency being generated by the vocal cords and the resonant frequency of the cavities, different tonal structure can be imposed on the sound by amplifying or attenuating different frequencies present in the sounds. The brain also controls these regions in volume and shape so as to select the desired tonal structure. The tongue, teeth, and lips play a critical role in articulating speech, since they are a major means by which the shape and volume of the mouth cavity is controlled.

Speech, when analyzed for frequency content, is found to have components that are multiples of a fundamental pitch. These are called *formants*. This fundamental pitch is determined by the vocal cords that are vibrating at that fixed rate. Sounds made by the vocal cords have a very large number of harmonically related frequencies present due to the wave shape generated. Because of the way in which the vocal cords oscillate, they create a waveform that is roughly a sawtooth. Fourier analysis of such a waveform shows that all multiples, both odd and even, of this fundamental frequency are present with gradually decreasing amplitude. Thus, a bass-sounding voice that has a fundamental pitch of 100 Hz will also have energy at 200 Hz, 300 Hz, 400 Hz, and so on. By changing the tension in the vocal cords, increases or decreases in pitch can be created by the speaker. By shaping the mouth and nasal system, the speaker is able to select the frequencies to be amplified or attenuated, thus allowing a rich set of sounds.

Figure 2–1 shows the distribution range of fundamental frequencies for male and female speakers. For men, the range of fundamental pitch is generally 50 to 200 Hz, with an average of 130 Hz. Women have more high-pitched voices in which the fundamental ranges from around 150 Hz to 440 Hz. The average for women is around 220 Hz. Furthermore, speakers can modulate their voice to higher frequencies by tensing the muscles of the larynx and controlling the various cavities of the nasal passages. In general, most people can modulate their speech over a range of two octaves above their fundamental, a factor of four in frequency. As people age, their fundamental pitch becomes lower.

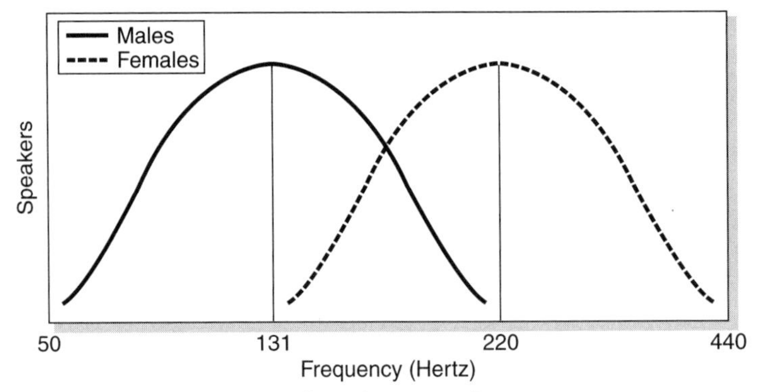

FIGURE 2–1 *Fundamental pitch in speech.*

The consequence of this is that the frequency range needed to represent the average speaker is quite wide, ranging from around 130 Hz to carry the male fundamental to frequencies as high as 1760 Hz for an average female. In the case of operatic sopranos, pitches as high as 3136 Hz have been recorded. Even higher frequencies are actually present as harmonics, as high as 8000 Hz in some speakers, but their inclusion is not necessary for good intelligibility and speaker recognition. For these reasons, telephone systems have been designed to transport a range of frequencies from around 300 Hz to about 3200 Hz. This is the first in a series of degradations necessary to transport speech.

Digitization of Speech

Transport of speech today is most often done using digital transmission, as shown in Figure 2–2. This involves conversion from analog signals, the natural representation of speech coming from a transducer, such as a microphone, into a digital signal constructed of bits of information. Normally, we wish to limit the frequencies transmitted by the system to values below 4 kHz. So, the initial analog audio processing makes use of filters with an upper cutoff frequency somewhat below 4 kHz to ensure that sounds above this range made by the talker or present in the talker's environment will be attenuated rather than transmitted. Using Nyquist's sampling principle, we find that to accurately reconstruct signals restricted to less than a 4 kHz bandwidth, we must sample the signal at an 8 kHz rate. Conceptually, this will allow at least two samples per cycle of a sinusoidal wave at the maximum frequency and allow the original sinusoid to be reconstructed at the receiver.

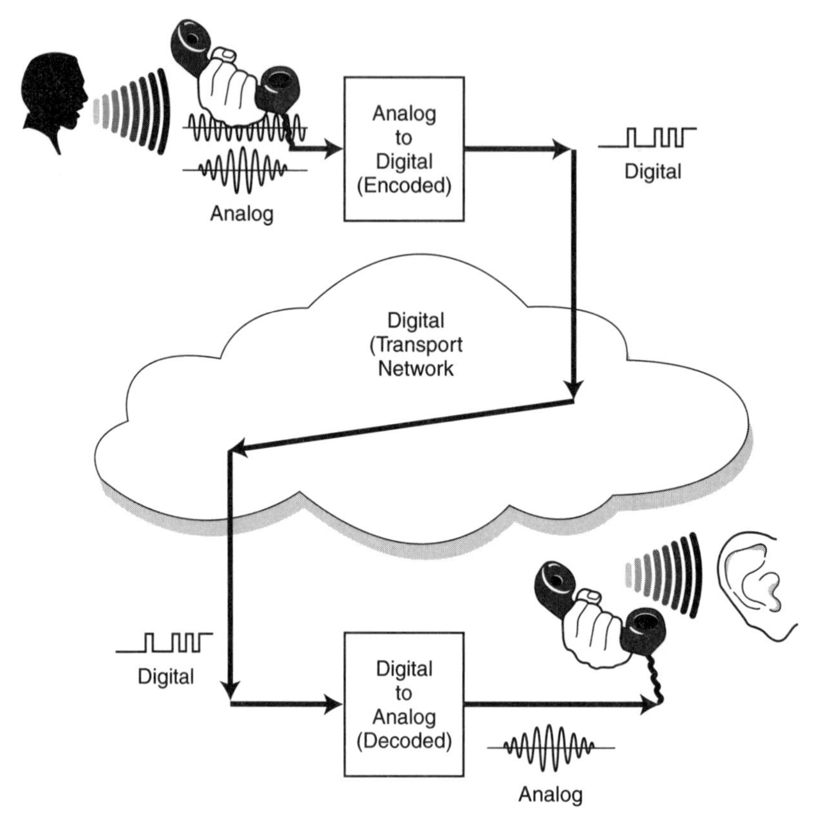

FIGURE 2–2 *Digital transport of speech.*

The samples will be encoded using digital representation in which the numeric value of the sample is encoded into a set of bits. Speech samples in North America, Japan, and other parts of the world are represented using an 8-bit form of floating-point representation known as μ-law. Europe and some other countries use a similar scheme called "A-law". Together, these coding schemes have been standardized internationally by the ITU[2] as recommendation G.711. The μ-law and A-law coding schemes have a 1-bit sign indication (S), a 3-bit exponent (L), and a 4-bit mantissa (V) that operate

2. International Telecommunications Union (ITU) is part of the United Nations. Technical experts from around the world negotiate technical details of international recommendations that are published by the ITU.

as a form of floating-point representation. This allows the reconstructed signal to have a relatively constant signal-to-noise ratio independent of amplitude, because as the signal becomes larger, the steps between discrete values also increase due to the choice of the exponent, L. If a fixed-point method were used, the signal-to-noise ratio would be significantly higher for small signals than for large ones. The conversion from analog to digital inherently introduces some level of noise and distortion, yet another means by which the speech channel is degraded.

Since each sample consists of 8 bits, and the digitizing system creates samples 8000 times per second, the transmission of μ-law voice channels requires a 64 kilobits-per-second (Kbps) transmission rate. Ordinarily, these are transmitted serially, one bit at a time, through telephone systems. Inside these systems, sometimes the samples are moved about in 8-bit groups or even in large blocks of information. It is important to maintain the order of these samples in time, and it is also important that systems always maintain the order of the bits so that S, L, and V are properly interpreted.

Today, silicon integrated circuits perform this conversion in both directions. Such devices are called codecs, an acronym for coder/decoder. These are actually two functions: the coder that takes the analog signal and generates its digital representation and the decoder that performs the reverse operation. The space required for such a device is very small, allowing the codec to be integrated along with other parts of a system or to allow many codecs on a single integrated circuit. This is important, since all users will have one or more codecs as part of their connection path. Later, when we consider evolution, the placement of the codec will be one consideration that must be decided. Because G.711 is the world's end-to-end standard for voice encoding and has been used in the worldwide market for so many years, it represents the yardstick by which all other schemes are measured. The quality that users perceive in today's wire-line network is that of G.711, an ITU standard.

Pauses in Speech

Individuals trained in speaking are able to articulate uninterrupted speech for periods approaching 1 minute, after which it is necessary to breathe. Also, even during active speech, sound is not generated continuously since there are very short intervals between words, phrases, and sentences that allow the listener to delineate the sounds being generated back into words, phrases, and sentences.

In 1938, A. C. Norwine and O. J. Murphy observed this effect in telephone networks, and researchers at Bell Labs sought to find a way to exploit these silences to increase the capacity of systems transporting voice. The proposition was simple: If there is nothing to be transmitted because a speaker paused in speech, the channel could be used for the transport of a different conversation. Besides the short pauses during speech, there is the very lengthy interval when the speaker stops to listen to a response. If one person listens when the other speaks, roughly one-half of the transport capacity is wasted. Of course, this rule does not always hold, and there is occasional double talk during conversations.

In a landmark set of studies, P. T. Brady carefully examined the characteristics of speech with regard to the duration of pauses and bursts of speech. He made a number of findings, including a key problem associated with speech detection. In order to switch a channel between various speakers, we must decide if speech is present or not. So, how shall we go about this? In a simple speech detection mechanism, there are two parameters that can be controlled: volume and duration. If sound is present at or above a specific volume threshold and continues for some minimum duration, then the detector indicates that speech is present and the equipment must arrange for its transport.

When speech is carefully examined, it is found that there are some sounds present that are not very loud and that have very short duration. Depending on the thresholds selected, these sounds will be discarded. No doubt, some of these signals are noise and do not require transmission. But others probably contribute to the more subtle factors in intelligibility or to the context of the conversation. This adds to the growing list of tradeoffs we can make, all of which reduce in some way the quality of the end result.

One pair of useable thresholds is 5 milliseconds and –40 dB. That is, if the speaker's volume level reaches at least –40 dB anytime during an interval of 5 milliseconds, the speech detector will make a positive indication that speech is present. If this occurs, the interval will be transmitted; otherwise it is discarded. Note that in order to utilize this scheme, it will be necessary to delay the speech by whatever time interval is used to make this determination. The effects of delay will be considered later in this chapter. A necessary consequence of this method is that any utterance shorter than 5 milliseconds will be discarded. A complementary problem due to the simple nature of this detection scheme is that the last interval of a burst may not be fully utilized since the threshold for transmission may have been satisfied at the very beginning of the interval but most of the interval consists of silence. As a result, we will waste a bit of our transmission capacity sending intervals that are only partly filled with speech. Brady found the statistics listed in Table 2–2 regarding speaking and silent intervals using a simple detector with the thresholds mentioned previously.

TABLE 2-2 *Speech Statistics*

Total conversation time	51.57 minutes
Percent time both speakers are silent	18.2%
Percent time double talking	7.2%
Percent time average speaker talks	44.3%
Number of bursts	2042
Median burst length	0.77 seconds
Mean burst length	1.34 seconds
Number of pauses	2054
Median pause	0.72 seconds
Mean pause	1.67 seconds

From Table 2–2, it is clear that considerable savings can be realized, since both directions of transmission are utilized only around 44% of the time. Of course, this is an average case and individual conversations may vary from these statistics. Additionally, because we cannot perfectly predict when the speaker is entering a silent period, some time will be wasted in our system by transmitting silence. In early systems, 74 users shared 36 channels, a reduction to 48.6%, but modern sophisticated speech detectors can achieve 40% or less.

Speech Compression

Besides the elimination of silent intervals in speech, it is possible to reduce the transmission rate required from 64 Kbps to lower rates. This will reduce the perceived quality of the speech, but for certain algorithms, it will remain at an acceptable level. Many different algorithms have been created for this purpose, and most have gone through international standardization to allow compatibility between manufacturers and networks around the world.

Figure 2–3 shows a typical modern approach to speech compression. There are two parts, the encoder and the decoder. In a modern digital network, these elements can be placed at any point along the path used for the communications, but most often they lie at either end of expensive long-distance trunks. In mobile systems, they are actually included in the customer's handset. As will be discussed later, this would be the case to achieve the greatest benefit in a packet-based system. If the encoder is examined closely, it can be seen that it contains its own copy of the decoder.

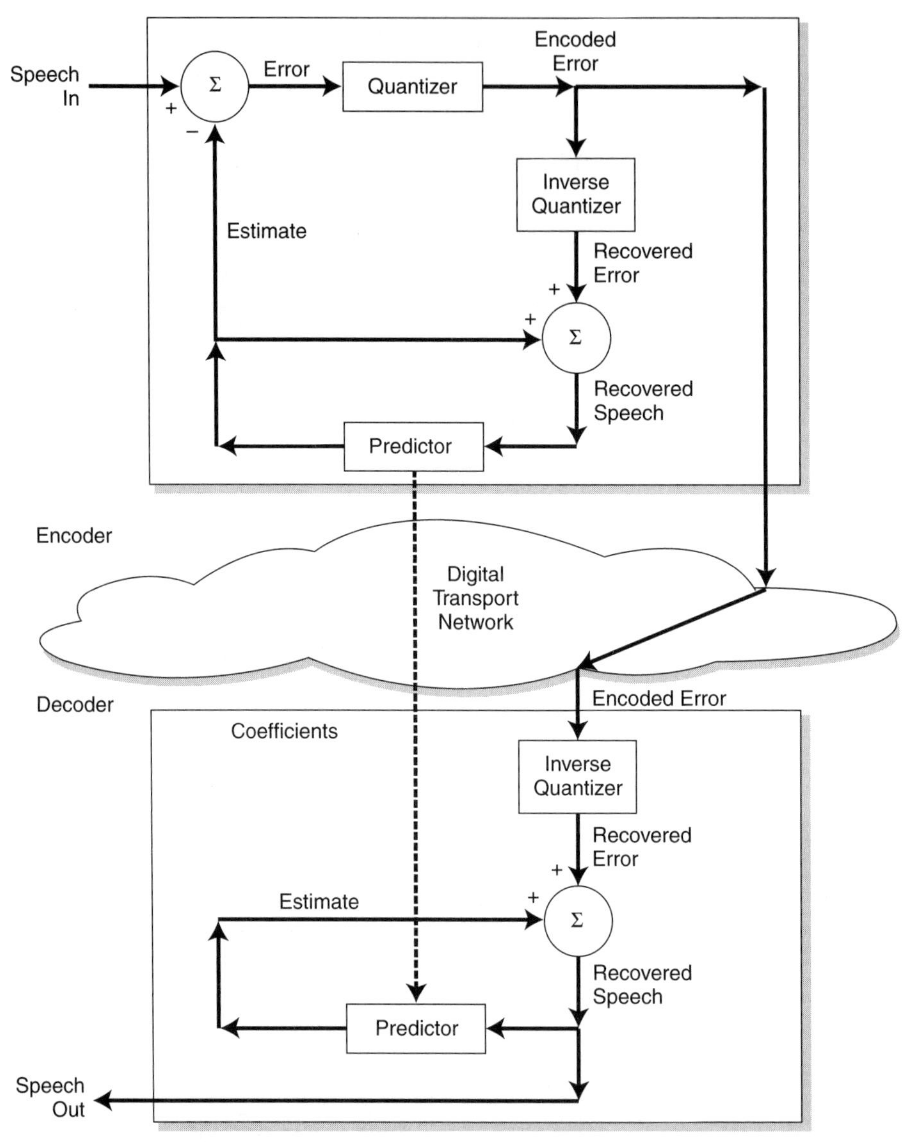

FIGURE 2–3 *Predictive coding system.*

The encoder includes a predictor that produces estimates of the input signal based on previous values. These estimates are subtracted from the actual current input signal value to produce an error signal. The error represents the difference between the estimated value of the input and the actual value. The error signal is quantized and encoded into a set of codes that represents the error. If the predictor produces good estimates of the input, the error signal will be small in magnitude and can be represented by considerably fewer bits of information than the original input. This encoded error signal is transmitted to the receiver. The receiver reverses the encoding operation to obtain the quantized error signal. This is then added to its value of the estimate in an attempt to reproduce the original input. The recovered speech signal is used at both the encoder and the decoder to adapt the predictor. In some algorithms, quantization and encoding are adaptive and change during the course of operation of the encoder/decoder. But in other cases, it is a fixed arrangement. The predictor itself may be adaptive, in which case a set of internal coefficients used for prediction must be sent to the decoder to synchronize the two predictors from time to time.

There are numerous schemes similar to that described here. Among them are many international standards adopted by ITU. G.721, G.726, and G.729 are just a few of these standards. Table 2–3 shows some of the rates produced by these systems and the MOS for each. G.711 is included for reference.

TABLE 2-3 *Speech Quality for Several Compression Standards*

Standard	Bit Rate	MOS
G.711	64 Kbps	4.2
G.726	16, 24, 32 or 40 Kbps	2, 3.2, 4 or 4.2
G.723.1	5.3 or 6.3 Kbps	3.7 or 3.9
G.729	8 Kbps	4.0

Because the predictor is imperfect, there is always some error produced by the encoder/decoder pair, but the reduction in bandwidth used for a connection is considerable. If we are seeking a toll quality service in the range of 3.5 to 4.0, we see that G.723.1, G.726 (at 32 Kbps or higher), or G.729 would all be suitable, at least based on MOS for quality.

In evaluating these coding standards, we must also consider their overall delay. Each of these, except for G.711 and G.726, takes a block of speech samples, processes it, and produces a corresponding block of values to send to the receiver. This is referred to as *frame delay.* As a result, there will be a delay caused while the encoder collects the samples. In addition, G.723.1 and G.729 include speech detection capability that requires a look-ahead buffer to determine when the user has started speaking. These delays are shown in Table 2–4.

TABLE 2-4 *Delay for Some Compression Standards*

Standard	Look-Ahead Delay	Frame Delay	Total Delay
G.711	0 msec	125 μsec	125 μsec
G.726	0 msec	125 μsec	125 μsec
G.723.1	7.5 msec	30 msec	37.5 msec
G.729	5 msec	10 msec	15 msec

The effects of these delays cause additional problems for the user if the delays are not kept under control. This is compounded by other sources of delay, such as propagation and switching. Ultimately, these delays will all be accumulated and will have impact on the users of the telephony service.

Effects of Delay

Voice conversations are sensitive to delay. If the signals are delayed sufficiently, conversation can become quite awkward, because when the talker stops talking, some form of response is expected. It matters not if the delay is due to propagation across the network or due to speech processing systems. If no response is forthcoming, the talker may think the listener is not there and abandon the call. Or, the talker may query the listener to see if she is actually there and that the call is intact. One-way delays of 150 milliseconds or less are tolerated by most people, but at 250 milliseconds (one-way), a significant number of people become uncomfortable without knowing exactly why. And long delays approaching 1 second or more can become practically unusable. When all the various sources of delay, including compression, propagation, transmission, and switching, are considered together, it is possible to accumulate a large overall delay.

Effects of Echo

In addition, because there are reflections of the signals in most telephone instruments and because both directions of transmission are combined in two-wire loops, echoes can be created when delay is present. Depending on the amount of delay and the volume of the reflections, these echoes can present problems to the talker, the listener, or to both parties. This is depicted in Figure 2–4, which shows a talker, a listener, and two points of reflection where echoes are generated. The talker hears an echo reflected back from a far away point in the network. This is called *talker echo*. The listener hears the talker's speech directly, but the speech is reflected first at the listener's end of the connection and then a second time at the talker's end, so the listener hears the speech a second time. This is called *listener echo*. In both cases the speech is attenuated at each of the reflection points, so it gets smaller at each pass. Normally, subsequent reflections are below the threshold of audibility.

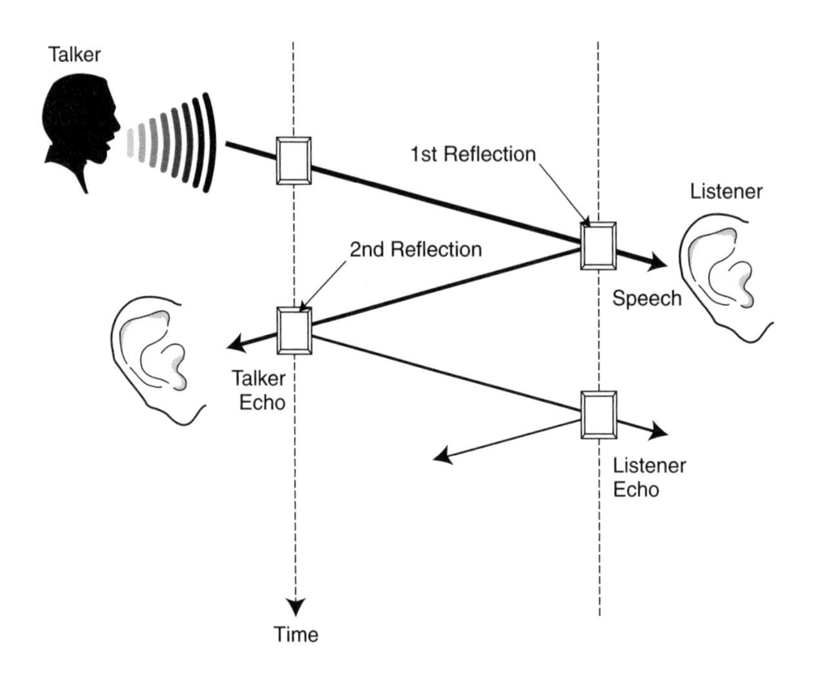

FIGURE 2–4 *Echoes due to reflections.*

Figures 2–5 and 2–6 show the percentage of talkers and listeners rating a connection as "good or better," depending on the time delay of the echo in milliseconds and its attenuation in decibels. In Figure 2–5, the talker echo opinion model, we see the scoring when the talker hears his own voice echoed back to him with varying delay and attenuation. As the duration of the delay and the volume of the echo increases, the talker has a lower and lower opinion of the connection. As the echo delay path increases, it is necessary to have higher attenuation of the echo to achieve the same perceived quality for the connection. Depending on the length of delay associated with the echo, several different impairments are recognized by talkers. If the delay is quite short, up to a few milliseconds, it has the desirable effect of reinforcing the talker's speech. People are accustomed to hearing this sort of feedback while speaking, and if none is present, they suspect the network is not operating properly. This form of feedback is called *side-tone* and is an essential part of voice service. If the delay is in the range of a few milliseconds to a few tens of milliseconds, the talker's voice takes on a hollow sound, as though he is speaking into a large barrel. Indeed, this sort of delay has been dubbed the "rain barrel" effect. Once the delays are beyond a few tens of milliseconds, the talker becomes uncomfortable hearing his own voice delayed and will pause, believing the other person is trying to interrupt him. This leads to jerky, erratic speech patterns and a bad experience for the user.

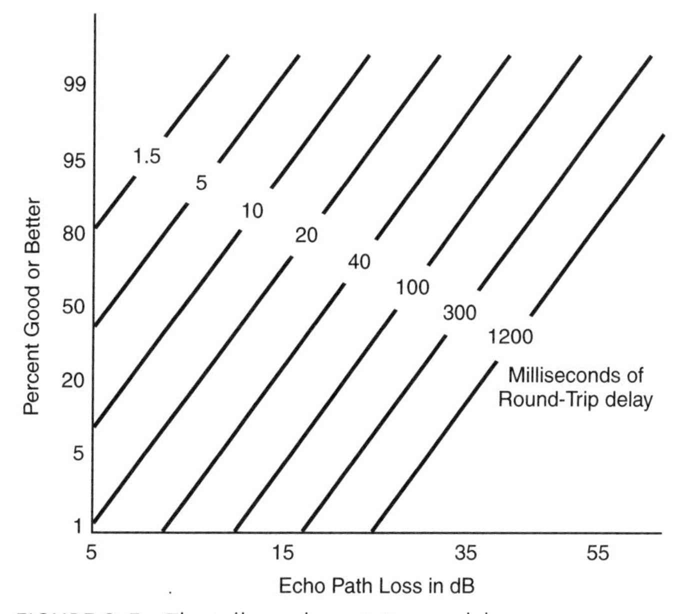

FIGURE 2–5 *The talker echo opinion model.*

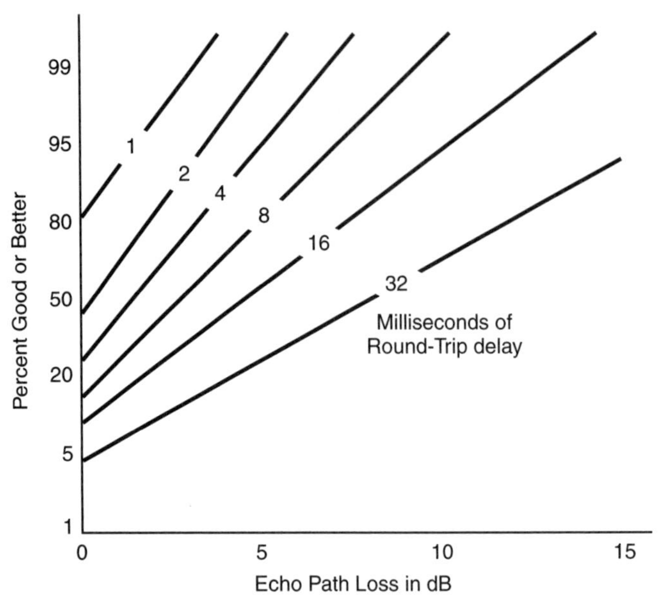

FIGURE 2–6 *The listener echo opinion model.*

Listeners also perceive echoes when speech is heard directly and then heard a second time with some attenuation. The listeners rate such connections as shown in Figure 2–6. As can be seen, even short delays can cause the listener to have a lower opinion of the connection. As with talkers, attenuation of the echo causes the score to improve even if delay is present.

It is worth noting that if the entire network is digital end-to-end, then echoes can be eliminated by making telephones such that the transmit and receive signals are carefully isolated from each other. Thus, even if there are long delays, any echoes are greatly or entirely attenuated. Since this is not the case today, systems to cancel echoes must be present in some parts of the network where delay and echo volume are sufficient to degrade the communications.

Today's network has been carefully designed to avoid precisely this sort of problem. A national delay budget has been created through requirements and standards that specify the maximum delay allowed by various network elements. Network operators pay close attention to delay and echo cancellation when planning networks and selecting equipment. Remember that if the network performs poorly, the network operator will receive complaints from customers. It will cost money to deal with the complaints, and customers may transition to other network operators resulting in a loss of revenue.

Echo Control

In a network that has separate paths (known as four-wire) for the end-to-end transmission of speech in each direction and has reasonably constructed telephones that isolate the two directions of transmission, there would be no source of reflections. As a consequence, there would be no echoes. However, today's network has locations where both directions of transmission are combined into a single analog media called *two-wire*. Most prominent of these locations is the so-called local "loop" reaching the customer's telephone. This will be discussed in detail in a following chapter. Wherever the network converts between two-wire and four-wire, there will be a point of reflection that will result in an echo. This point is known as a *hybrid*.

Because there is frequently some level of echo present in a connection, it is necessary to have some means for controlling echoes. Figure 2–7 shows two echo-canceling circuits at opposite ends of a connection within a network that has two reflections, one at each end. Ordinarily, reflections occur where the network hybrid converts the two-wire telephone to or from a four-wire digital circuit. The cancellation system at each end of the connection cancels echoes that would otherwise be returned to the opposite end due to the reflection point at their end. Thus, echo canceler "A" cancels the reflections from reflection point "A." These circuits are called *near-end echo cancelers* because they reduce the echo returned to the opposite end of the connection.

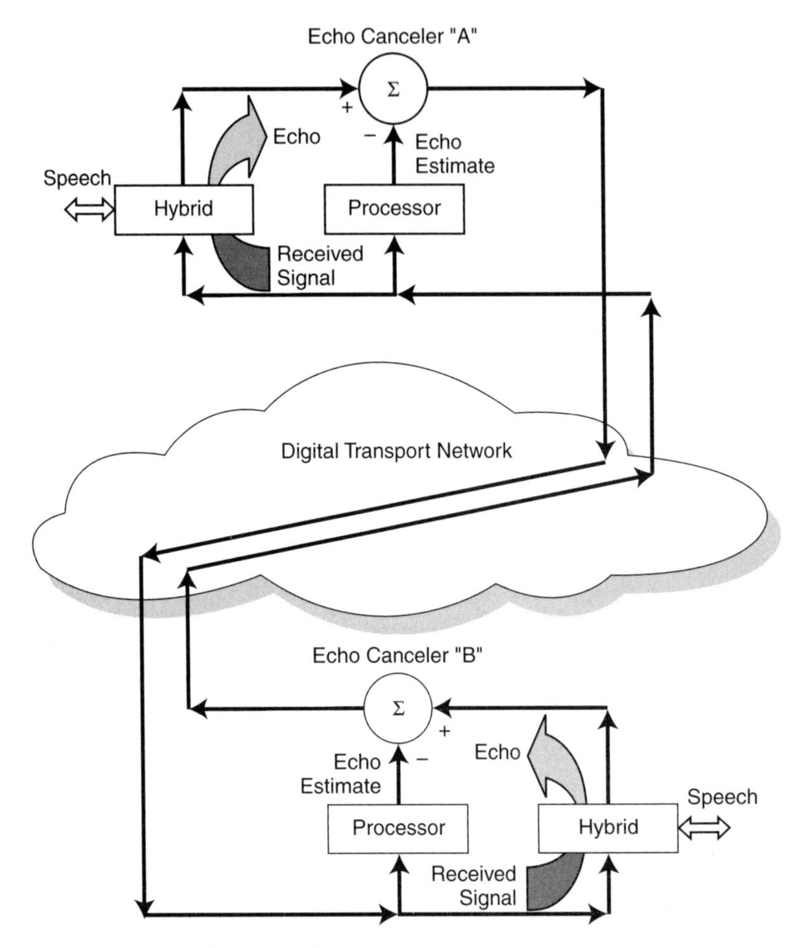

FIGURE 2–7 Echo control.

In both systems, the received signal passes to the user through the reflection point. The reflection point produces an altered version of the received signal that would normally be returned to the far end of the connection. The echo-canceling circuit simply creates its own estimated signal that approximates the echo. It does this by modeling the function of the hybrid and whatever may be attached to the hybrid with a processor. This estimate is then subtracted from the transmitted signal coming from the reflection point. If the processor's model of the hybrid generates estimates that closely approximate the reflection, the transmitted signal will show little or no echo.

Since the circuit will be used for many different connections that have quite different hybrids and terminating systems at their endpoints, it must adapt each time it is used. So, in order for the echo-canceling circuit to properly cancel the returned signal, it must adjust the coefficients of the model that the processor uses. The circuit will go through a training period in which it transmits a short tone burst and measures the delay and attenuation of the tone in its receive side. It then sets its internal values to the measured results and begins operation. As an alternative, the echo-canceling circuit can be made to adapt to connections. Whenever its received signal is large, it will adjust its delay and attenuation to minimize the output signal. By making small incremental changes in these parameters, it will gradually adapt to cancel any returned signal.

Echo-canceling circuits can be incorporated at any location in the network. Ordinarily, it is common practice to assign them to the long-distance network operator, who will use them as needed for connections exceeding a certain distance. The distances are estimated based on area codes dialed by the users. A pool of these systems can be kept available, and connections will be routed through them if required.

Circuit-Switched Transport

Today's Public Switched Telephone Network (PSTN) is based almost entirely on circuit-switching techniques. The basic concept in circuit-switched transport is that each digital sample is carried carefully to the destination and delivered in the exact sequence and timing that was present at the transmitter over a route that has been previously established and is entirely dedicated to this particular call. Prior to actually connecting two users and allowing information to flow in the connection, a signaling system is employed so the caller can indicate whom she wishes to connect with. This is accomplished when the caller indicates a phone number to the signaling system, usually using touch-tones. The network then locates the user, selects a route through the network, rings the user's phone, and completes the end-to-end connection when the user answers. In a perfect circuit-switched network, only delay is present. The amount of delay will depend on the precise means by which the network is implemented, the number of switches and transmission elements encountered along the route, and the distance being traversed.

Since the network is not perfect, some impairment may appear in the channel. Both switches and transmission devices will occasionally cause individual or multiple bit errors in the channel. This is usually caused by electrical disturbances such as lightening or by timing errors in decoding the channel by the equipment. Ordinarily, these errors seldom occur, and bit error rates on the order of one bit in every billion or even every 10 billion bits are commonplace.

Besides occasional errors in information content, there is delay. The most fundamental source of delay is distance. Connections that traverse long distances will encounter greater delay than those that are local in nature. This is because the propagation of electrons and photons is limited by speed of light for the media in which they travel. Light travels at 3×10^8 meters per second in a vacuum, but electrons in a copper wire or photons in a fiber optic travel at speeds closer to 80% of this value. This is around 150 miles per millisecond for typical media. So, for a national connection traversing 3000 miles of copper wire or fiber optic, a propagation delay of around 20 milliseconds would be experienced. A geo-synchronous satellite connection of 44,600 miles would have nearly 300 milliseconds of delay present. Note that the satellite is only 22,300 above the earth's equator but that the signal must travel both to and from the satellite to go from talker to listener. The round trip delay for these connections, an important consideration for echo, would be on the order of 40 milliseconds for the ground-based network and 600 milliseconds for the geo-synchronous satellite network. Because of these large delays, satellite systems using Low Earth Orbits (LEO) have been attempted, but these systems have other complexities, such as rapid motion of the satellites and complex requirements for routing between satellites. As a result, satellites are rarely used today for voice transport but are heavily utilized for video and data traffic that is not degraded by the additional delay.

Besides propagation delay, the transmission and switching equipment also requires some time for synchronization and processing of the channel. Usually these delays are in multiples of 125 microseconds, the duration of a single sampling interval. Typical transmission equipment such as multiplexing or cross-connect apparatus can introduce two frames of delay, while switching equipment will add around five frames of delay. Since a connection will be carried through many pieces of this equipment, measurable delays can occur. For example, if a national connection traversed 8 switches and 12 transmission systems, as shown in Figure 2–8, it would be delayed by 50 frames of 125 microseconds each for a total of 6.25 milliseconds. Round-trip delays would be double this value. This is in addition to propagation delays due to the physical locations of the originating and terminating users. In the example, there are two switching points in each local carrier and four switching points in the long-distance carrier. In addition, there are digital cross-connect systems used for managing trunks in the network, which break the transmission path into segments.

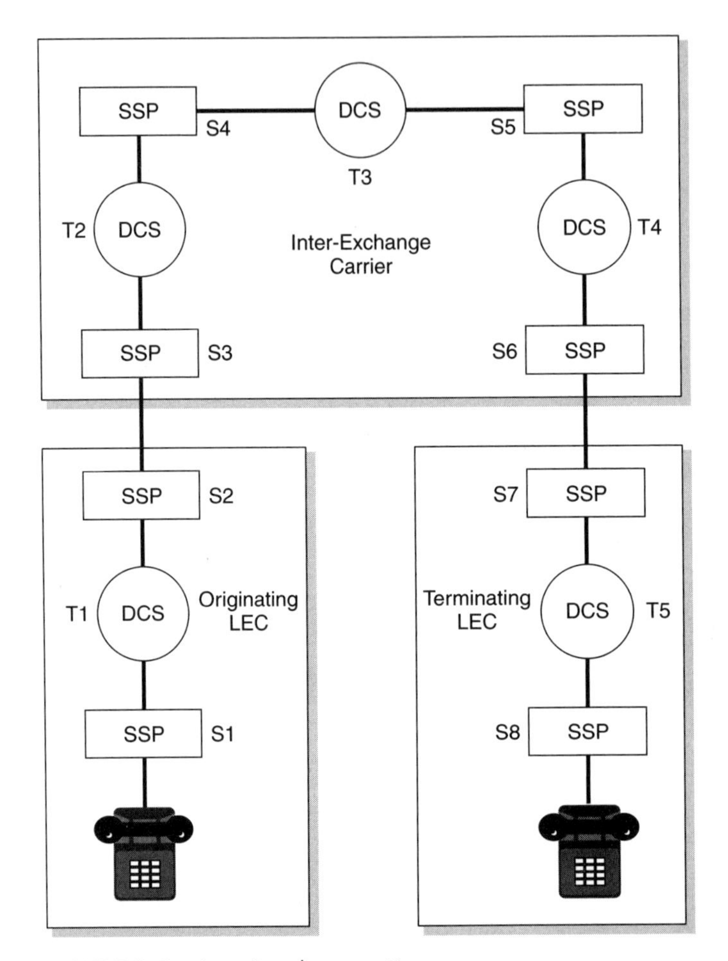

FIGURE 2–8 A national connection.

For terrestrial networks, we see that a national connection can experience delay on the order of 28 milliseconds due to the combined effects of propagation, transmission, and switching. Round-trip echoes would be on the order of 56 milliseconds. As can be seen from the previous table, the delay of the connection is low enough that normal conversations would be considered excellent, but measures must be taken to control the volume of any echoes.

As might be expected, in a coast-to-coast connection, the route the connection takes can have a significant impact on the delay experienced by its users. If a connection from Chicago to San Francisco were routed via Denver, it would have considerably less delay than if it went via Nashville and Kansas City. Ordinarily, the call control systems of a network would choose the shortest path for the connection, since this would tend to minimize the use of network resources. But if the shortest path is not available, the network will utilize alternates in order to complete the call and collect the revenue it will generate. Thus, the end-to-end delay in the network will generally vary according to how busy the network is. Besides covering greater distances, an alternate route is likely to include additional switching systems and their incumbent delay.

Of course, there will be times when the call simply cannot be completed because there is no available capacity by which the destination can be reached. This is called *blocking*. In this case the network will simply have to provide a busy signal to the user, who will probably attempt again and again to complete the call. Blocking a new call attempt will have no effect on any calls in progress already; however, a state of extreme congestion when a lot of calls are being blocked represents a source of dissatisfaction with the service as well as lost revenue for the network operator. If this occurs often enough, the users will complain to the network operator, who will have to respond in some manner. The network operator will also have to increase network resources, an action it probably should complete before complaints begin to roll in. In network systems and operations, it is normal to monitor the ratio of call attempts to call completions and the reasons for blocked calls. This allows the network operator to adjust routing procedures in the network or to plan to increase the capacity on busy routes.

The most appealing characteristic of circuit switching for voice services is its deterministic nature. Once the call has been established, the delay is fixed and the circuit is very reliably delivering samples of speech from the sender to the receiver. Echoes may occur, but these can be controlled. Issues such as congestion, the time to establish a connection, and other problems may arise in setting up a call. But the basic transport of speech is easy in a circuit-switched network.

The primary problem with circuit switching is that it is a very poor match to data, and if the network operator wishes to provide integrated voice and data services from a single network, circuit switching will not work very well. This is because of the dynamic nature of data information that is inherently variable in nature and is highly unpredictable. The idea of establishing a simple fixed bandwidth channel between two data sources is very unappealing as a service. In Figure 2–9, circuit transport is depicted as a set of soda straws that are aggregated to make a transport facility. The soda straw channels are used continuously in time from the start of a conversation until it finishes. Each soda straw is a small fraction of the overall transport capacity. The inflexibility and fixed bandwidth of circuit switching that are its greatest strength for voice services are the root cause of its poor match to data.

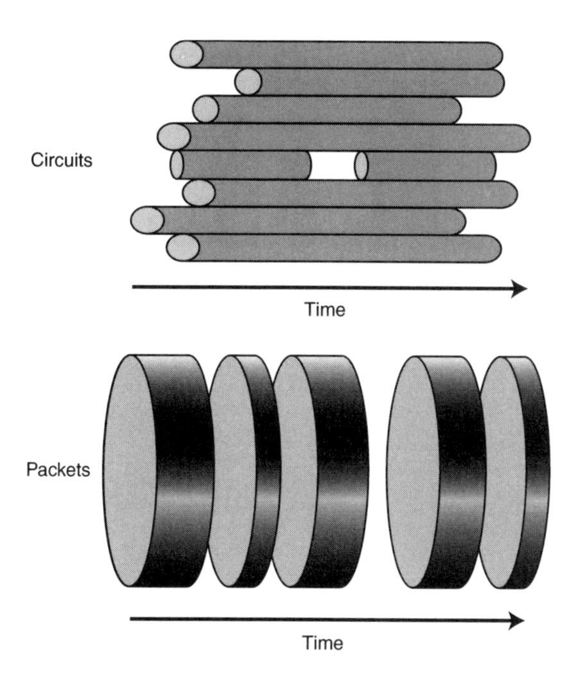

FIGURE 2–9 *Circuits and packets.*

Packet-Switched Transport

Unlike circuit-switched networks, packet systems transmit information in large blocks that are usually originated by computers. There are actually two forms of packet switching in common use today: *connection-oriented* and *connectionless*. Both rely upon the transport of a block of user information that is preceded by a header indicating the destination to which the information should be delivered. In connectionless networks, such as IP (Internet Protocol), every packet carries the full destination address, which will be a large field. However, in connection-oriented packet networks, such as X.25 or ATM (Asynchronous Transfer Mode), the destination is indicated by a much smaller field that has been negotiated with the network through a signaling system much like the circuit-switched network.

An easy analogy to understand connectionless networks is the postal system. Every destination in the world is given a name, street address, city, state, and country (please ignore the zip code concept, which will be discussed shortly). The sender simply places information inside the envelope and puts the complete destination address of the desired receiver on the outside of the envelope. The post office does not examine the interior of the envelope; it simply delivers it to the desired destination based on the address provided by the sender. Incidentally, other phenomena in the post office, such as lost letters and congestion during busy times of the year also occur in connectionless packet networks. In connectionless switches, it is necessary (and possible) to translate destination addresses into routes very quickly. Usually, the first time a destination address is used at a switch, it will take some time to establish the route. However, this information will be cached locally, enabling the switch to very rapidly route subsequent packets.

Connection-oriented networks operate much as if the sender made an agreement with the post office in which the sender told the postal system a value that would be used to mean a particular destination. For example, the sender might inform the post office that for the time being, the value 17 represents Telcordia Technologies, 331 Newman Springs Road, Red Bank, NJ. Thereafter, the sender would simply put something in an envelope, write the number 17 on the outside, and hand it to the postal system. The postal system would know the true destination and would deliver it there. This shorthand method saves space in the packets and also allows the network to pre-establish a route for the packets before they start to flow. In a connection-oriented network, this negotiation would involve a signaling system and the switches that would select an end-to-end route through the network when the user initially indicated a destination.

The zip code concept combines aspects of both these methods. A zip code represents a geographic region that contains the destination address. This allows the postal system to immediately forward the letter close to the destination, ideally to the nearest post office, so that only a single post office will have to examine the full address of the letter. Without the zip code, it would be necessary to examine the full address on the letter and select a route at every point along the way to the destination. But with the zip code, all these points need to do is examine a short numerical field to make the routing decision, and this system also allows the network to bundle together all the letters going to the same zip code. Just as this concept makes the post office faster and more streamlined, it can do the same for networks, and methods quite similar to this are in use today.

These methods of packet switching have received endless debate within the telecommunications research and engineering community, and there are steadfast proponents and opponents of each method, because each has some advantages and disadvantages. The Internet uses a connectionless approach overall, but here and there some connection-oriented thinking has started to creep into the IP camps to help solve some issues associated with voice and other delay-sensitive services.

With any of these schemes, some of the basic issues mentioned for circuit switching appear as well. Namely, there will be delay as the packets traverse the network. However, for either type of packet technology, the delay will be somewhat different from circuit switching, since the delay is variable. The reason for this is simple. Packet switches operate basically as queuing devices. A packet arrives, its header is examined for the destination or route, and the packet is then forwarded to an output headed in the right direction. If there are other packets waiting to be transmitted on the same output, then the new packet will have to wait its turn. The number of packets ahead of it depends on the traffic in the network coming from other sources and headed for other destinations. Since there is no way to predict the volume of traffic that will occur at any given point in time, it is impossible to predict with any certainty the delay any given packet will incur. It is, however, possible to estimate average delay and to accommodate delay up to some particular maximum. However, if the delay exceeds even this value, the usefulness of the connection will be degraded.

As mentioned previously, packet networks also experience congestion when more traffic is submitted than can be routed and delivered by the network. In this case, a switch will discard packets arriving at its inputs because there is no space left to store them for transmission. In this circumstance, it is necessary for higher level protocols at the sender and receiver to resolve this problem by either re-sending the packet, ignoring the loss, substituting one in its place, terminating the application, or taking whatever step is most appropriate. Most data applications take the action of re-sending the information, and elaborate protocols such as Transaction Control Protocol (TCP) exist, which number each packet so the receiver can tell if one is missing and which use acknowledgements and timers to detect when something is amiss. This leads to some necessary functions at both the transmitter and the receiver, since packets will have to be saved by the sender until it is certain that the receiver has received it. In connectionless packet networks, such as the Internet, the packets may not be delivered in order. It is up to the higher layers of protocol to resolve this issue. Again, the packets will be numbered by the transmitter and placed in sequence at the receiver.

However, voice applications do not have the luxury of re-sending the information, because it will arrive too late to be of any use. As a result, the receiver will have to do its best with whatever packets do arrive. In some systems, it will be best to substitute silence for the missing packet. In others, it may be possible to generate an estimate of the information that was in the packet by examining the packets that preceded and followed the missing packet. Thus, congestion in packet switches leads to degradation of service, a quite different situation than in circuit switches, where established calls are unaffected.

If the packet network is used in conjunction with existing telephones, there will have to be conversions between the two-wire analog telephone and the two-way packet system. This will introduce circuits that have the possibility of generating reflections. Thus, we will also have echoes to deal with in our packet network—unless, of course, we choose not to use existing analog telephones, in which case echoes would not be a problem for our service. This decision will have tremendous impact on the market we attempt to serve and will be considered more deeply later.

Many of the fundamental aspects of voice are excellent matches to packet technology. Speech naturally occurs in bursts. As described earlier, there are silent intervals when a person is not speaking and there are pauses during speech. These bursts can readily be turned into packets for end-to-end transport. Speech compression technology is also a ready match to packet systems, since most compression schemes invariably take a block of speech and reduce it. These processed blocks make very natural packets, and G.723.1 as well as G.729 operate in exactly this manner.

So, the major issue for packet networks and voice services is one of delay and delay variation. We must plan the packet network in a way that minimizes delay and makes it as bounded and deterministic as possible under normal operation. In short, we would like for the packet network to emulate a circuit network for a portion of its traffic. And, as mentioned previously, we shall also have to deal with echo control issues. In many ways, this is no different than the circuit-switched network; however, the variability of these delays and the loss of packets must be carefully controlled and dealt with if an acceptable service is to be provided. And unlike the circuit-switched network, the delay and loss of packets within a connection will increase as the network load is increased. So, a careful balance must be struck between the dimensioning of the network, the traffic load that is offered, and the end equipment that must accommodate variability in the reliability of the connection. In Figure 2–9, packet transport is contrasted with circuit switching. Instead of resembling a package of soda straws, packet transport gives each user the full capacity of the transport media, but for short periods of time. This method has tremendous advantages for transporting data information, since each block can be sent at the highest possible rate. By breaking large blocks of information into segments, other information can be interleaved, allowing all users to share in the capacity of the media.

But the most appealing aspects of packet switching are its low cost, its ability to simultaneously handle data and other media for communications, and the ability to rapidly deploy new features and capabilities. These factors make its adoption inevitable, but some care must be taken to avoid adding expenses and technologies to the network that will make it unattractive for data. This might happen if, for example, the cost of the network drove up the price of providing basic "bare bones" data services. We must never forget that one reason today's data services are inexpensive is because of the reduced requirements in transporting data as compared to voice. Once these services are integrated, it also seems inevitable that the price of data service will rise as operators amortize costs over all services provided. If the introduction of voice services over the data network demands a higher overall quality of service, data users may find themselves paying for a better network than they need.

Other Telephony Service Impairments

There are additional impairments associated with telephony service that apply to any form of network, whether it be circuit or packet switched. These include:

- **Unavailability** – The user attempts to make a call, but the network does not respond. This would be quite serious in an emergency situation, possibly resulting in loss of life or property.
- **Dial-tone delay** – The user picks up the phone and does not immediately receive dial tone. Users who have to wait any appreciable amount of time for dial tone will quickly become annoyed with the service, since they will wonder if the network has become unreliable or unavailable.
- **Cut-through delay** – The user dials the called party phone number but does not hear ring-back within a reasonable time. Again, the user who must wait may assume that the call did not go through and may abandon the call.
- **Blocking probability** – The user completes dialing the called party phone number but receives a fast-busy tone, indicating that the call did not go through. This has wasted the time of the user, who will have to redial the call. If this happens frequently, the user will consider the carrier service unacceptable.
- **Disrupted calls** – The call is disrupted due to poor transmission quality or because the parties are completely disconnected. Occasional faults in the network can cause this to occur, but it should not be frequent, or the carrier will receive a high number of complaints.
- **Poor speech quality** – If the transmission path alters or discards information from the actual channel of communication, the users may notice the degradation.

Each of these impairments, and others, can cause unacceptable service for the user and could result in increased expenses for the network operator. As such, the network operator would like to avoid these problems. This is best accomplished by careful surveillance of the network's operation, use of a fault-tolerant network, quick repair of any problems, and good forecasting of network resource needs. As we shall see later, this is more easily said than done, and for packet networks, solutions to some of these problems are still under development. In any case, avoiding these problems will also cause expenses for the network operator, because either more resources or a higher quality resource is needed for both the network equipment and the technicians maintaining it.

Summary

Speech has definite requirements for transport that are independent of the network offering the service. Transport of an adequate portion of the frequency spectrum is necessary to achieve an acceptable level of service. Delay and delay variation are key problems for users of voice services, and there are several sources of delay, including the scheme for digitizing the speech as well as the end-to-end distances involved in a connection. Because of end-to-end delay, any reflection of the speech at the distant ends of a connection will result in echoes that will annoy the talker, the listener, or both. Echoes must be controlled if users are to have an acceptable experience with the service.

The key advantages of circuit-switched networks are their simplicity, their fixed delay, their well-understood operating rules, and the fact that these problems have long been solved for the circuit-switched approach to telephony. Circuit switching is wasteful of bandwidth because users do not continuously utilize connections. Also, circuit switching is a poor match to data services because of its fixed bandwidth.

In concept, packet switching is a better match to the voice traffic because it tends to naturally occur in bursts. However, packet switching has inherently longer delays, which can lead to problems for telephony. Further, packet networks will discard packets when congestion levels are reached, which will disrupt the speech being transported. Engineering plans and rules for network operation are needed to provide a good telephony service.

Besides addressing these issues, a successful service must meet other requirements if it is to be widely accepted. These include continuous availability of the service, the speedy completion of calls, infrequent unexpected disconnects, and other such matters that will influence the customer of the service. Network operators must carefully monitor these sorts of malfunctions in their network and make rapid corrections to avoid complaints. Forecasting demands placed on the network when new markets are entered or special promotions are offered are essential to avoiding problems.

These issues are key to the successful deployment and operation of any network, whether it utilizes circuit-based or packet-based transport. The successful transport of voice over circuit-switched networks is well understood and has complete solutions to these issues. Packet systems, on the other hand, are relatively new, and solutions to these problems have not completely been formulated. Even in cases where solutions do appear to be available, they do not have the long history of use and experience that proves their validity. Nevertheless, the advantages of packet systems are clear, even for voice services, and are the inevitable choice for any network operator wishing to approach both telephony and data services.

References

Brady, P. T. "A Technique for Investigating On-Off Patterns of Speech," *Bell System Technical Journal,* vol. 44, Jan. 1965.

Brady, P. T. "A Model for Generating On-Off Speech Patterns in Two-Way Conversations," *Bell System Technical Journal,* vol. 48, Jan. 1968.

Brady, P. T. "A Statistical Analysis of On-Off Patterns in 16 Conversations," *Bell System Technical Journal,* vol. 47, Jan. 1968.

Collins, Daniel. *Carrier Grade Voice over IP,* McGraw-Hill, 2000.

Hersent, O., D. Gurle, and J. Petit, *IP Telephony,* Addison Wesley, 2000.

Norwine, A. C., and O. J. Murphy. "Characteristic Time Intervals in Telephone Conversation," *Bell System Technical Journal,* vol. 17, Apr. 1938.

Telcordia Technologies, Inc., *Notes on the Networks,* 5th ed., 2000.

Zemlin, Willard R. *Speech and Hearing Science: Anatomy and Physiology,* 4th ed., Allyn and Bacon, 1997.

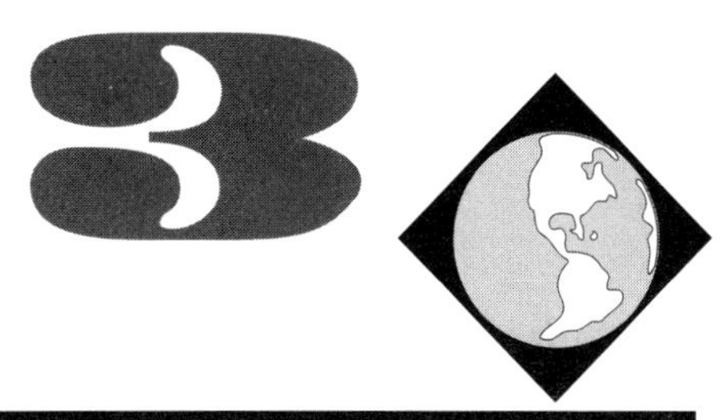

THE OLD TELEPHONY

When the Bell System dominated the U.S. voice telephony industry, there was a logical technical design for the network that focused primarily on achieving very high reliability, excellent service quality, and universal service availability. Most countries around the world tended to adopt this design because it was a very logical way to organize a network for voice services and because the United States was a major source—some would say the dominant source—of research in this area. This, coupled with the known excellence of the Bell System and its services, made the U.S. network architecture and technology the primary model by which all carriers planned their networks and organized their businesses. The Bell System worked, and it worked well. As a consequence, much of the content of this chapter applies to networks all around the world. The Bell System service is widely known as POTS, which stands for Plain Old Telephone Service, and it represents the "old telephony" yardstick by which any new telephony will be measured.

The old Bell System's business model was built on a century of regulation. To be sure, there were changes introduced all through the lifetime of the Bell System, but at its core was a regulated monopoly receiving a guaranteed rate of return. The old Bell System had to justify every rate increase to its federal, state, and local regulatory bodies. Nevertheless, it was able to provide solid blue-chip values to the investment community because of its enormous size, the certain knowledge that it would stay in business, and its ability to guarantee a profit from quarter to quarter. It also ensured lifetime employment for its staff. The Bell System was primarily concerned with providing a complete high-quality solution that could be used in any location at a reasonable cost. Bell Labs engineers worked to achieve the lowest cost that did not compromise the quality and performance of the system. In addition, new apparatus deployed generally had a long lifetime, resulting in lengthy depreciation schedules, and could not be rapidly replaced with more modern systems. This led to slow, careful deployments of new technology and methods that assured high quality and universal service.

Today, there is little to be seen of the old Bell System business model, which has rapidly disappeared due to many factors and pressures in today's regulatory and business climate. But the network architecture and technology has been much slower to evaporate for many reasons. The massive capital investment made by carriers in their network and operating infrastructures, particularly in local loops and local exchange switches, cannot be quickly replaced by them. As long as their business is successful, they are satisfied to make incremental improvements in their networks and to expand them as needed. Most of the large carriers' focus since the major deregulation of 1984 has been to reduce operating costs through higher degrees of automation. This has been a major tool in maintaining operating margins and profitability for shareholders when faced with competition.

Today's public switched voice network consists of several disparate networks operated by different carriers. The car-

riers have business arrangements between themselves and their customers that are the result of many years of regulation and business practice. Carriers subject to various federal and local regulatory bodies have, in some cases, been prohibited from using certain technologies and architectures due to legal decisions in the court system. They have also been prohibited from offering some specific services to their customers and from various pricing strategies. But this has had little impact on the technology or the network architecture. Instead, the existing technology and network architecture has forced regulatory bodies and carriers to simply reorganize around the existing network. It is for this reason that we have long-distance carriers and local carriers—it is an obvious separation of the architecture of 1984, when the basic business and regulatory decisions were made. So, a key point to remember when trying to understand both today's network and its possible future evolution is that the network is what it is because of its history and original design objectives. Today, it is proper to reconsider whether those same design objectives are appropriate in today's business and social environment. But we should not be naïve in forecasting how quickly these enormous investments can be displaced by a competitor nor how slowly incumbents saddled with these enormous assets will move to upgrade them.

The Overall Network

Figure 3–1 shows the key components of today's modern Public Switched Telephone Network (PSTN). The PSTN in the United States consists of Local Exchange Carriers (LEC) who provide service in local areas, designated as Local Access and Transport Area (LATA), and Interexchange Carriers (IXC) who provide services between LATAs. It is intended that through deregulation, competition will be introduced in both these areas. However, at present, the primary competition with incumbent LECs for voice services is in the business market. IXCs are a different matter, however, and there are numerous competing carriers for all long-distance services.

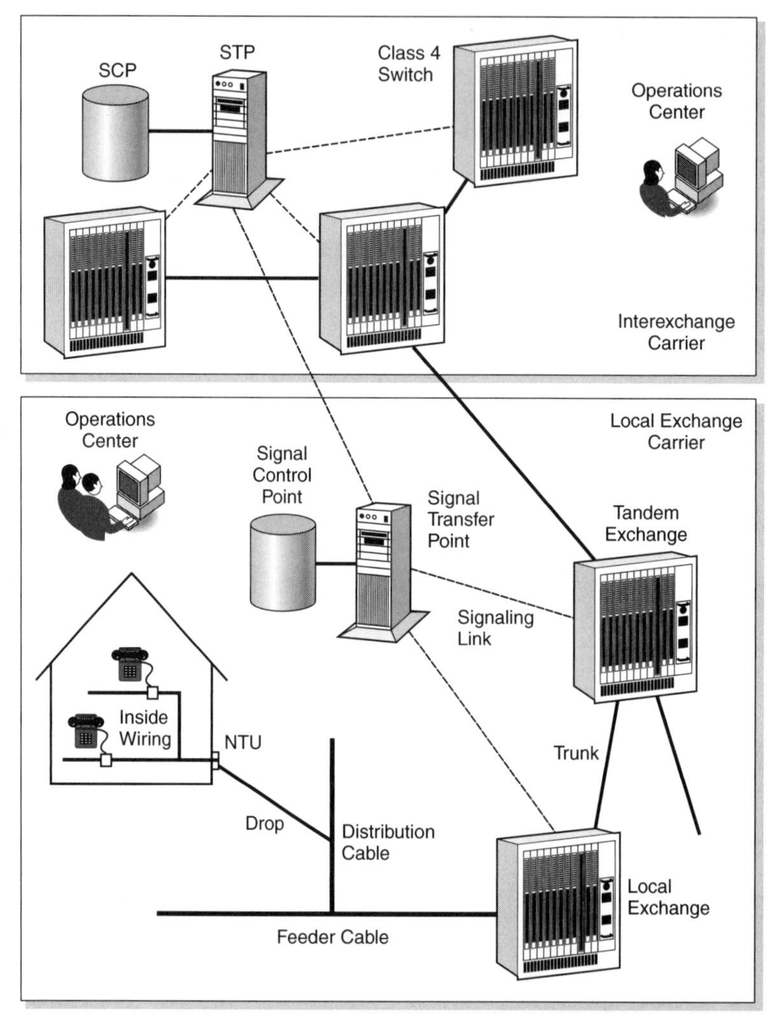

FIGURE 3–1 *PSTN components.*

The major parts of the LEC network are:

- The telephone that resides at the customer's location.
- The local exchange that provides service to the telephone and switches calls to their proper destinations.

- The local loop that connects the telephone to the local exchange.
- The interoffice network that provides connections between local exchanges.
- Tandem exchanges that provide a switching point for calls between local exchanges that are not directly connected or that have fully utilized all direct connections.
- The SS7 (Signaling System 7) network made up of Signal Transfer Points (STP) and Service Control Points (SCP) that provide the control of the network and its services.
- Operations centers where the health of the network can be monitored and technicians dispatched to repair faulty equipment, bills can be rendered, new orders can be taken, and all the other necessary functions for maintaining both the network and the customer can be managed.

The IXC network consists of:

- Switching centers arranged according to the service demands placed upon the IXC, sometimes in a hierarchical system.
- Interoffice facilities that interconnect the switching centers and connect to the LEC network.
- Operations centers similar to those of the LEC.

The goal of this chapter is to explain each of these components in greater detail, beginning with that most humble of all systems, the telephone.

The Telephone

This familiar instrument embodies more functions than is obvious to the casual user. Figure 3–2 shows the major components of the telephone. These include the transmitter, receiver, handset, hybrid, touch-tone generator, hook-switch,[1] and ringer. To operate, the telephone requires a single pair of wires, which must reach from the telephone to the switching center where service is provided. The wires in this pair are referred to as *tip* and *ring,* a throwback to the days of cords and jacks. The basic functions of the telephone exist much as they did over 100 years ago. New technology has improved it, and it has a slick modern appearance, but the fundamentals are much the same.

1. Some readers may know this item as the switch-hook. Historically, this switch was associated with the hook on early telephones (those wall-mounted wooden boxes now seen only in museums) on which the receiver was hung. Thus, it was known (I surmise) as the "hook's switch" or "hook-switch." How these terms became reversed is a matter for other scholars, but I shall use the term hook-switch.

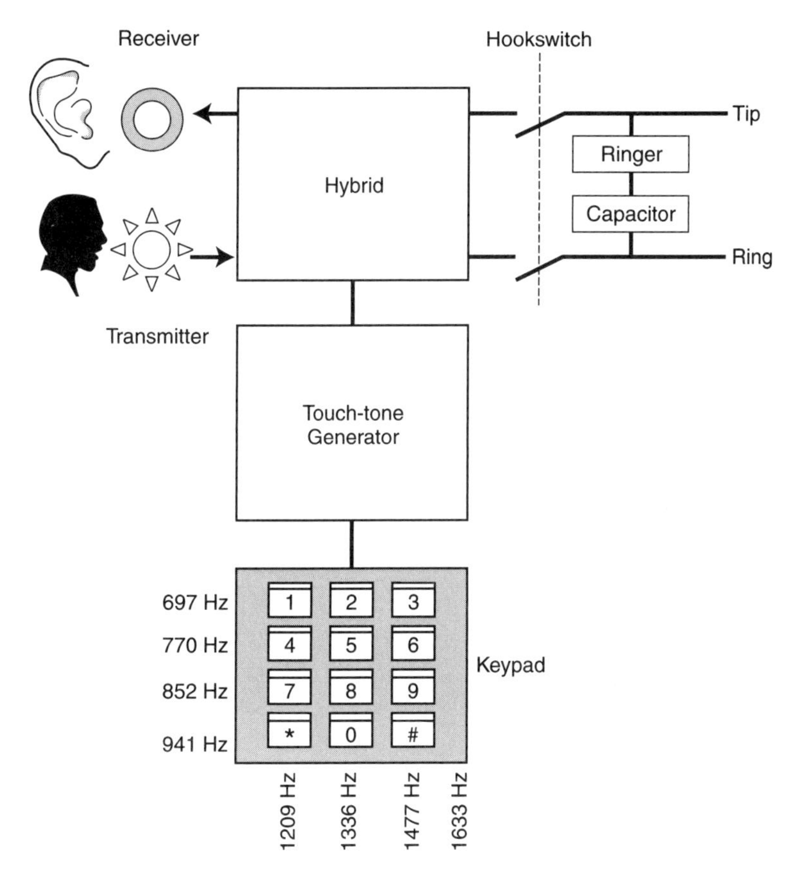

FIGURE 3–2 *Telephone functional diagram.*

When the handset is laid in the cradle of the telephone, the hook-switch operates so that only the ringer is connected to the wire pair. To ring the phone, the network equipment at the far end of the customer's wires simply places a low frequency AC voltage across the wire pair. This ringing current is typically in the range of 90 volts alternating current at 20 Hz and is pulsed on for one second and off for three seconds. As can be seen in the diagram, the ringer has a series capacitor that prevents the flow of DC current.

The network equipment applies the ringing current through a circuit that superimposes DC current at 48 volts and can detect the flow of DC current. Figure 3–3 shows a simplified version of a network interface. When the user lifts the handset from its cradle, the hook-switch changes positions, causing the hybrid to be connected to the wire pair. The actions of the hook-switch are referred to as supervisory signals; on-hook means the user is not using the phone, and off-hook means the user is present at the phone. At the network, on-hook is signified by the fact that DC current is not flowing to the phone, while off-hook has a closed DC loop of approximately 600 ohms, allowing a DC current to flow.

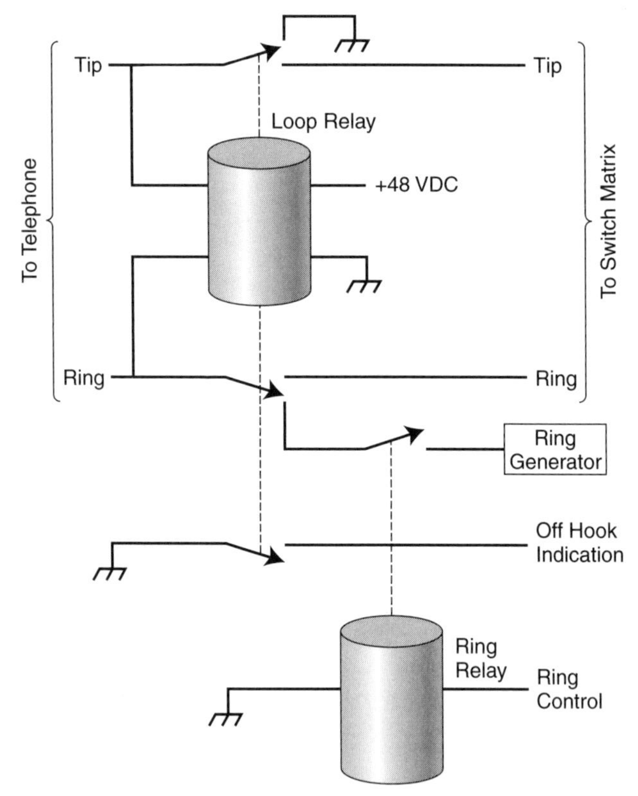

FIGURE 3–3 *Network interface.*

The hybrid serves two purposes. First, the hybrid presents a 600-ohm DC circuit to the wire pair so the network equipment can detect that the user has lifted the phone. Should this be in response to an incoming call, the network

will cause the user to be connected to the calling party. Should this be the origination of a new call, the network will provide dial tone to the caller. Second, the hybrid causes the transmitter into which the user will talk, the receiver at which the user will listen, and the touch-tone generator that is used to indicate phone numbers to all be combined in appropriate levels on the wire pair.

The hybrid cancels most of the transmitter's power in the path to the receiver so as to minimize echo. Because signals at this point have extremely low delays, this is the location for controlling side-tone, which has essentially zero delay. A very small amount of side-tone is created directly in the handset that houses the transmitter and receiver because of sound transmitted inside the housing. In a similar manner, a small amount of the sound generated by the receiver makes its way to the transmitter and appears as an echo; however, it will be heavily attenuated. The hybrid couples as much of the transmitter's energy to the wire pair as possible, and it couples as much of the signal on the wire pair to the receiver. In doing so, it cancels most of the transmitter's component that would otherwise reach the receiver, leaving only a trace of side-tone. Finally, it couples the touch-tone generator's energy to the wire pair while allowing only a little side-tone. Levels of all the signals have been standardized for the telephone.

The touch-tone generator creates a dual-tone signal wherein two tones of different frequencies are combined to represent a number. The two tones are selected from each of four high frequency tones and four low frequency tones. Using a pair of tones, one from each group, allows easier decoding at the network. In all, this represents 16 possible combinations of tones; however, a normal telephone uses only 12 of them to represent the digits 0 through 9 and two special codes, *' and #. This scheme is called Dual Tone Multiple Frequency (DTMF). In lieu of the touch-tone generator, older phones utilized a rotary dial to generate on-off pulses in the DC voltage to signal the numbers. These phones are becoming rare today, but they can still be found in some locations.

Later, when we consider a new means for providing telephony, the telephone will be a special-interest item. On the one hand, it is an antique, and if we were starting completely from scratch today, very different devices could be designed to interface with the user. We could make a superior phone that would still look and operate the same from the user's perspective but would use modern schemes for conveying the signals and controls. Or we could build a sophisticated new phone that would look and operate completely differently. On the other hand, there are several billion telephones installed and operating around the world today. It would be very limiting in a business plan to ignore these and build a new telephony network that could not use or interface with these phones. If our new service cannot work with the existing base of telephones, we must either be satisfied with a niche market or accept a very slow migration to the new instruments. This will be an important consideration in any business plan for a new telephony service.

The Local Loop and Inside Wiring

For every customer, there is a pair of physical wires reaching from the telephone to the local exchange or to an intermediate point where electronics can be located. The local loop is intended to carry the analog signals originated by the telephone. The loop length depends very much on population density but can be quite long. In the 1983 Bell Operating Company Loop Survey, it was found that 65% of all loops surveyed were 12 kft or less, 90% were 18 kft or less, and that some loops were as long as 42 kft. Although there is an increasing amount of fiber being used as part of the local loop, most of this facility consists of large cables made of copper wire. This is a physically large and financially expensive asset that the local carrier has created over many decades of operation. These facilities have a very long lifetime and, correspondingly, a long depreciation schedule.

The local loop begins inside the residence or business location with inside wiring. In most installations, the inside wiring consists of a 2-pair, 4-pair or 26-pair cable that runs around the user's home or offices. Each individual telephone in the location can be placed on an individual circuit consisting of one pair of wires, or several telephones can be placed in parallel on the same wire pair. An example of this inside wiring scheme is shown in Figure 3–4. The inside wiring terminates on an element called the Network Termination Unit (NTU) that is the official demarcation point between the network and the customer. All wiring and equipment that is inside the customer's facility belongs to the customer and, in the United States, is the responsibility of the customer. Everything from the NTU outward towards the network is the property and responsibility of the carrier. In business locations, there may be many sets of cables running around inside the business location and also a small switching system known as a key system that allows the customer to make calls inside the building. This will be discussed later in this section, after the basics of switching have been explained.

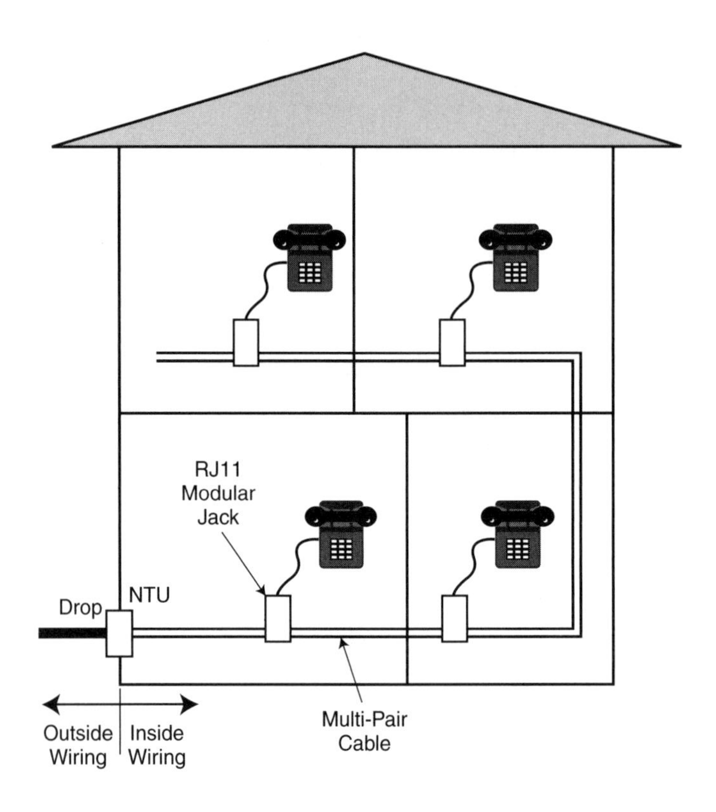

FIGURE 3–4 *Inside wiring.*

The section of wiring that reaches from the NTU to the telephone pole or pedestal is known as the *drop*. Along the street in residential neighborhoods or business locations, there is a *feeder* cable containing a large number of wire pairs. This cable winds past buildings in a way that makes it as easy as possible for each building to connect to it at various access points along the cable. Figure 3–5 shows an example of this for a neighborhood. This is analogous to the path that inside wiring takes inside a building. As the cable winds its way down the street, additional distribution cables will be tapped onto the various wire pairs in the main cable so as to reach sidestreets and buildings off the main line. These are called *bridge taps*. As a result, a single wire pair in the original main cable may be extended several times down sidestreets in a way that there are various stubs in parallel with it. The basic strategy of the local carrier is to have many wires available in the serving area that can be attached to at multiple points. This gives the greatest flexibility to the use of this physical asset, the outside wiring, because it allows the drops to be connected from the customer to the cable plant at many different points. This is important, since the customer and the service provider will want to activate and deactivate service rapidly. The time required to install a new cable is far too long, so customer locations typically have drops attached and left in place even when the customer discontinues service.

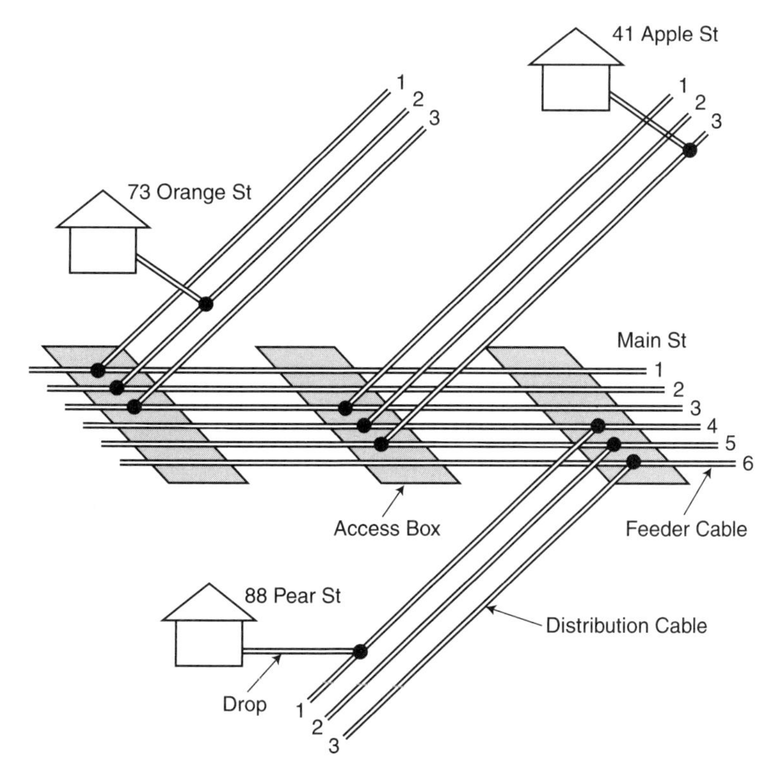

FIGURE 3–5 *Outside plant cabling.*

A few special conditions of the outside plant and inside wiring deserve extra consideration. First of all, each wiring element utilizes different gauge wires. Typically, inside wiring is 26 gauge, while the main cable is 22, 24, or 26 gauge.

This may not seem important, but the result is that each wire pair has slightly different characteristics which, when connected to each other, cause the signals to be reflected back and forth between the ends. The result of these reflections is that some frequencies being transmitted along the wires will be attenuated differently than other frequencies. For voice services, these differences are not noticeable because the cable plant has been engineered to provide adequate performance. But when high-speed digital signals are transmitted, these differences distort the digital signals and cause difficulty in extracting the signal at the receiver. Special signal processing techniques are required to circumvent these problems. Furthermore, when a transmitted digital pulse reaches the ends of the "stubs," shown in Figure 3–6, reflections are generated that travel up and down the wire pair. These can confuse the receiving electronics. Again, sophisticated signal processing methods can improve the receiver.

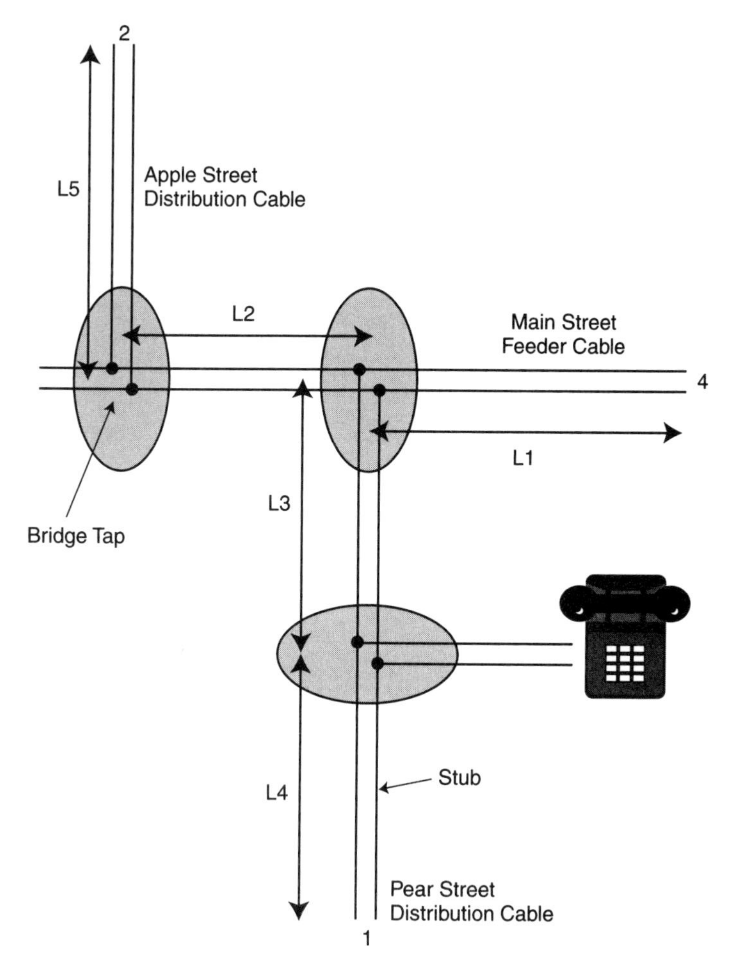

FIGURE 3–6 *Bridge taps and stubs.*

A receiver can compensate for all these impairments except for the notorious loading coil. In installations that have exceptionally long cables greater than 18 kft, it was found that the audio quality deteriorated to a point that even voice conversations were affected due to high frequency attenuation. As a result, the loading coil was introduced to boost the performance of the loop by placing a small coil in between two sections of the cable. This coil adds additional attenuation to the lower frequencies, thus bringing the loop back to a more balanced condition with respect to frequency response, albeit with high attenuation. These coils do not allow the transmission of high-speed digital signals at all and must be removed if the loop is to be used in this way.

Interoffice Facilities and Fiber Optics

Besides the wiring connecting users to their local exchange, there is cabling interconnecting the local exchanges. Often, these can be quite distant, and in the long-distance network, city-to-city distance will approach several hundred miles. But even within a municipal area, these distances can be considerable, ranging from a few miles up to several tens of miles.

As the distance between endpoints increases, copper cables have distinct disadvantages that limit their usefulness in the interoffice network. As their length increases, so do the impairments such as cross-talk, attenuation, high-frequency loss, and noise. To deal with these problems, it is necessary to place repeaters or amplifiers at points along the route of the cable to regenerate the signals. These additional access points to the cable represent locations where moisture can enter the cable, further degrading its performance, and the electronics at these sites require power and maintenance. These difficulties create added expense for the operator and lower quality for users.

Long ago, it was recognized that many of these problems could be eliminated if digital transport is utilized. Once the user's voice has been converted from analog to digital, it is only necessary to discern the difference between a 1 and a 0 at the receiver to reconstruct the original signal. If noise or attenuation impair the signal, as long as the receiver can discern these two values, it can reproduce the original speech, free of all the impairments. As a consequence, virtually the entire interoffice network has been digital for many decades. However, digital transport utilizes the higher frequency portions of the cable's bandwidth that receives considerable attenuation, requiring repeaters to regenerate the digital pulses. Thus, the use of digital transport will improve the quality of the connections but will still require many repeater sites with their incumbent cost. In most networks, repeaters were required every few miles or so to regenerate the signals.

A further benefit of digital transport in the interoffice network is that when extra capacity is needed, the electronics can be modified to operate at higher speeds, allowing the transport of more and more channels. This is known as time-division multiplexing, and it is a powerful tool in expanding networks because it allows the operator to avoid the extremely expensive construction programs to place additional cables on overhead poles or beneath the ground. Besides the expense, such programs require many years to complete. Thus, such additions must be planned years in advance and cannot be used to respond to quick changes in demand for service.

Fiber optic cable simply carries the digital signals as pulses of light along a tiny strand of glass. By making the glass extremely pure, there is very little attenuation of the light pulses as they travel along the cable. Thus, fiber optic cables can reach greater distances without the use of repeaters. An example fiber optic system is shown in Figure 3–7. This creates savings in operating expense, since the electronics and their maintenance at all the former repeater points can be eliminated. Furthermore, the fiber optic cable is less subject to impairments such as crosstalk, noise, moisture, and electromagnetic disturbances.

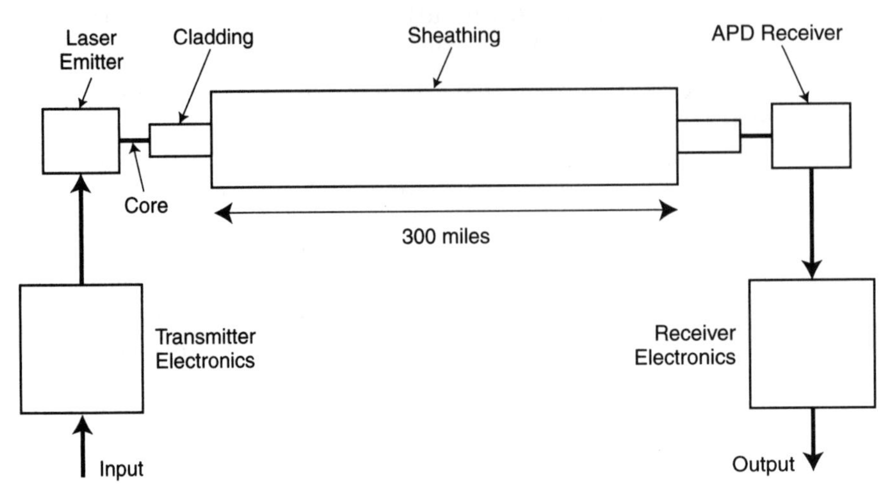

FIGURE 3–7 *Fiber optic system.*

As a result, fiber optics has come to dominate the longer distances between local exchanges, and it has even penetrated parts of the local loop. The fiber cable has two main parts: an outside protective jacket and the interior fiber optics. There is an armored jacket that protects the fibers inside from damage. Normally, there are multiple fibers inside this jacket, and the number varies quite widely, ranging from as low as 12 or so up to several hundred fibers. Each fiber has a core of very transparent glass that is surrounded by a second type of glass known as the cladding. By design, the index of refraction of the cladding is different from that of the core so that all light that is coupled into the cable is completely reflected by the interface created by these two differing glasses.

SONET Transmission Systems

The transmission system of choice used on fiber optics today is the Synchronous Optical Network, or SONET. Internationally, this system is known as the Synchronous Digital Hierarchy (SDH). The two are largely the same, although some small differences exist between them, primarily regarding the lower level multiplexing structure and operations control. SONET allows for the easy aggregation or multiplexing of lower speed transmission circuits into a single circuit operating at a higher speed. Figure 3–8 shows a SONET multiplexing device, a fiber optic media, and a demultiplexing device, as well as other key parameters. At either end of the media are the various lower speed transmission channels, called tributaries, that are to be aggregated and carried through the multiplexing device, transported through the fiber optic media, and then demultiplexed back into the original channels. There is an operations interface to the system (or systems) that is used for provisioning various features of the system as well as for monitoring performance, alarms, and other indications. Should one end or the other be located remotely, the remote operations interface can be accessed from the other end system interface. This allows flexible deployments of SONET and easy operations.

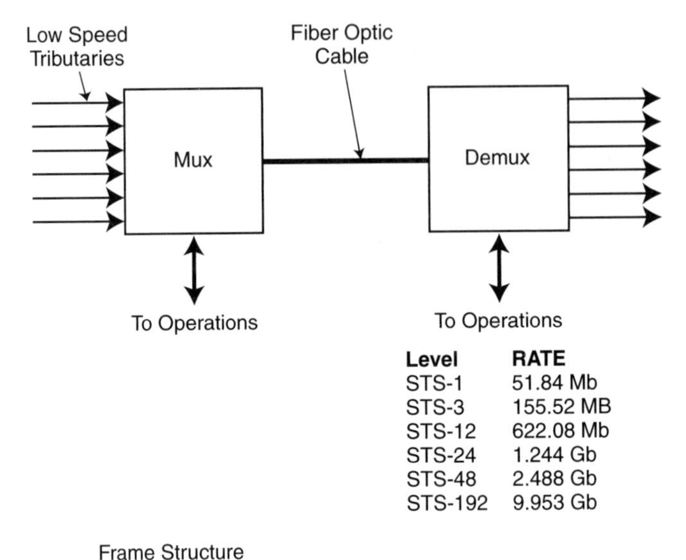

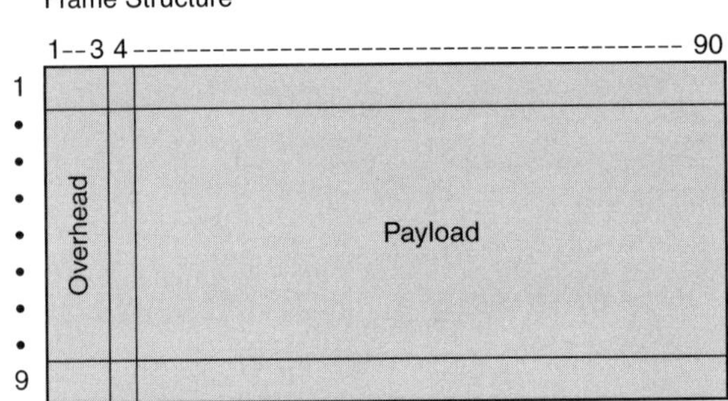

FIGURE 3–8 SONET.

Like all transmission systems, information to be transported by SONET is organized in a pattern containing the tributaries that are interleaved with certain specific patterns. These patterns are used to synchronize the endpoints and are called a framing pattern, while the overall pattern containing both the framing and the tributary information is called a frame. Figure 3–8 shows the basic SONET building-block frame structure as a two-dimensional pattern with nine rows and 90 columns of 8-bit bytes. The frame structure shown is that of the basic STS-1 building block signal at 51.84 Mbps. Higher level signals are simple byte interleaves of this basic signal. The leftmost columns are called the transport overhead and consist of section overhead and line overhead and are used for controlling synchronization and multiplexing functions. The remaining columns comprise the path overhead and synchronous payload that is used to carry information through the system. In actual transmission, these bytes are transmitted from left to right and top to bottom. The bytes are sent least significant bit first. Thus, the overheads are interleaved with the payload information.

Section overhead provides for frame synchronization between the transmitter and receiver present at the ends of the optical media. This is accomplished by repeating a specific pattern that can be recognized at the receiver and will not occur so deterministically within the payload. Section overhead also provides the ability to monitor the availability and performance of the underlying fiber optic media and its lasers and receivers. Section overhead also includes a data communications channel that is used between operations systems at either end of the media. These operations systems are used to provision various aspects of the SONET system and to report failures of the end equipment of the fiber optic media.

Line overhead provides for performance monitoring of the individual multiplexed tributaries for errors. It also provides a channel for communications similar to that contained in the section overhead but which is carried end to end. There is a pointer that indicates the first byte of the synchronous payload. There is a protection switching indication that indicates the use of an alternate fiber optic media, should one be present. Line overhead includes alarm indications, which activate in the case of equipment failures, and a far-end receive failure indication that notifies the far-end system that its transmitter is not being received.

Path overhead is carried as part of the overall payload from end to end. It includes a pointer to the first byte of the individual tributary channel, a status indication to show if it is in or out of service, and a field for monitoring the performance of the individual tributary. In SONET, it is possible for the payload to be organized as the interleaving of lower speed tributaries or as a concatenated payload that operates as a single high-speed path. In the former case, SONET works well for transporting either aggregated 64 Kbps voice channels or single high-speed data information. This flexibility has proven to be a key feature of SONET that is being utilized by carriers entering the high-speed data market.

The use of pointers in SONET deserves some special mention. In earlier transmission systems, information being multiplexed was assigned specific positions within the transport frame structure. The first bit of a tributary was assumed to be located at that specific position. But the first bit of a tributary will arrive at some arbitrary time due to propagation and other forms of delay. As a result, it was necessary in these systems to first synchronize with the tributary and locate the beginning of its frame. Then, it was necessary to store the frame in a buffer that could be read and placed in the outgoing transport frame at the proper time. In this way, the tributary would be properly aligned. Naturally, this operation adds delay and complexity in the form of additional hardware to the transport system. And this function had to be provided for every tributary being multiplexed.

But with SONET, the tributary can be placed in the outgoing frame without buffering or otherwise synchronizing the tributary with the transport system. By including a pointer in the line overhead, the synchronous payload can start in any position within the frame. And by including a pointer in the path overhead associated with each tributary, that tributary can be interleaved anywhere within the payload. This reduces the multiplexing delay and simplifies the SONET products. The pointer concept, which has deep roots in software and computer programming, has revolutionized transmission systems engineering.

A second important concept in SONET is that of the concatenated payload. This simply means that the entire payload is available as a block to carry information. The line

overhead pointer can still be utilized to indicate the starting point of the payload within the frame, but the payload can be organized in any manner desired and does not have to be an interleaved set of tributaries. This capability allows most of the capacity of the fiber optic media to be used for carrying data. The table contained in Figure 3–8 shows the capacity of the various SONET interface rates. When used in this manner, the SONET overheads continue to allow the operator to monitor the health of the equipment, the fiber optic media, and the overall condition of the transmission system. This is an important capability, since it allows SONET to be used for carrying data or other services that may not be of a continuous circuit nature, especially information organized as packets.

Many different types of products and applications can be constructed from the basic SONET concept. The basic multiplex/demultiplex explained above, cross-connect systems, and add/drop multiplexing systems are but three of the SONET family of systems that can be built. These are shown in Figure 3–9.

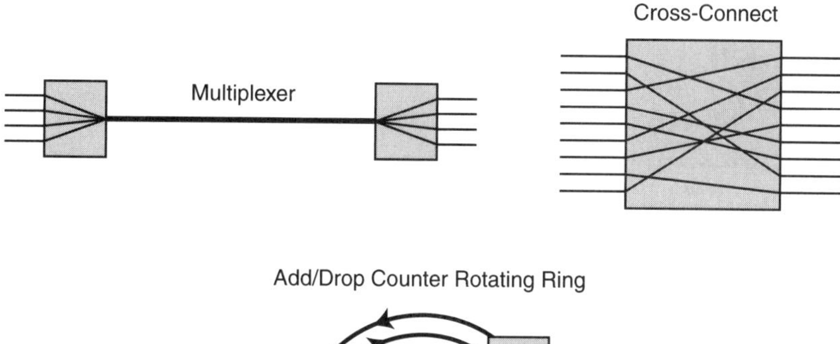

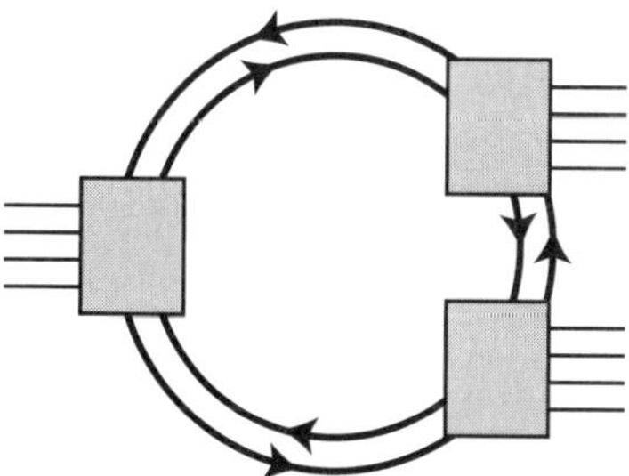

FIGURE 3–9 SONET systems.

Cross-connect systems simply allow the rearrangement of circuits within tributaries and between tributaries. This is a primitive form of circuit switching; however, these connections are usually established on a semipermanent basis. Changes to the cross-connect mapping are usually as a result of adding new equipment or a new route, or to some change in network demand. Cross-connect systems are an important element of any circuit network for managing capacity between the various switches and other network equipment.

Add/drop multiplexing systems are ordinarily used in ring architectures that allow the system to survive any single fiber cut by simply reconfiguring the direction in which information is being sent. Rings of this type are becoming widely deployed in metropolitan areas to reach digital loop carrier systems and to provide high-speed transport directly to large customers. Ring configuration algorithms are available, which can rearrange the system in a few milliseconds, thus providing very high availability and reliability. Such systems not only provide good service to users, they also allow the operator to defer repairs until such time as is convenient for the technicians, a capability that reduces operation cost.

SONET deployment today has reached enormous proportions. At this time, virtually the entire interoffice facilities consist of fiber optic media and SONET systems. One reason for this is that the original purpose of SONET was to provide a fiber optic interconnection standard to use between LECs and IXCs. This interface was standardized in U.S. standards committee T1 and the international standards group ITU. A predecessor to SONET that was standardized but never deployed was SYNTRAN.[2] With the availability of an international standard and the business pressures to rapidly interconnect LECs with an ever-increasing number of IXCs, the

2. SYNTRAN stands for Synchronous Transmission and embodied most of the final standardized concepts of SONET.

SONET interface has been widely deployed. SONET has proven popular within the networks as well, mainly due to the desire to have a single form of transmission system and media within a carrier's network. This reduces costs, inventory requirements, and technical skills needed to maintain and operate the equipment. Hence, the broad deployment of SONET for loop access and other interconnection requirements has occurred. SONET systems operating at 51.84 Mbps, 155.52 Mbps, 622.08 Mbps, 2.488 Gbps, and 9.95 Gbps are in daily operation.

Due to its ubiquity and its ability to move to higher and higher transmission rates, SONET is a key asset for operators. SONET is easy to operate and, like the local loop, has well-established procedures and a force of technicians. Because it can be used to transport either 64 Kbps voice channels or concatenated high-speed channels, data can be effectively transported over SONET systems. IEEE has defined a method for transporting Gigabit Ethernet over SONET. However, newer optical networking approaches based on wave division methods are moving away from reusing SONET concepts.

The Local Exchange

Figure 3–10 shows a simplified block diagram of a local exchange, also called a central office, an end office, or a Class 5 switch. There are several parts, including Line Termination Units (LTU), Trunk Termination Units (TTU), the switch fabric, the call processor, and the operations processor. The local exchange terminates the user's local loop and is frequently the first system the user utilizes in making a call. The local exchange provides dial tone, collects and analyzes dialed digits, rings the phone for incoming calls, and performs many other services, such as three-way-calling and call forwarding. The user's loop is used to carry signaling information about the call as well as the user's voice. All of these signals are represented as analog signals on the user's loop and the outside cable plant, but are expressed as digital messages between various elements in the network. The loops are terminated on the line termination unit. Trunks are circuits leaving the switch, which go to other distant switches, including the long-distance network. All of today's local exchanges rely on time-division multiplexing and circuit-switched technology architectures developed 30 years ago for the transport and switching of voice. Several processors are part of the switch, including the call processor (which performs all the necessary computing for routing calls and setting up connections in the switch fabric) and the operations processor (which is responsible for maintenance aspects of switch operation, including billing, alarms, traffic monitoring, and the like). Next, let's examine each of these key points in more detail.

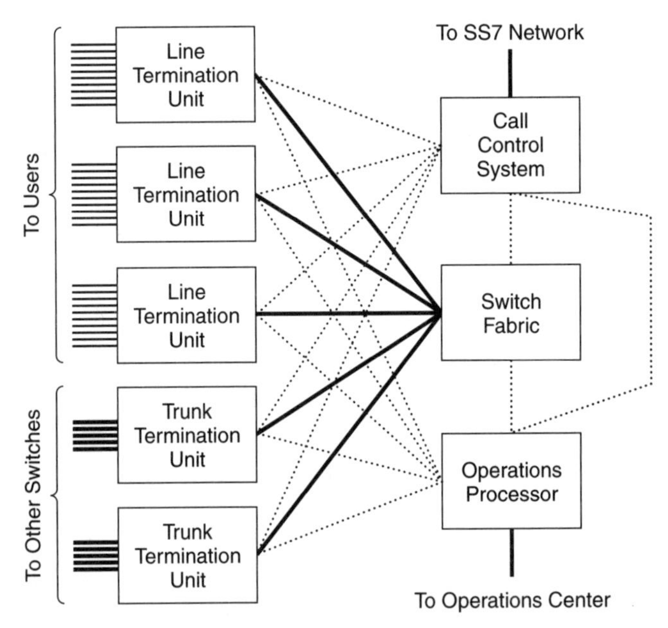

FIGURE 3–10 *Local exchange functional diagram.*

The LTU provides all the needed functions associated with the user's telephone. These functions include:

- Detecting when the user lifts the handset to originate a call.

- Powering the telephone.
- Providing dial tone to the originating user.
- Receiving Touch-tones or dial pulses from the user's telephone.
- Converting the user's voice signals from analog to and from digital representation during a call.
- Ringing the phone to indicate an incoming call.
- Detecting when the user has lifted the handset to answer the call.
- Providing various call progress tones and signals, such as ring-back tone, busy signal, and the like.
- Providing a concentration function that limits the number of simultaneous callers originating from a group of users.

The LTU also provides the important function of concentration. Because the switch terminates the lines of a very large number of users, it is engineered to accommodate a reasonable number of simultaneous calls, but it will not be able to complete all call requests if every user originates an outgoing call. In fact, in such a situation, not every user will even receive dial tone. Typically, switches are engineered to allow between 10% to 20% of its users to originate calls at any given time. This is a key difference between the local exchange and all other switches in the network. The concentration ratio is simply the ratio of the number of lines terminated at the LTU to the number of circuits leaving the LTU to the switch fabric. If, for example, an LTU terminates 4,000 telephone lines but has only 400 circuits leaving it for the switch fabric, then only 10% of the users could simultaneously originate or receive calls, resulting in a concentration ratio of 10 to 1. If 800 circuits were provided, then the concentration ratio would be 5 to 1. This function is critical because it would be prohibitively expensive to build a network that allowed every user to simultaneously make a call using Time Division Multiplexing (TDM). Conversely, if the exchange cannot handle enough simultaneous calls, users will experience poor service, since they will not be able to make or receive calls during peak busy hours. Switching systems must be carefully engineered for the traffic they experience. This is known as blocking probability. Based on the call attempt rate of subscribers in a local exchange, an appropriate number of paths from line to trunk side must be provided to achieve an acceptable blocking probability. Similarly, the number of trunks leaving the exchange must support the calling patterns of the customers. Also, the average duration of calls affects the blocking probability, and as average call duration increases, the engineered blocking probability will be maintained only if a lower concentration ratio is used. This has occurred due to dial-up Internet access. Typically, local exchanges are engineered to allow 20% of the customers to make simultaneous calls in a local exchange serving mostly residences. Local exchanges serving businesses are engineered for a higher capacity, around 30%. We shall revisit this issue later when we consider the implications of packet technology for transporting voice.

The TTUs provide similar functions for digital trunks leaving the switch as part of the interoffice network. In most cases, these trunks are digital and are simply used to carry the digitally encoded speech of the user. In this case, all call control information is carried by the SS7 system as digital messages between call control systems. Unlike LTUs, TTUs do not provide any concentration. However, they may be connected to the switch fabric in a way that spreads any focused traffic situations that may arise across the entire switch fabric rather than place it all on a single group of circuits reaching the switch fabric. This will also provide greater reliability for the switch as a whole because access to any given trunk can be performed from many places within the switch. A key function of the TTU is to monitor the state of health of the trunk and provide maintenance information to the technicians who are maintaining the switch. The condition of a trunk is more important than the state of a loop, because if a trunk is having problems or is removed from service, all the customers using the switch will be impacted in some way, whereas a loop problem will only affect a single customer. For this reason, most trunks use a concept known as protection switching to protect against failures wherein a spare circuit can rapidly replace any of the trunks.

The switch fabric is simply a matrix that connects the circuits of one LTU to another LTU (or a TTU) under the control of the call processor. Many different schemes are possible for building the switch fabric, but most use some form of time-division multiplexing and the exchanging of information in time slots. One such system is the time slot exchange system that simply receives the channels in order and places them in a memory. The channels are read out of the buffer in a different order based on the content of a table. The exchanger simply cycles through this table over and over, storing information in one place and retrieving it from another. In this way, the content of one time slot is moved to another position so the information is switched to a different destination. Using several of these systems and other variations, it is possible to build a switch fabric wherein any input can be transported to any output.

The call processor is simply a computer that receives requests from users at their telephones and takes actions based on the current state of their line and content of their request. For example, when the user goes off hook, causing a DC current to flow in the loop, the line termination unit indicates this occurrence to the call processor. In turn, the call processor causes dial tone to be supplied to the user's line. This is provided that the customer has subscribed to service. When the customer enters digits, the call processor receives, collects, and analyzes them for completion of dialing. If a complete number has been accumulated, the call processor will determine the proper route for the call based on the phone number. It then causes messages to be sent to reach the distant switch through the Common Channel Signaling (CCS) network or, if the dialed number is within this local exchange, it simply rings the line. The call processor takes all these actions and many more not apparent to the user. Traditionally, the call processor has been tightly integrated into the local exchange equipment but could, in fact, be separated. In the emerging new telephony architectures, this is the case.

The operations processor monitors the switch components for failures or abnormal conditions such as high blocking of connections, and is the primary interface for technicians to administer the switch. Diagnostics are resident throughout the switching system that can be invoked either on command or automatically when problems are detected. The operations processor also connects to other operations systems where overall network operation is monitored and administered. Many of these administration systems are concerned with functions such as activating services for new customers, billing, monitoring the performance of the network and the quality of its operation, and predicting the need for additional capacity in parts of the network.

Because a switch may serve a very large number of customers, usually between 10,000 and 100,000 lines, it is necessary for it to have very high reliability. Should the switch fail entirely, no user will be able to make calls. Since telephone service can be a lifeline in the event of fires, health crises, crimes, and other serious events, reliability is paramount. As a result, line terminations, trunk terminations, and switches can only be unavailable for, at most, 18 minutes/year, 12 minutes/year, and 2 minutes/year respectively. Because a year contains 525,600 minutes, 2 minutes/year of down time is equivalent to 99.99962% availability. This is the frequently quoted[3] "Five-9's" heralded when discussing availability of the circuit-switched network. To achieve such high reliability, special designs are used, including duplication of critical elements, such as the call processor, and

3. The Five-9's requirement for switching is frequently misquoted. This requirement applies only to an *entire* switching system, not to individual components of a switch or to the availability of the service.

having redundant elements such as a spare trunk termination unit that can be immediately substituted for a defective termination in a group of trunks. This allows the switch to continue operation even when several parts have failed completely. The defective systems can be repaired or replaced by technicians without disrupting the operation of the switching system. But these functions have significant impact on the cost of the switches.

The Tandem Exchange

Within a geographic area, there are likely to be several local exchanges that switch calls between local users. Even though users in every local exchange make calls to other users in every other local exchange within a region, it is not practical to establish trunks between every pair of local exchanges. Instead, a tandem exchange is provided that switches connections between the local exchanges. Tandem exchanges are different from local exchanges because they only terminate trunks. Also, they experience much higher call attempt rates because the traffic has already been concentrated. Trunks are sized to accommodate peak busy hour calls between local exchanges, so the tandem exchange will be kept quite busy processing connections during this period.

In some cases, there are direct trunks between local exchanges due to their geographic placement and the volume of traffic between them. A direct trunk is installed between two switches when a high volume of traffic is found to occur on a daily basis and if the distances are not excessive. But users can call anywhere in the world, and it is not practical to have a trunk directly from every switch to every other switch, so it is necessary to have more levels of switching.

This is shown in Figure 3–11, where we can see an example metropolitan area with several local exchanges and a tandem exchange. Should a user attempt to reach another user who is not at the same local exchange, the originating user's local exchange may route the user directly to the other switch if a direct trunk is available. If a direct trunk is not available, or if it is completely utilized, the switch will route the call through a tandem trunk to reach a tandem exchange that provides connections between local switches and to the long-distance network. For example, if user A attempts to call user B, the 42nd Street local exchange would prefer to use the direct trunk between it and the 49th Street local exchange where user B is terminated. But if there are not any idle circuits in this trunk, it will route the call to the 53rd Street tandem exchange that will then route the call to the 49th Street local exchange. All the trunks, whether tandem trunks or direct trunks, are carefully sized to accommodate the volume of traffic experienced.

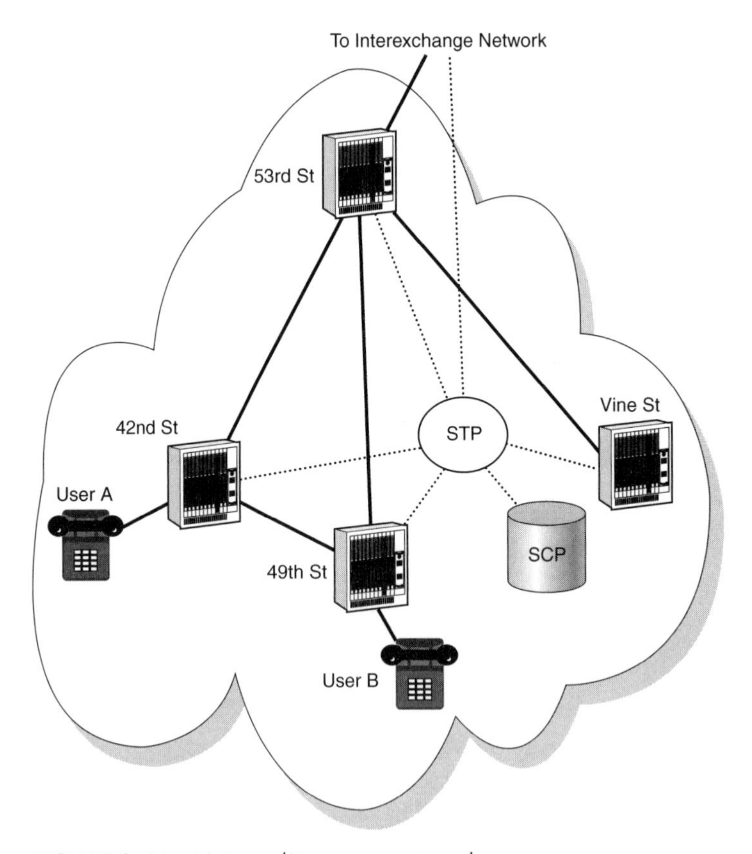

FIGURE 3–11 Metropolitan area network.

Sometimes, there are several tandem exchanges that serve to interconnect the local exchanges. Thus, when a local exchange must choose a route, it will select either a direct trunk, a preferred tandem exchange, or an alternate tandem exchange. Sophisticated routing schemes, including Dynamic Non-Hierarchical Routing (DNHR), have been created to get the maximum performance in completing calls. These routing schemes operate in the call processors of local exchanges and tandem exchanges.

Common Channel Signaling

The local exchanges and tandem exchanges must communicate very quickly and with great reliability to rapidly set up connections. Some local exchanges can experience over 1 million busy-hour call attempts. If the processing becomes bogged down, calls will be completed slowly, and some users will abandon the call before it is completed. This can lead to complaints about service. To facilitate call processing and to introduce additional services, a signaling network allows the call processing systems at the switches to communicate.

Figure 3–12 shows the basic CCS network interconnecting several local exchanges and tandem exchanges. The latest protocol that specifies the messages and transfer procedures within a CCS network is SS7. SS7 is in wide use today throughout the North American network and most of the world. Operation of the CCS network is monitored and controlled by a Signaling Managing System, or SMS. The SMS is connected to the larger world of operations that is described later in this chapter.

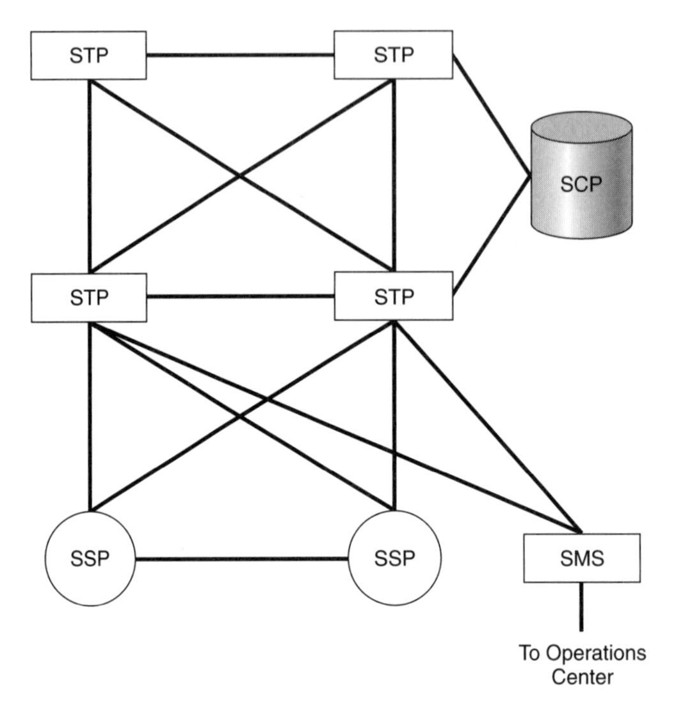

FIGURE 3–12 *Signaling System 7 network.*

At the base of the network are the Service Switching Points (SSP). These are the various local and tandem switches within the network where calls originate and terminate. These systems use the SS7 signaling protocol to indicate to each other the various parameters of a phone call, such as calling party and called party phone numbers. These SSPs generate messages that must be carried by the CCS network to the indicated destination (SSP).

One component of CCS is the Signal Transfer Point (STP), which relays messages between the call processing units of the various switches. Every switch is assigned an address known as a point code that uniquely identifies it within the CCS network on a national basis. The STP simply receives messages on one of its links, looks up the destination point code route, and then forwards the message out the appropriate link for that route. Sometimes this means further routing and forwarding by subsequent STP switches. As such, an STP is a connectionless packet switch, and each message is simply a datagram from one local exchange to another.

To achieve reliability objectives, each local exchange has dual links to the STP so that should one fail, an alternate can be utilized. The systems automatically select a working link for message transfer. Furthermore, each local exchange is connected to not one but two STP switches. This is so that service will continue should an STP fail. Internally, the STP has high levels of reliability built into its processors and systems to minimize failures. STPs operate in clusters of four and can achieve extremely high reliability goals. During periods of high traffic, STP switches can discard signaling messages. For this reason, it is necessary to have an additional protocol to assure the correct end-to-end transfer of the messages.

A protocol known as Message Transfer Part (MTP) operates between endpoints to assure the proper transfer of messages by the STPs. Each message is numbered in ascending sequence, has a Cyclic Redundancy Check (CRC) computed and appended to allow the message's content to be checked for errors, and is transmitted in sequence to the receiver and stored in case a retransmission is needed. At the receiver, the message's CRC is recomputed to determine if the message is error–free, and the sequence number is compared to the expected value. If there are no errors and the message is in the proper sequence, an acknowledgment will be sent to the transmitter that will then discard its retained copy of the message. If, however, there were errors or a message was lost, causing the sequence numbering to be violated, the receiver will provide a negative acknowledgment, which will cause the transmitter to re-send the message. At both ends, timers are operated to detect transport and system failures. MTP has been carefully designed to ensure error-free transport of messages, the rapid detection of failures, and rapid reconfiguration in their presence. It automatically bypasses failures by using alternate systems and paths. Since each local exchange has dual links to two STPs, there are actually four possible routes by which messages could flow into an STP cluster, four routes by which it could be delivered, and many routes inside the cluster. These combine to make a staggering number of possible paths between local exchanges. In the event of transport or STP failures, MTP will automatically reconfigure to make use of a functioning alternate route.

A key system in SS7 is the Signal Control Point, or SCP. The SCP provides various database services and was first introduced for "800" number translations. However, the functional use of the SCP has greatly expanded since the advent of the Intelligent Network (IN) and the Advanced Intelligent Network (AIN), and many new value-added services based on capabilities such as variable time-of-day routing, screening and other concepts have been created. These include local number portability, a capability that allows a user to retain her telephone number when switching between local carriers. SS7 is the backbone of any carrier's voice services because it provides the means by which calls are completed and stores the information by which services are created.

Digital Loop Carrier Systems

Several decades ago, it was recognized that some of the LTU's functions could be implemented for a modest number of lines and placed in a remote location near a group of customers. By using either a fiber optic or other digital transport back to the local exchange, loops could be shorter, which would reduce costs and improve quality. The basic scheme is that when a customer demands service by going off-hook, the remote electronics would detect this indication and take a few simple actions. It would simply place the customer's channel into an idle circuit and send a message to the local exchange indicating which customer had gone off-hook and into which circuit the customer had been placed. The local exchange would then handle the customer as though there were a direct connection via a loop to the local exchange. When the call was complete, the local exchange would inform the remote electronics that the circuit was no longer needed, and the remote electronics would then disconnect the customer from the circuit and mark the circuit as idle again. The electronics at the remote point would have to provide some of the LTU functions, such as powering and ringing, but the local exchange would still perform most of the call control functions.

Figure 3–13 shows a Digital Loop Carrier (DLC) system that is serving 100 customers from a single 24-circuit digital transport system. DLC systems are widely deployed in North America, especially in regions having low population densities. This is because in low population densities, it is far more cost effective to concentrate the users near their location and only transport active call requests than to provide a complete loop to every customer from the quite distant local exchange. Naturally, the operation and maintenance of the remote electronics must be considered, but DLC easily proves to be a cost-effective approach in a wide-ranging set of deployment situations. One reason for this is that as electronics and software have improved in performance, it has become possible to build larger and larger local exchanges that are able to serve greater numbers of customers. Naturally, this leads to having more and more loops to terminate at the local exchange, which must be longer and longer to reach the additional customers.

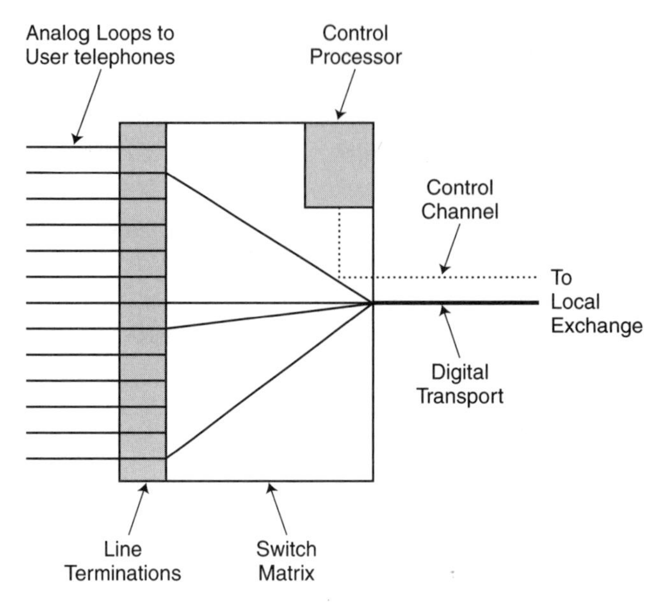

FIGURE 3–13 Digital Loop Carrier system.

Mobile Networks

No description of today's voice network would be complete without discussing wireless mobile networking. Unlike the wire-line network, mobile networks have been subject to competition from their very beginning. As a consequence, there is a far faster pace in adopting new technology and new business postures than in the wire-line networks. Later, when business directions are considered, this will be an important consideration. Also, wireless access is beginning to invade the Internet, and in some countries, such as Japan, wireless data has already become a successful service.

Figure 3–14 shows the architecture of a mobile network. The network consists of one or more Mobile Switching Centers (MSC) that have access to both a signaling network and a switching network for trunks. The signaling network, usually SS7, is used for message passing between MSC and other switching elements as well as for data storage and retrieval. Mobile networks rely heavily on the use of SS7 signaling for controlling calls, achieving hand-offs, and supporting roaming services. These signaling and switching elements can belong to or be leased by the mobile carrier, or they can be elements of the PSTN. The trunk and signaling interfaces are used for receiving and originating calls by the MSC to and from the mobile users. The MSC is connected to several Base Station Controllers (BSC), and each BSC manages multiple Base Stations (BS). The BS is the radio frequency element of the system and includes transmitters, receivers, and antennas on a tower that overlooks its serving area. Mobile Stations (MS), whether handheld or otherwise, communicate over a radio frequency (RF) link to the BS. This RF link uses Frequency Division Multiple Access (FDMA) to allow carriers to share the radio frequency spectrum. This is combined with either Time Division Multiple Access (TDMA) or Code Division Multiple Access (CDMA) to allow multiple MS to share the capacity available. The actual frequency spectrum used varies between countries and serving areas, but ranges between 850 MHz and 1990 MHz according to the particular standard used.

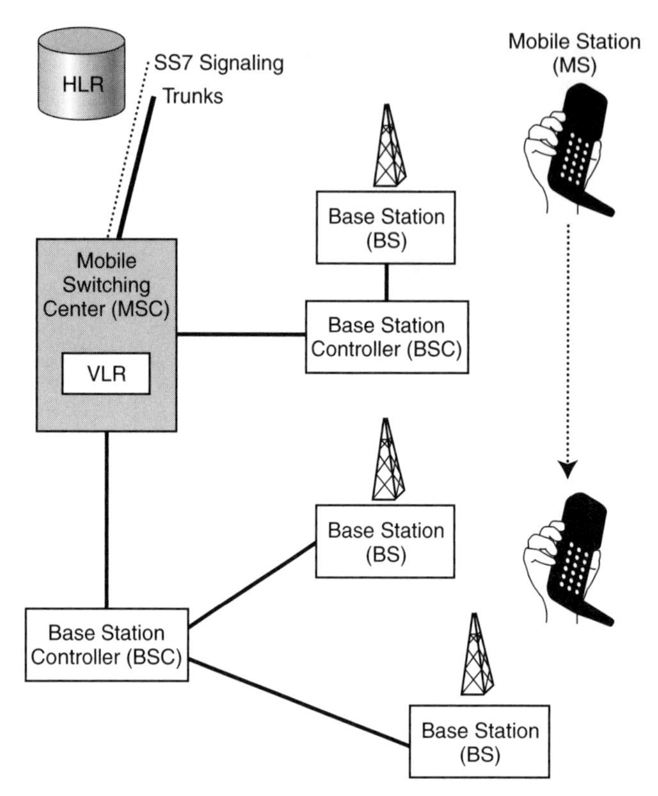

FIGURE 3–14 *Mobile network.*

A basic principle of mobile networking is that the serving area is divided into "cells" that are served by a radio frequency transmitter and receiver using antennas on a tower that communicate with the mobile stations within their range. Except for CDMA systems, adjacent cells use different frequency spectrum to avoid interference, but cells that are separated by enough distance can use the same spectrum. This means that within any given cell, only a portion of the available frequency spectrum allocated to a carrier for the service can be used. This principle of frequency reuse was introduced with the earliest analog cellular systems and is used today for TDMA systems. However, with CDMA, the carrier uses its entire spectrum allocation within every cell because channels are extracted using correlation methods. This allows users to all transmit on the same frequency band and expands the spectrum available within cells. A critical aspect of this technique is that the power level of the users must be carefully managed so that maximum capacity is achieved.

Depending on the specific way in which either TDMA or CDMA is used, different digital channel rates can be created. Usually, rates around 8 Kbps are used for carrying compressed speech or low-speed packet data, but it is possible to support higher speeds. There are various control channels that are used for command and control messages to manage the links, power levels, and other aspects of the MS.

One key to the operation of the mobile network is that each MS has a unique identification that allows the network to directly address it. This can be supplemented with a Personal Information Module (PIM) that can be moved between mobile stations in some countries. Also, each MS performs a registration procedure when activated that informs the network of this identity and other parameters used for its operation. This is important, since the BSC and MSC could not otherwise distinguish between the MS operating with a cell.

When an MS moves about during an active call, it may migrate from one cell to another, requiring a transfer of the call to a different BSC. This transfer is referred to as a *hand-off* and requires special functions using a series of messages to transfer the call. Once the decision is made to move the user's talking path from the original BSC to the new one, the MSC will simply create a second connection to the new BSC so that the MS can begin using it. This is accomplished by the MSC without making any changes to the network portion of the connection. Once done, the connection to the original BSC can be released and the RF capacity at the original BS reallocated for new call requests. If the acquiring BSC is on a different MSC, the original MSC first establishes a network connection to the new MSC so the call can be continued. If the user moves into the serving area of a different carrier, a new connection through the PSTN must be established to the MSC of the carrier within the new serving area. This hand-off is more complex and lengthy, and will only be performed if the carriers involved in the hand-off have agreed on contractual terms to support it.

When users move between locations, there are two important registers known as the Home Location Register (HLR) and the Visited Location Register (VLR) that allow the network to keep track of the user's profile and location. The HLR is normally stored in a database that is on the SS7 network, but the VLR is inside each MSC. The HLR stores the user's profile and knows where the user is currently registered. This is critical for routing incoming calls to the user, for maintaining service when the user travels to a different region, and for billing purposes. When the user roams to a different territory, a VLR entry will be created in the MSC that serves that territory. This occurs when the MS is activated and registers with the network. The MSC sends messages to the HLR so that it can be updated with the user's new location. Then, incoming calls for the user can be correctly routed to the new MSC.

Mobile networks are rapidly absorbing voice users. In some countries, new users do not obtain a normal telephone. Instead, they simply subscribe to mobile service. This has begun to erode the traditional telephone service revenues in some serving areas. Today, mobile is a high-growth business and there are many competing carriers offering services.

The Interexchange Network

The interexchange or long-distance network usually consists of two or more levels of switching, which are utilized much as the local exchange and tandem exchange are in the local serving area. However, these switches receive traffic that has already been concentrated by the local exchange. At this level in the network, the switches are generally routing calls between cities. In essence, all these switches are equivalent to the tandem exchanges in the local exchange network. Within a given city, there may be many so-called Points of Presence (POP) where the long-distance carrier can interface with local carriers or directly with large customers such as corporations. Should there be multiple carriers within a city, the long-distance carrier will carefully size its trunks to the carriers as well as the trunks reaching the higher level of switches so as to ensure that calls can be completed. Should users migrate from one local carrier to another, this must be reflected in the sizing of the IXC's trunks. Figure 3–15 shows a typical long-distance network as an IXC might configure it.

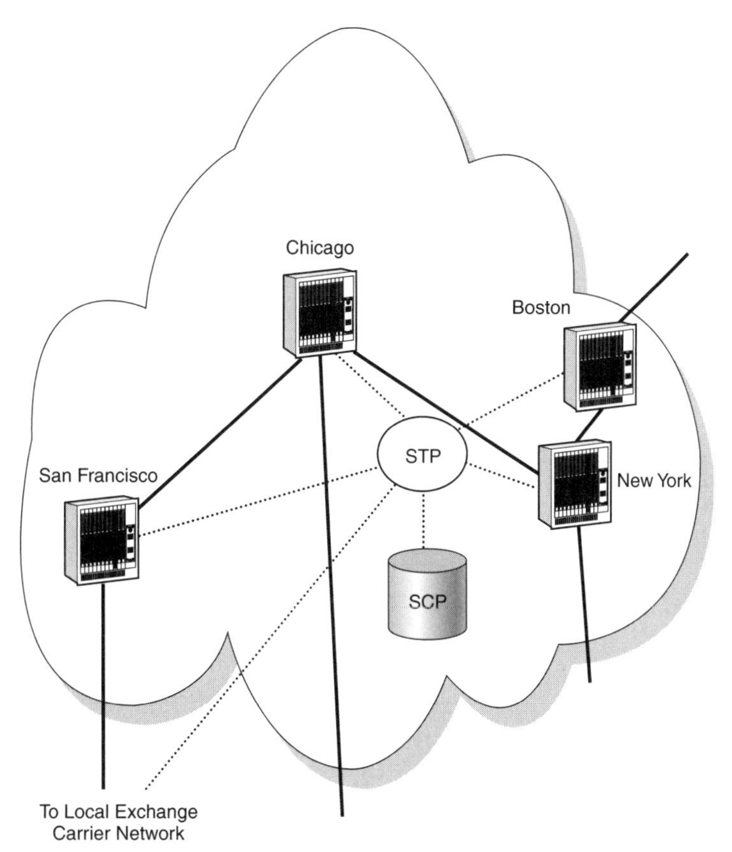

FIGURE 3–15 *Inter-LATA network.*

The switching systems used by IXCs are similar to the tandem exchanges described earlier. IXCs also make extensive use of SS7. The key difference between the LEC and IXC switching systems and signaling network are the nature of the services offered. Also, IXC switching centers have a very high call attempt rate and must be engineered accordingly for adequate capacity. This is because the traffic has been highly concentrated by the local exchanges and tandem exchanges of the LEC. Consequently, trunks to and from IXC switching centers are almost continually busy. Due to this high traffic load and the subsequent impact on revenues should a failure occur, these switching centers are designed to the highest possible reliability.

The operations and maintenance center for an IXC is similar to that of an LEC; however, there is a greater concentration on switching system operation and maintenance because the IXC has no loops. Thus, they need few if any outside plant technicians. Often, IXCs lease their transport facilities from other carriers, especially fiber optic cables, because of the high cost of construction and the need for right-of-way to do the construction. On the flip side, many companies who own right-of-way, such as railroads, have launched telecommunications companies based on installing fiber systems. In turn, these companies lease facilities to other carriers as needed.

Routing

In the PSTN, routing is geographic in nature and depends on the area code and exchange code. Of course, phone numbers can be preceded by a carrier selection code, which is used to route the call to the long-distance carrier of the customer's choice. So, routing can be broken into two problems: the LEC's routing decision and the IXC's routing decision. While there are similarities, there are also differences. It should be remembered that routing is only performed one time per call. Once the route is selected and the call is established, the connection remains frozen in the chosen circuit for the duration of the call. For the moment, consider only the overall case of the basic routing problem.

When a calling party enters a phone number, it is organized into three fields. In North America, there is a three-digit Numbering Plan Area[4] (NPA) followed by a seven-digit number, which represents a three-digit exchange code and then a four-digit station. Thus, a phone number such as 732-758-2994 represents the "732" NPA, the "758" exchange, and the "2994" station. In this case, a two-digit exchange code could be used and each exchange could have up to 99,999 lines. However, a three-digit code could be used, which would only allow 9,999 lines per exchange.

The problem a switch faces when given such a number is to first get the call to the proper NPA and then, within that NPA, to the proper local exchange. That exchange then faces the trivial problem of translating the station code into the proper line termination and then ringing the correct station. The central office where the call originates will examine the number and determine how it can route the call. Remember that this switch knows its own NPA code and exchange code. If it finds that the destination matches these values, then this is a local call to be handled within the exchange, and it will simply direct the call internally to the correct line appearance for that station number. Usually, for a local call, the user only dials the exchange code and the station code by entering seven digits. In this case, only the exchange code need be tested for the match. If the user is calling someone in a different exchange, then the exchange code will be different. In some cases, the central office will have a direct trunk to the desired exchange. In this case, the central office will choose an idle channel in that trunk and send a message to the destination exchange through the SS7 network, informing it of the incoming call and the channel selected. But if there is no

4. Otherwise known as area code.

direct trunk or if all the channels are utilized, the switch will forward the call to a tandem switch that has trunks to all the local exchanges. The tandem will examine the number and determine if it is within its NPA code. If so, then the tandem will have a trunk to the correct end office, so it simply selects an idle channel in the appropriate trunk and notifies the end office using SS7. If the NPA is not local, then the tandem will route the call through a trunk to reach an IXC. The carrier selected could be the calling party's presubscribed long-distance provider, or it could have been specified explicitly as part of the number dialed. At any point in the route, if there is no idle channel or an alternate route, the call will be blocked. This is called progressive routing. Each switch makes a local determination about what route to follow and, once chosen, passes the call to the next switch along the route.

Within an IXC's network, routing is more complex. DNHR is used to get the greatest number of calls completed by the network. The network is more complex, and while it is possible to use fixed routing schemes such as was just described, it is far more efficient to route calls in ways that utilize alternative paths when the primary route is fully utilized. In these networks, the routing processors have many alternate routes, and when a call is blocked along the chosen route, a "crank-back" message will be sent that causes the previous switch to try an alternate route. In this way, primary routes between endpoints will be used until they are filled to capacity, and then alternate routes that are not yet fully utilized will be chosen. The result is a greater resilience to unusual traffic circumstances such as routinely occur on Mother's Day and other events, such as disasters.

Operations

Besides having all the necessary switching and transmission equipment to complete calls between customers, the successful operator must also have the capability to manage the network and to respond to customer requests. This is realized through business processes, management functions and information, and operations systems that scale with service features, the network size, and its complexity. Human resources include maintenance technicians for inside plant equipment, such as switches, and for outside plant equipment, such as fiber cable systems, as well as operators and administrators. These people are needed to operate the network, interact with customers, oversee the business, bill customers, and collect payments. Naturally, these operations have a high degree of automation, using computers and databases to store, retrieve, and manipulate the information associated with administering a large network with many customers. These are the so-called "FCAPS" functions of Fault, Configuration, Accounting, Performance, and Security that are part of the Telecommunications Management Network (TMN) architecture.

Figure 3–16 shows an example of the operations systems used to administer large networks. Lest you forget, these systems are at the core of managing an enormous business, often in the region of $10 billion or more in annual revenue. Managing such a large business is a complex matter, as can be seen from the figure. Within the figure, functions are divided into four key layers: Service Management Layer, Network Management Layer, Element Management Layer, and Network Element Layer. This partitioning of functionality provides a structure within which operational flows can be defined and follows a logical partitioning of the needs of the business. In addition, within each layer there are key functional groups. These include Customer Care, Interconnection Services, Activation, Assurance, Planning, Workforce, and Element. Within each group is a set of functional blocks. Each functional block represents a software system or automated function that interacts with the operator's staff, with other systems, and with the network elements, as needed to perform its specific function.

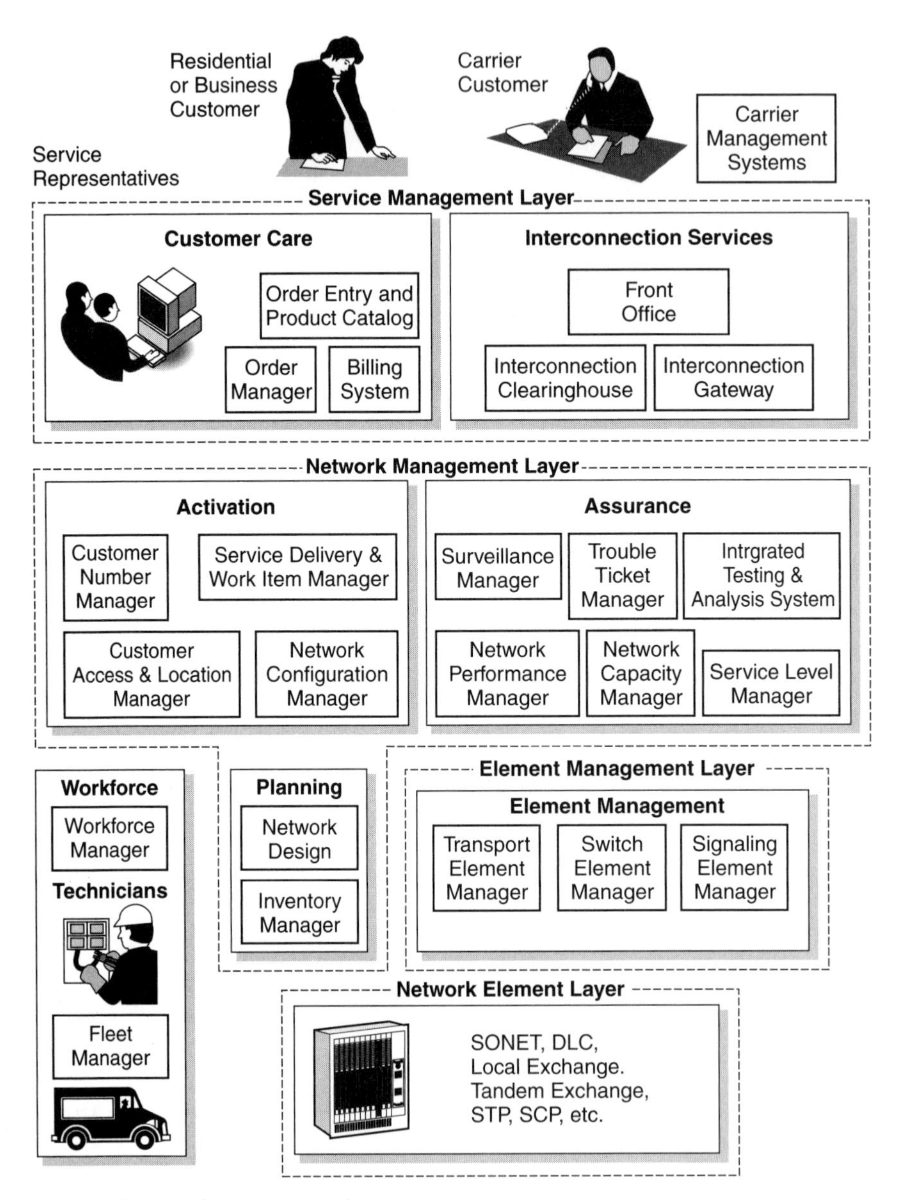

FIGURE 3–16 *Carrier operations.*

Within the Customer Care grouping, there are three key functions: Order Entry & Product Catalog, Order Manager, and a Billing System. When a customer contacts the carrier, the Order Entry & Product Catalog system is accessed by a

service representative who negotiates the service order with the customer over the telephone. This system is used to determine the appropriate service choice and its necessary parameters. As required, this system may interact with others in the course of the interaction with the customer. Once negotiated, Order Manager will receive the completed service order and will automate the sending of all necessary requests to other systems, such as to the Activation group, to complete the service request. The Billing System will also be notified once the service has been activated, and billing will commence. Besides interfacing with the customer using a service representative, carriers are increasingly providing Web-based access systems that allow a customer to directly interact with these systems using online services.

The Interconnection Service is focused primarily on services provided to other carriers. In some circles, this is known as "wholesale." One example of this is the access between an LEC and an IXC for providing long-distance services to customers. In this grouping, there are four systems: the Front Office, an Interconnection Clearinghouse, an Interconnection Gateway, and an Advanced Service Management System. The Front Office supports direct online access by customers to obtain preorder information and to query the status of orders and services. The Interconnection Clearinghouse accepts electronic orders and queries from customers in various e-commerce interchange formats that can vary from customer to customer. It then processes and transmits these in the appropriate format to internal systems or to other business partners as required. The Interconnection Gateway interacts with customers and allows the controlled access to the carrier's operations systems to examine data or query status of various services and equipment involved in the customer's service.

Within the Network Management Layer, there are three groupings: Activation, Planning and Assurance. Activation includes those functions necessary to configure and acti-

vate a new service. Since new services are constantly being introduced, the Activation group of systems requires a high degree of both full flow-through automation and rapid customization to accommodate the needs of a new service.

Within the Activation grouping, there are four key functional blocks: Customer Number Manager, Service Delivery & Work Item Manager, Customer Access & Location Manager, and Network Configuration Manager. The Customer Number Manager is used to allocate and track phone number assignments to customers, including vanity numbers, ISDN numbers, Local Number Portability assignments, Centrex numbers, bulk number requests, wireless numbers, and other numbering needs. The Customer Access & Location Manager maintains the customer location information, including service address, as well as network inventory of equipment involved in the customer's service. Service Delivery & Work Item Manager is a key component of activation that dynamically assigns orders to technicians and other operations systems based on customer information and service requirements. The Network Configuration Manager is able to locate and assemble the necessary network equipment elements for the Service Delivery & Work Item Manager to provide a particular service to a particular customer. The Network Configuration and Service Delivery functions directly access the Element Managers to actually "turn on" service automatically.

The Assurance grouping includes functions required to monitor the network for proper operation and to respond when problems occur. Assurance includes Surveillance Manager, Trouble Ticket Manager, Integrated Testing & Analysis System, Network Performance Monitor, Network Capacity Manager, and Service Level Manager. The Surveillance Manager continually monitors the operation of the network and coordinates fault messages from the equipment and interprets the problems indicated. The Trouble Ticket Manager creates and administers trouble tickets from individual customers and coordinates these reports with known network problems identified by Surveillance Manager to avoid duplicate dispatches of technicians. The Performance Manager collects network traffic data from multiple systems involved in a service to detect potential problems and determine the quality of service being provided. When problems are found, the Trouble Ticket Manager is notified. The Network Capacity Manager examines the utilized and available capacity of network systems, including transport and switching systems, to determine current and future requirements to meet quality of service objectives. The Service Level Manager compares the quality of service levels found by other systems to negotiated Service Level Agreements and monitors other key metrics, such as mean time to repair, to determine if the carrier is meeting the needed service level and if rebates should be provided to the customer.

The Planning grouping includes Network Design and Inventory Manager. Network Design assists the carrier in engineering additions to its network or entirely new networks by creating optimal placement and sizing for equipment such as switches and transport facilities. The Inventory Manager keeps track of spare equipment and plug-ins for the various systems within the network so technicians can quickly locate replacements and so stocks can be replenished.

The Element Management Layer provides functions that are tightly coupled with the actual network equipment. It is necessary for the Network Elements to provide functions for alarm generation, performance monitoring, configuration management, and billing to this layer. In some cases, Network Elements may bypass the Element Management Layer and communicate directly to higher layers. Element Management consists mainly of systems typically provided by equipment manufacturers that support a uniform protocol suite of command and control to the higher layer systems as well as managing multiple instances of the network equipment. For example an Element Manager may be built that makes multiple Network Elements appear as a single large element, a function that can aid in operating distributed networks.

Other systems needed to operate the business include a Workforce Manager that can assign the various technicians to installation orders or trouble tickets based on skills needed and problem type and that can also create optimal scheduling of problem repairs. In carriers that have outside plant equipment, there will be a fleet of vehicles for the technicians to use, and a Fleet Manager system is needed to schedule the use of the vehicles, track their assignments, and schedule maintenance. Some systems not shown in Figure 3–16 but that are commonplace include forecasting tools, call center management systems, a directory assistance service manager, as well as various market information systems to analyze and predict the response to a new service and to target the advertising for services. Like any other business, the carrier needs various other information systems to handle its payroll and the like.

Next, consider the interaction of these systems for a simple service order to activate a service. The customer calls into the call center and the call center management system will assign the customer to a specific service representative. The service representative will retrieve the information regarding the customer service location from the Customer Access & Location Manager and will assign a telephone number using the Customer Number Manager. Once the order is completed, the Order Entry & Product Catalog system passes the completed service order to the Order Manager system. The Order Manager system will generate a set of work items needed to activate the service that it will transmit to the Service Delivery & Work Item Manager. This system will request network port assignments as needed to fulfill the service requirements from the Network Configuration Manager, will generate any installation orders needed to the Workforce Manager, and will transmit activation orders to the various Element Managers depending on the particular service being activated. The Workforce Manager will optimally select and dispatch the required technicians, while the Element Managers transmit activation messages to the specific equipment involved, such as SONET multiplex systems and switching systems. Finally, the Service Delivery & Work Item Manager will transmit service and circuit data to the Assurance group of systems so the new service, once activated, will be maintained.

While this may seem a complex process to the uninitiated reader, it must be remembered that without this structure and automation, chaos would reign within the carrier's business world. These systems operate tens of thousands of pieces of equipment, interface with millions of customers and provide for hundreds of thousands of daily requests by customers. To perform these tasks manually is unthinkable. The logical separation of the operations into the categories and functions shown gives a framework wherein new services can be prepared and existing services can be analyzed. As carriers begin to move towards a new telephony network, they will modernize these operations systems and streamline their processes. Only by employing these systems can a large carrier remain profitable and provide an acceptable level of responsiveness to customer requests.

Summary

This concludes the introduction to the PSTN in which all its key technologies have been briefly described and their interrelationships explained. In a later chapter, we will further consider these systems as assets or liabilities of the incumbents that provide the PSTN. The scope of the PSTN is easy to overlook, and its reliability easily forgotten. The PSTN provides a high quality of service because of its architecture and the attention that it has received over many decades of operation. This is not to say that it represents the only way or the best way in which telephone service

could be provided. In fact, in a later chapter, we will show several radically different means by which telephony service could be deployed.

But the PSTN represents a yardstick by which all new approaches will be measured by customers and investors. Does the new approach have equivalent service quality? Does it have the same or better profitability? If so, is it because users are paying more, or is the new approach of lower cost? How will the new approach be operated? Does operations require more or less staffing to succeed? A successful attack on the telephone industry will need to deal with these and many more issues. To do so, the attacker should understand the basis on which the current service is being provided, for it may have strength and flexibility that can be used in a response that defends the market from an interloper.

References

Ash, Gerald R. *Dynamic Routing in Telecommunications Networks,* McGraw-Hill, 1997.

Bell Telephone Laboratories, *Engineering and Operations in the Bell System,* 1977.

Bell Telephone Laboratories, *Transmission Systems for Communications,* 5th ed., 1982.

Garg, Vijay, K. Smolik, and J. Wilkes. *Applications of CDMA in Wireless/Personal Communications,* Prentice Hall, 1997.

Garg, Vijay and J. Wilkes. *Wireless and Personal Communications Service,* Prentice Hall, 2000.

Goralski, Walter. *SONET,* 2nd ed., McGraw-Hill, May 2000.

McDonald, John C. (Editor). *Fundamentals of Digital Switching,* 2nd ed., Plenum Press, 1990.

Personick, Stewart D. *Optical Fiber Transmission Systems,* Plenum Press, 1981.

Russell, Travis. *Signaling System #7,* 2nd ed., McGraw-Hill, 1998.

Talley, David. *Basic Telephone Switching Systems,* Hayden Book Company, 1969.

Telcordia Technologies, *Notes on the Networks,* Issue 4, October 2000.

Thompson, Richard A. *Telephone Switching Systems,* Artec House, 2000.

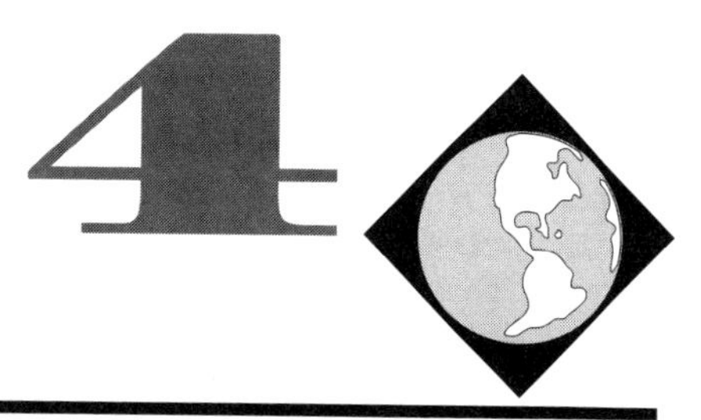

Inside the Internet

The Internet has a marvelous history and set of objectives. It began in the late 1960s when the Advanced Research Project Agency (ARPA) funded ARPAnet. This research project was intended to support organizations within the Department of Defense and other government agencies. It involved many university faculty and students as well as technical experts from a number of corporations. Its goal was to provide a seamless packet network for communications between computers that could use a wide variety of physical media such as radio, satellite, and telephone links. Two major creations specified early in this program, which are still alive and well today, are Internet Protocol (IP), which defines the basic capabilities of the Internet, and Transmission Control Protocol (TCP), which makes possible the reliable transfer of information between computers. Together, TCP and IP set the stage for the creation and evolution of the Internet based on very simple concepts and capabilities.

Since the original definition of TCP/IP, both have gone through major evolution as the demands on the Internet have increased and the knowledge of its creators, based on experience, grew. The early Internet was unpredictable in its performance and was primarily utilized by those researching data communications. Applications, such as email, were quite primitive, and delivery of information transiting the nation sometimes took days. By the late 1970s, this had begun to change, and applications, especially email, became commonplace among Internet-savvy users, mostly researchers working in funded institutions.

The National Science Foundation funded a set of national supercomputer centers in 1985 and wanted to make them widely available to members of the research community around the United States. To accomplish this, they funded a 56 Kbps network known as NSFnet to link the five supercomputer centers and allowed university computer centers to connect to this network. Now, users who were not data communications experts began to use the Internet to access the supercomputers. Many of these users were scientists doing research in other disciplines, such as visualization, cancer treatment, and weather prediction. By 1988, traffic had grown to such a level that the original 56 Kbps trunks were replaced by 1.5 Mbps T-1 links allowing users in approximately 170 computer centers connected to NSFnet to more quickly access the supercomputers. This capacity was quickly outstripped by traffic demand, and in 1991 the links were upgraded again to 45 Mbps trunks, and the number of access sites increased from 5 to 16. By this time, the access had grown to 3,500 Local Area Networks (LANs) consisting of computers and user workstations.

In 1993, as commercial interest increased, the government determined that it would no longer fund the NSFnet Internet backbone. A new architecture was created, which allowed multiple backbones to be interconnected by four Network Access Points (NAPs). Using this model, users who are connected to different backbone networks could still communicate via the NAPs. This was necessary, since an increasing number of Internet Services Providers (ISPs)

had begun to provide dial-up access to the backbone in various markets around the nation. These ISPs could not connect directly to every backbone to ensure that their users could reach any point in the Internet. Along this same line, Metropolitan Area Exchange points (MAEs) were deployed to provide interconnection between ISP points of presence, national backbones, and large end users on a statewide or citywide basis. These perform the same function as a NAP.

Today, most traffic exchanges occur directly between carriers. This is called *peering,* and most large carriers have established peering agreements between themselves. The content of these agreements is not usually disclosed, and it includes terms such as whether or not transit traffic will be accepted and what rates will be charged. The establishment of peering agreements is essential to an Internet carrier. The Internet is truly a network of networks.

The most recent innovation of the Internet is the World Wide Web. The WWW was instituted in 1991. Once the HyperText Transfer Protocol (HTTP) and its companion, the HyperText Mark-up Language (HTML) was specified and implemented, the concept of Web browsing became possible, and Web sites sprang up all around the world. By 1995, WWW traffic became the largest volume of packets carried on the Internet. The rest, as they say, is history. But the future of the Internet is unbounded. Besides capturing telephony, the subject of this book, the Internet has begun its initial foray into instant messaging, music-over-IP, and video-over-IP. An "Everything-over-IP" future seems certain.

Figure 4–1 shows this architecture. Today, there are over 7,000 ISPs, 36 national backbone providers, and 11 NAPs. There is price competition at every level; ISPs struggle to acquire end users, while backbone providers struggle to acquire ISP customers (and large business customers).

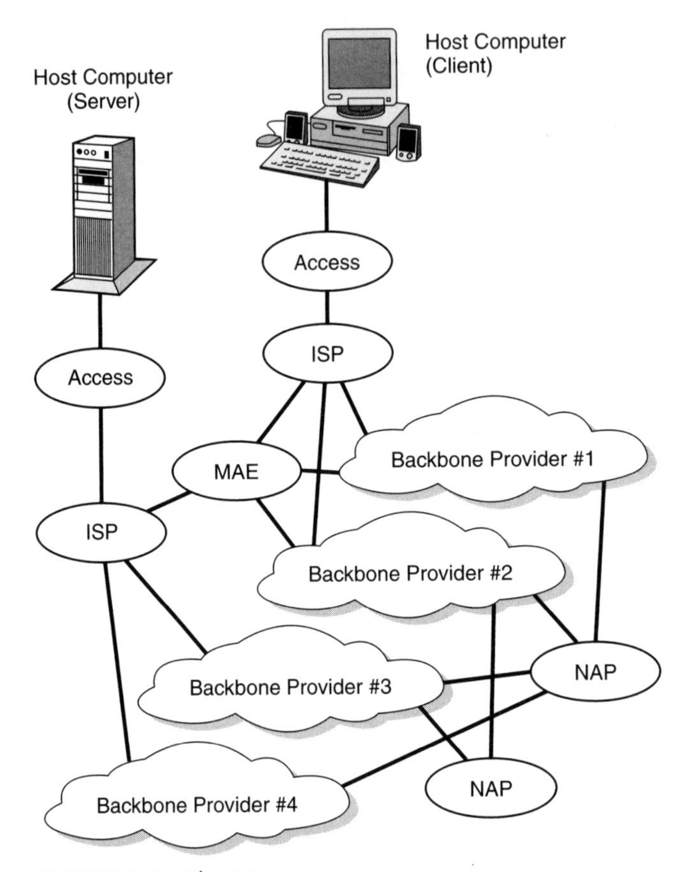

FIGURE 4–1 *The Internet.*

This massive endeavor is founded on two very simple principles, one technical and one business:

- The network provides a single service, the unreliable transport of connectionless packets. Designers must not assume good behavior by the network and must be prepared to recover from random delays, undelivered packets, packets delivered out of sequence, packets delivered to the wrong destination, and any other form of misbehavior that is possible.
- Open competition assures low pricing and ever-increasing quality of service, and there is no government regulation or intervention in business. Prices are

not fixed, and competition is based on free-market principles. Service providers at every level compete for customers and make the best business deal they can.

These two principles dominate everything that occurs in the Internet, whether it relates to technical specifications known as Request for Comments (RFC) created by the Internet Engineering Task Force (IETF) or the price for monthly Internet service. The Internet Society, a coalition of interested companies, provides some level of direction and steering of the Internet's future but, overall, the Internet is now operating primarily in the commercial sector, and its future will be determined by economic forces, customer demands, and possibly government regulation.

How the Internet Is Organized

The primary elements of data communication consist of a host computer running an application program that generates and receives packets, an access arrangement that can be chosen from several possible systems, and a set of interconnected networks composed of routers that forward packets from one location to another. Unlike the PSTN, there is no strict hierarchy of carriers. The goal of the network connectivity is to allow packets addressed to any computer anywhere in the world that is connected to the Internet to be delivered. Figure 4–1 shows a high level view of how this is implemented.

The first level of network encountered is the access network that can consist of different technology solutions. Sometimes access is as simple as a dial-up connection, or it may consist of a more complex networked arrangement. The next network level is the ISP, who provides the termination of the access arrangement. The ISP will provide some basic services to the user, usually consisting of email, Web hosting, and access to the Internet. The ISP connects to the wider Internet through a Backbone Service Provider (BSP), which is connected to many ISPs on a broad national or international basis. Some ISPs are also BSPs and have large backbone networks, and most large BSPs are also ISPs, at least in some regions. The primary distinction is whether or not they have a backbone network or simply lease capacity from someone else. Since ISPs have learned that BSPs can sometimes have failures, they usually connect to two or more BSPs to ensure reliable access. Sometimes, within a state or region, ISPs will connect to each other or, to reach their own local nodes, through an MAE.

For a long time, there was a single BSP for the Internet, the NSFnet. Users, no matter which ISP they subscribed to, could be sure of universal access to all systems in other ISPs because everything met at the backbone. However, when NSFnet was opened for commercial competitors, it became apparent that unless the BSPs were interconnected, it might become commonplace that one ISP was on a particular BSP while another ISP would be on a different BSP. In this case, the users in the two ISPs could not access each other. Thus, it was recognized that an interconnection between BSPs was needed. NAPs provide this needed interconnection.

So, summarizing and referring once more to Figure 4–1, the user's computer is connected through an access arrangement to an ISP, which in turn is connected to one or more backbones. The backbones are themselves interconnected through NAPs. Each of these entities, the access provider, the ISP, the BSP, and the NAP service provider, play an important role in establishing what we call the Internet. Each entity is serving its customers and seeking to be profitable. In later chapters, we shall explore the relationships between these players and the telephone companies. But for now, let's explore the technology and understand how it works.

Protocol Principles

In order to understand how a network operates, we must consider how software functions when interacting with

networks. The application software does not directly manipulate the network. Rather, there are layers of software that have been designated to perform specific tasks in the communication function. These layers are called a *protocol stack*. A generic representation of these layers and their functions is given in Table 4–1.

TABLE 4-1 Protocol Stack

Layer	Function	Example
Application	Performs a specific function for the user; the source and destination for information	Web browser, email
Transport	Multiplexing and reliable transfer of information	TCP (Transmission Control Protocol), UDP (User Datagram Protocol)
Network	Transfers data across the network	IP (Internet Protocol)
Link	Access, transmission, framing, and error control over a link	Ethernet, ATM, Frame Relay
Physical	Interfaces with specific media	Twisted wire pairs, coax, optical fiber, radio, satellite

The use of this layering for communications greatly simplifies the construction of computer software when new technologies are introduced. By isolating the key issues into these layers, most of the existing protocol software can be reused with no change at all when introducing a new technology. An example is when a computer is switched from using a modem over a twisted pair of wires to a fiber optic interface. To do this, the physical layer circuits and software interface drivers would be changed completely, but it is possible that no other layers would be impacted. In order to take advantage of some aspects of a new media like fiber, an improved link layer might be introduced, but most of the old link layer as well as all higher layers could be retained intact.

Within the host computer, all of these layers, as well as other functions necessary for the computer to operate, are run as simultaneous processes under the management and control of the Operating System (OS). The OS performs many important functions for the processes, including time and memory management, but a key function it provides is message passing between processes. Thus, an application like email can pass a message to a lower process such as the transport layer by sending it through the OS. In this way, all the layers are operating independently and in complete ignorance of the other layers. The only uniform agreements necessary are on what functions each layer provides, what data it requires from higher or lower layers, and how to invoke these functions. Given such agreements, each process or layer can be fabricated by different parties and used with any other layer. It is even not specified how these layers are to be built. Each layer could be software running in the computer or a special external hardware assembly within the computer. This layered model has made possible a steady evolution of improved networking protocols and applications for networked computers.

This model is very generic and can be applied to both connection-oriented and connectionless communication protocols. These were explained in Chapter 1, but here we must note that there is a profound difference in the functions assigned to each layer, depending on which type of protocol is being developed. At some stack level, it is essential to introduce the requirements of addressing, connecting, segmenting and reassembly of information, and reliable delivery. These critical issues must be determined and will have considerable impact on implementations. For example, if the physical layer provided reliable delivery, then it would not be necessary to introduce this requirement at a higher layer. However, most physical layers do not provide reliable delivery, because errors in transmission can occur, so a mechanism to detect such errors and recover from them is needed. If a mechanism is placed at the physical layer, then every new physical layer must have it. But if it is placed at a higher layer, then a multitude of simpler physical layers having no recovery mechanism could be used. This is good logic and will lower the cost of implementations. The protocol designer must decide how far up the stack to place error detection and recovery functions and how to distribute it among the various layers. Yet another issue to consider is where to place segmentation and reassembly of information blocks, such as files, that are too large to be sent as a single packet. Otherwise, systems across a network would have no idea how large buffers need to be to accommodate a transfer. The placement of these and other functions within the stack will affect what exactly is done in each layer.

The IETF specifies the necessary details required to solve a particular problem while generally adhering to this layered structure. Furthermore, there are many networking issues, such as route calculation, address resolution, and network management functions, that do not fit so neatly into a layered model. Usually, these items are tacked on as needed. IETF ignores these irregularities and focuses on a good engineering solution rather than having an elegant stack.

Figure 4–2 shows the layout of a generic packet. There are three major areas within any packet: the header, the payload, and the trailer. However, the trailer, and sometimes the payload, may not be used or may not be present. This is the principle of encapsulation—namely, that information coming from a higher layer protocol will be carried in its entirety inside the payload field while the particular protocol layer adds some information in front of and behind the payload. Always, the information coming from the higher layer is carried transparently and without any modification. The header is the most important portion of the packet so far as the protocol is concerned, since it will contain data vital to the processing of the packet. Examples of data contained in headers include source address, destination address, sequence numbers, and other items needed to process the packet. The trailer is not always present, but some protocols require them. The most common examples of data used in trailers include checksums and padding fields, but sometimes other information will be found there.

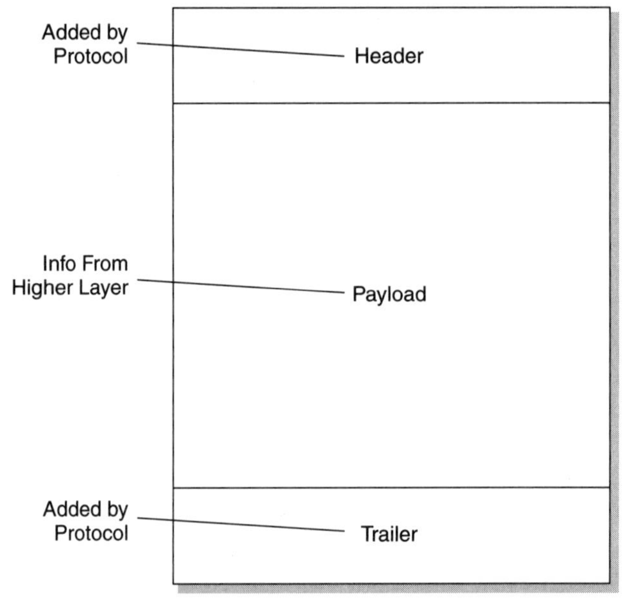

FIGURE 4–2 *Generic packet format.*

Internet Protocol Suite

While the Internet uses the world's most famous protocol—the Internet Protocol or IP—there are an enormous number of protocols operating in the Internet today. In order to understand the technical operation of the Internet, a partial list of these protocols must be examined. Among these are:

- IP, the Internet Protocol and its integral addressing scheme, which is responsible for the basic routing and delivery of packets
- ICMP, the Internet Control Message Protocol, which is used to examine and control the network's operation
- ARP, the Address Resolution Protocol that maps IP addresses into physical media addresses
- RIP, Routing Information Protocol, which establishes the routes for packets inside a particular network
- OSPF, Open Shortest Path First, which is the new emerging routing protocol for internal routing
- BGP, Border Gateway Protocol that routes across external networks
- DNS, the Domain Name Service that translates domain names into IP addresses and many other data translation functions
- TCP, the Transmission Control Protocol that provides reliable transfer of information over the unreliable IP layer
- UDP, the User Datagram Protocol, which gives TCP-like direct access to the raw IP transfer capability but without providing reliable transfer
- PPP, Point-to-Point Protocol, which is used to establish an end-to-end link and provides user authentication
- RSVP, the Resource Reservation Protocol that manages resources to meet quality of service requirements
- DiffServ, the Differentiated Services concept, which also meets the service requirements
- FTP, the File Transfer Protocol that can transfer files from computer to computer
- HTTP, the HyperText Transfer Protocol used by Web browsers for transferring files containing HyperText Markup Language documents for creating those lovely World Wide Web screens
- SMTP, the Simple Mail Transfer Protocol that is the basis for electronic mail

- SNMP, the Simple Network Management Protocol that allows network managers to monitor and control the various elements inside the network

In the next chapter, a few more protocols that are essential to telephony service over the Internet will be added to this list. These will include:

- RTP, the Real-time Transfer Protocol that supports delivery of information in a suitable form to support services such as telephony or video
- RTCP, the Real-time Transfer Control Protocol that is the companion to RTP and is used to manage the RTP sessions
- NTP, the Network Time Protocol that provides reliable timing for transfers and an accurate clock
- H.323, a set of protocols based largely on ISDN that can be used for providing telephony over IP
- MEGACO, the Media Gateway Control Protocol that is yet another means for doing telephony over IP
- SIP, the Session Initiation Protocol that is yet another means for doing voice over IP

We begin our exploration of the Internet with a discussion of each of these Internet protocols and their relationships. As we will see, some of the protocols make use of others within the suite. For example, the FTP will use the TCP to ensure that its transmitted packets arrive correctly. TCP in turn will use IP to transmit the information across the network. So, these protocols are interdependent. Figure 4–3 shows some of these relationships.

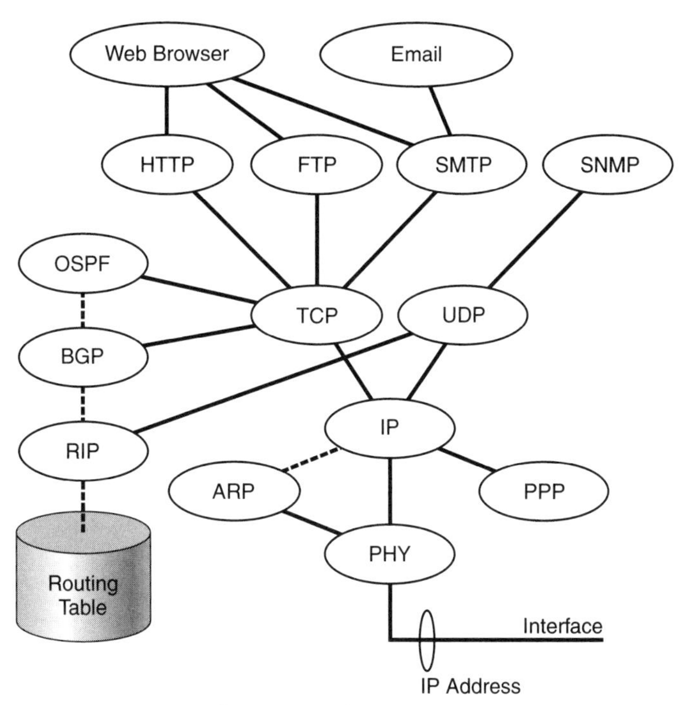

FIGURE 4–3 *Partial IP protocol suite.*

Internet Protocol Version 4 (IPv4)

Figure 4–4 shows the layout of the now famous IP packet. In fact, there are a variety of IP packet formats, but the one shown here is Version 4 from RFC-791,[1] which was specified in 1981. This is commonly referred to as IPv4. The most recent version is IPv6, but this protocol has not yet been widely accepted, and IPv4 is the most popular packet format of all time. The various fields of the packet are filled out at the originating host and in some cases are modified as the packet moves through the network.

1. RFC stands for Request for Comments and is the name given to specifications created by the IETF. RFCs are created by groups in the IETF, and when work is complete, are given draft status. Once implementations meeting certain criteria appear, they can become an Internet standard.

Version	Header Length	Type of Service	Total Length
Identification		Flags	Fragment Offset
Time to Live	Protocol	Header Checksum	
Source IP Address			
Destination IP Address			
Options			
Payload			

FIGURE 4–4 *IPv4 packet format.*

As we will see, IP makes no assumptions about the behavior of the network itself. Because there can be transmission errors, IP must be able to detect these errors if they occur in its header. And if errors are detected, IP will discard the packet. Because routers may send packets destined to reach the same point by different routes, it is not assumed that the network will deliver the packets in the order in which they were sent, so the layer above IP that receives the packets must be able to reorder them. If a packet that is too large for transmission is passed to the IP layer, it will be broken into multiple fragments and then reassembled at the receiver before being passed up to the higher layer. Never forget that IP does not provide reliable transfer of packets. If they become corrupted, spend too much time in the network, have missing fragments, or any other problem, they will be discarded.

The fields of the IP packet and the number of bits used to represent each field follow:

- **Version** (4 bits) – The version of IP for this packet. Note that earlier and later versions have entirely different formats and fields. For this reason, this field is given first and must be checked before applying any processing to the packet. The value is (naturally) 0100 for IPv4 and 0110 for IPv6.
- **Header Length** (4 bits) – The length of the entire header, not including any payload, expressed as the number of 32-bit words. By having 32-bit alignment, a great deal of time can be saved in processing the packets, since a 32-bit computer can move the packets around without the need to mask and shift information about.
- **Type of Service** (8 bits) – This is a complex field containing a 3-bit Precedence subfield and a 5-bit Type of Service subfield. The Precedence field selects one of eight precedence values: Routine, Priority, Immediate, Flash, Flash Override, CRITIC-ECP, Internetwork Control, and Network Control, where Routine is the lowest precedence and Network Control is the highest. This subfield affects how the packet is queued by routers. The second subfield, Type of Service, consists of 5-bits specified as D, T, R, C, and spare. This subfield is intended to specify routing priority for the packet, where D requests low delay, T requests high throughput, R requests high reliability, and C requests low cost. Only a single priority can be specified, and it is intended that the router select a path that best supports the requested priority, if any. This field is little used today, although there has been some thought given to using this field for quality of service control.

- **Total Length** (16 bits) – The total length of the packet, including header and the payload, in octets.[2] Thus, the maximum size of an IP packet is 65,535 octets. However, if the lower media layer cannot support this size, IP will fragment the packet to accommodate the media.
- **Identification** (16 bits) – If a packet larger than 65,535 octets is passed to the IP processor, it will be segmented into several small packets at the transmitter that are then reassembled at the receiver. Because this might be going on for several packets at the same time, and because the network cannot be trusted to deliver the segments in order, it is necessary to identify the packet to which each segment belongs. Identification serves this purpose and can identify up to 65,535 packets undergoing reassembly.
- **Flags** (3 bits) – This field specifies if further fragmentation is allowed or not and whether or not more fragments are outstanding. This is done by two bits, the DF (Don't Fragment) and MF (More Fragments), while the third bit is set to zero. If DF is set, it is an indication that the packet should not be fragmented. If the packet is too large, it will be discarded in this case. If MF is set, there are more fragments outstanding, but if MF is cleared, this is the last fragment of a packet. The reassembling IP layer at the receiver uses this information to determine when all fragments have arrived. Once all the fragments have been received and are reassembled, the resulting packet can be passed to the higher layer.
- **Fragment Offset** (13 bits) – This field specifies the position within the original packet that the current fragment should occupy. The receiver will use this information to position the payload in the reconstructed packet. Because packets may not be delivered

2. Communications experts refer to the lowly byte of the computer world as an *octet*. Both these terms refer to an 8-bit combination of binary codes, meaning ones or zeros. This many bits can represent decimal values from 0 to 255.

sequentially in the order in which they were sent, the receiver must examine both the Fragment Offset and the Flag bits to determine if all the fragments have been received. As an example, consider the case that a packet has only two fragments but the second one arrives first. In this case, the receiver will know there is an outstanding fragment due to the Fragment Offset value and that the intervening fragments have not been received. Once the tardy fragment arrives, the packet reassembly can be completed.

- **Time to Live** (8 bits) – The time, in seconds, remaining before this packet should be discarded. The purpose of this field is to prevent packets from somehow bouncing around inside the network endlessly. Because an exact measure of the time spent in router queues is not practical, modern systems simply decrement the TTL field at each routing step. If the TTL field reaches zero at a router, the packet will be discarded.
- **Protocol** (8 bits) – Specifies which higher layer protocol should receive the payload when the packet reaches the destination. Some example values and their protocols are 0 = Reserved, 1 = ICMP, 4 = IP (encapsulation), 6 = TCP, 17 = UDP, 89 = OSPF, and 45 = IDRP.
- **Header Checksum** (16 bits) – The sum of the header as 16-bit words expressed in one's complement. This is computed at the transmitter and all systems that may receive and process the packet. Should there be any errors, the packet must be discarded, since none of the critical information needed for processing it can be trusted. While this scheme can be tricked and there are stronger protection means available, it has proven adequate in practice. Furthermore, it is easy to compute and serves and a universal means of checking packets in the IP suite. The checksum is regenerated at each router because it is normal to modify parts of the header (such as the TTL value).
- **Source IP Address** (32 bits) – The IP address of the originating system. IP addresses will be explained later in this section.

- **Destination IP Address** (32 bits) – The IP address of the desired destination. The network may or may not deliver the packet due to transmission errors, excessive time spent bouncing around inside the network, equipment failures, or any of a multitude of other reasons.
- **Options** (24 bits) – In the early days of the Internet, this variable length field was used to request various routing schemes, such as source routing and secure routing, but it is rarely used today, since there are better means to such ends.
- **Padding** (8 bits) – This unused field simply ensures that the entire header exactly occupies a 32-bit framework.
- **Payload** (As required) – The higher layer information that is carried end-to-end without modification other than possible segmentation into multiple IP packets. Even in this case, the packet is reassembled before it is passed to the higher layer protocol.

In operation, when an IP entity receives a data block and a destination from a higher layer protocol entity such as TCP, it simply fills out all the fields of the packet with the appropriate values. Key among these is the Protocol field that will identify the same higher layer protocol at the destination from which the IP layer received the request. Thus, the transfer will be from peer to peer. The higher layer protocol may also request certain treatment of the data by the IP layer, as specified by the type of service. The IP layer will also complete the version number, the source IP address, determine if fragmentation is needed, and calculate a checksum for the header. Once the packet is prepared, it will be passed to the lower layer for transport through the network.

IP Addressing

The IP address is a key element of the Internet. The IPv4 address consists of 32 bits that are generally written as four decimal numbers, each ranging from 0 to 255 to represent 8 bits, which are separated by decimal points. For example, my portable notebook computer's IP address is 128.96.70.83. This represents the 32-bit binary address 10000000 01100000 01000110 01010011. These addresses designate network interfaces, not host computers, a common misunderstanding. As such, a host computer may have a multitude of IP addresses, one for each of its operating interfaces.

In its earliest definition, the Internet address consisted only of a network identifier and a host number, but this was later modified to have three fields: network number, subnetwork number, and a host number, where the subnetwork address is found by applying a mask to the IP address. The Internet numbering authority (IANA) assigns network identifier values. Host numbers and subnetwork numbers are established locally by the network operator. Through the concept of subnetworking, the operator is able to organize the overall network. When creating subnetworks, the operator distributes the mask value to elements inside the network. Because the mask is not normally distributed outside the network, it will not be known to outside entities.

Prior to introducing Classless Interdomain Routing (CIDR), the organization of the address depended on the most significant bits of the first (highest) octet of the address. There were five cases, as given in Table 4–2.

TABLE 4-2 IP Address Structure

High Order Bits	Format	Class	Number of Networks	Number of Hosts
0	7-bit network ID 24-bit host number	A	126	16,771,214
10	14-bit network ID 16-bit host number	B	4094	65,534
110	21-bit network ID 8-bit host number	C	2,097,150	254
1110	28-bit multicast group ID	D	N/A	N/A
1111	Reserved	E	N/A	N/A

As can be seen in the table, these different classes were able to support different numbers of networks[3] and hosts. As the number of networks and hosts grew over the years, there was continual difficulty in assigning addresses. Since so few class-A and class-B addresses were available, they were quickly exhausted. Because each class-C address could only support 255 hosts, large organizations with many end systems required a large set of network ID values. This caused an enormous number of entries in routing tables which proved difficult to administer and also slowed down routing functions.

Using these address classes, the IP address is decomposed into a network number, a subnetwork number, and a host number by examining the upper bits of the address to determine the class type and then applying a mask of ones

3. Because the value all zeros and all ones are reserved, the number of hosts and networks are two less than what might otherwise be expected.

and zeroes to the original IP address. The mask, which is a contiguous set of ones followed by zeroes, is used to select that part of the address that is the subnetwork. The remaining bits are then the host value. For example, my notebook's IP address 128.96.70.83 is the 32-bit binary value 10000000 01100000 01000110 01010011. Because the first two bits are 10, this address has a 14-bit network ID of 000000 01100000, otherwise known as network 128.96. Devices outside this network do not know the subnetwork mask. But any IP device inside this network knows the subnetwork mask to apply. According to my notebook's IP parameters, the subnetwork mask for this network is 255.255.255.0, otherwise expressed in binary as 11111111 11111111 11111111 00000000. The host number is given by the lower 8 bits of the address. This means that the subnetwork number is 128.96.70, which is 10000000 01100000 010000110. So, a router in network 128.96 will forward the packet to a router in subnetwork 128.96.70. The subnetwork router will pass it on to my notebook at 128.96.70.83. Table 4–3 summarizes this addressing example.

TABLE 4-3 *Subnetwork Addressing Example*

Object	IP address	Comment
Network	128.96	This address refers to the Telcordia network. When routing, it will translate into the actual IP address of a gateway to this network.
Subnetwork	128.96.70	This refers to subnetwork number 70 in the Telcordia network. It will translate into the IP address of an interface to a router inside this subnetwork that can deliver packets to hosts within it.
Notebook computer (host)	128.96.70.83	My notebook computer is host number 83 in subnetwork number 70 in the Telcordia network.

Use of masks in this manner may seem confusing but it allows the managing organization to establish several subnetworks to manage their routing in an efficient manner. It also simplifies routing decisions outside the network. As we will see later, routers operating inside a network need to know the subnetwork mask and will route to the proper subnetwork by decomposing the address and finding a route. But routers outside any given network will be able to route only to that network and will not know how the network's subnetworks are organized or how to reach hosts within it.

Some addresses have special significance to network systems. For example, there is a broadcast address with a host number of all ones that can be used to transmit a message to all hosts within a network or a subnetwork. Messages sent to this address will be received and processed by all listening IP layers but will never be forwarded outside the network or subnetwork. Also, the value 0 can be used as either network identifier or host number whenever the true value is not known. This is generally used by hosts or network systems that are just coming online and have either forgotten their identifiers or are new systems being installed. Through a methodology known as *auto-discovery,* these systems can learn their identifiers from special servers in the network.

CIDR does not use the upper bits of the address to determine the class and the number of bits that make up the network address. Instead, CIDR uses a variable length mask that selects the correct number of upper bits in the IP address to identify the network. This mask is a series of contiguous ones followed by contiguous zeros and can have between 13 to 27 bits set. CIDR addresses are written with a suffix that indicates the number of bits in the mask. For example, 128.96.70.83/16 means the mask has its upper 16 bits set. When this mask is applied to 128.96.70.83, the network address of 128.96 emerges. Although used in a similar manner, this should not be confused with the subnetwork mask that still is used for routing inside a network. In fact, CIDR has been called "super-netting."

Use of CIDR supports two important capabilities in Internet addressing. First, it allows blocks of addresses to be assigned that are more in keeping with the needs of the organization requesting an address. This is because a CIDR address can serve between 32 to 524,288 hosts depending on how many bits of the address are left to identify hosts after the mask is applied. So, organizations having 32 or fewer hosts will use a mask with the upper 27 bits set. An organization having 8,000 hosts will have a mask with the upper 19 bits set. This flexibility allows more efficient assignment of the 32-bit IP address so as to extend its life. Second, the use of CIDR through address aggregation reduces the number of entries necessary in routing tables. This is important as more and more networks are added to the Internet. This occurs because routers only advertise their network identity. Smaller routing tables will also speed up the routing function, another useful benefit.

Internet Control Message Protocol (ICMP)

Any system running IP is required to also recognize ICMP messages. ICMP is used to manage certain aspects of IP operation. ICMP messages are carried directly over IP so their delivery is not reliable. The messages normally are used to provide diagnostic information about problems that occurred and to discover various aspects of the network's performance and operation. ICMP messages are carried over IP so they are addressed to a particular physical interface somewhere in the network that has been assigned an IP address. The message may be routed past many systems that ignore it because it is not addressed to them. When the message reaches the destination IP address, the ICMP protocol processor at that interface will process the message and respond if necessary. In responding, it only has to reverse the source and destination IP addresses so the packet will return to the originating ICMP processor.

ICMP has several message types, a few of which are given in Table 4–4. The header is shown in Figure 4–5.

TABLE 4-4 ICMP Message Types

Type	Message
4	Source quench
9	Router advertisement
10	Router solicitation
5	Router redirect
3	Destination unreachable
11	Time exceeded
8	Echo
0	Echo reply

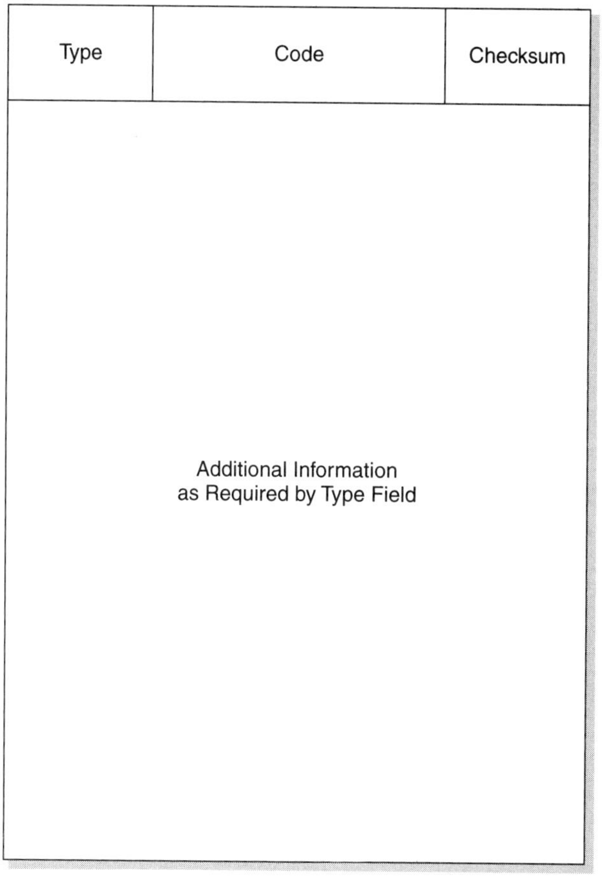

Type	Code	Checksum
Additional Information as Required by Type Field		

FIGURE 4–5 *ICMP packet format.*

As can be seen, ICMP messages provide important functions necessary to operate the network, such as congestion (source quench), routing (router advertisement, solicitation, and redirect), discarded packets (destination unreachable and time exceeded), and pinging (echo and echo reply). These are just a few of the ICMP messages. Furthermore, many of the message types have additional parameters and data included that can be interpreted by the receiving ICMP protocol processor. Besides the few examples given in the table, ICMP can synchronize clocks within the processing system and can trace the routes over which an IP packet has traveled.

Transmission Control Protocol (TCP)

Since IP does not provide any assurance that the data packets sent between applications will be delivered, it is necessary to have a means for doing so. Otherwise, every application would need to include such a capability if reliable data transfer is needed, so it is better to provide a common capability. For those cases when reliable transfer is not needed, applications could directly use the IP layer or a different protocol—UDP, described later—that otherwise mimics TCP. TCP provides this reliable transfer service for application layers. To accomplish this, TCP will place sequence numbers and acknowledgments in its header with the data and will store the data for possible retransmission until the receiver has acknowledged receipt of the data. Because the IP layer may not deliver the packets at all, TCP maintains a timer for each packet. If the receiver does not acknowledge the packet before the timer expires, it will be retransmitted. Because the packet may have been received but the acknowledgment discarded, TCP receivers must be prepared to receive multiple copies of data as well as to recover from missing ones.

When TCP is first requested by a higher layer to begin a transfer, it starts a session. This should be considered as a connection between the endpoint applications. The protocol will first synchronize the transmitting and receiving TCP layers and will then begin transferring data between the higher layers. When the higher layers have completed their interaction and inform TCP, the session will be terminated. All these operations are accomplished by piggybacking control fields with the higher layer data so as to maximize the transfer rates and minimize delay.

The TCP header can be seen in Figure 4–6 and its fields are described next.

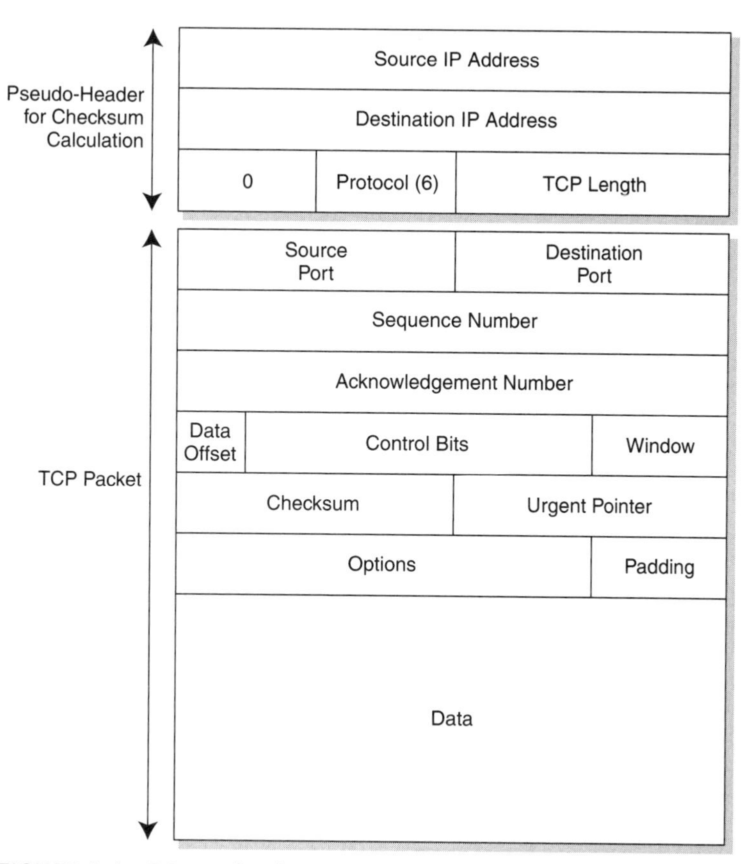

FIGURE 4–6 *TCP packet format.*

- **Source Port** (16 bits) – This value specifies what higher layer protocol originated the data where specific values in the range 0 to 1023 have been identified[4] for various applications. Among these are
  - 23 = SMTP
  - 25 = Telnet
  - 20, 21 = FTP [20 = data, 21 = control]
  - 53 = DNS
  - 80 = WWW-HTTP
  - 70 = GOPHER

4. Visit the IETF (www.ietf.com) and retrieve RFC 1700 to see a complete list of port numbers and the related application layers.

- **Destination Port** (16 bits) – This value tells the receiving TCP layer what higher layer to deliver the data to. As given previously, there is a set of well known values for key applications. However, values 1024 and above can be used however the developer wishes.
- **Sequence Number** (32 bits) – This value is incremented as each successive block of data is transmitted. At the receiver, this is used to determine if a data block is missing as well as where the received block belongs in the sequence (remember that IP may not deliver the packets in their original order).
- **Acknowledgment Number** (32 bits) – This value tells the transmitting system how far the receiver has gotten in correctly received packets. By checking these off, the transmitter can eventually discard data blocks being held in storage in case retransmission is needed. Because the packet carrying the acknowledgement is coming from the receiver, it may also be carrying data in the opposite direction. As such, the acknowledgement is piggybacked on the reverse information transfer. But if there is no information to send, the TCP receiver will generate a packet just to carry the acknowledgment.
- **Data Offset** (4 bits) – This field specifies the length of the header in 32-bit words. This allows the receiver to quickly access the user data for transfer to the higher layer protocol.
- **Control Bits** (12 bits) – This field contains 6 reserved bits and a set of flags for controlling the transfer. The flag bits include
  - URG indicates urgent data
  - ACK indicates that the acknowledgment number is meaningful
  - PSH indicates that the data should be "pushed" promptly to the destination
  - RST indicates that errors have occurred and the session should be aborted

  - SYN causes the layers to synchronize at the beginning of a session
  - FIN indicates the normal closing of a session
- **Window** (8 bits) – This field indicates the amount of buffer space available at the receiver for receiving payloads. This allows the sending side to manage its transmissions in a way that it will not overrun the receiver with information.
- **Checksum** (16 bits) – As with the IP layer, this is a simple sum of all the fields of the header. However, a pseudo-header consisting of three extra words is included inside the checksum. These three words include the source and destination IP addresses for the packet and a word containing the protocol value (6) and the TCP length. This allows for strong checking of the IP delivery mechanism at the receiver.
- **Urgent Pointer** (16 bits) – This field contains an offset and the length of urgent data contained in the data block, if any. This allows critical information to be passed to the user application as soon as possible.
- **Options** (24 bits) – The only option specified for this field is the maximum length of data that the receiver can process.
- **Padding** (8 bits) – Not used for any processing function, this field simply ensures 32-bit alignment for fast transfer within processors.
- **Data** (as required) – This is the data block from the higher layer protocol.

Using these fields, TCP will utilize the unreliable IP layer to provide reliable transfer of data. Remember that IP will take care of fragmenting the TCP packet if necessary. TCP must allow for the fact that IP may discard packets randomly, it may not receive them in the order in which they were sent, and the packet may have its data corrupted with errors. Using the fields in its header, TCP is able to withstand most of these assaulting conditions and, like the pony express rider, get the data through.

One special feature of TCP is its reaction to congestion and the way it is engineered to avoid congesting the network. During operation, timers are used to estimate the statistical delay of acknowledgments. TCP will pace its transmission speed to the rate of acknowledgments received. It employs a "slow start" in its transfer and then gradually increases its packet submission rate until the acknowledgment rate stops increasing. Also, when congestion is detected, it will back off to a low transfer rate. This allows TCP to gracefully operate at or near the highest possible speed but without congesting the network.

User Datagram Protocol (UDP)

Because some applications do not require reliable transfer of their data, a protocol complementary to TCP is available in the IP suite of protocols. UDP utilizes the same port structure as TCP but without providing reliable transfer or any other service. It simply uses the IP layer in as direct a means as possible. It is the higher layer protocol's responsibility to deal with the issues of lost packets, out of sequence packets, delay and delay variation in delivery of packets, and so forth. There are many applications for which this is an appropriate strategy. Nearly any application that makes very short transactions during a session would prefer to use UDP rather than TCP because the overhead of establishing a session for such short transfers would slow down the protocol. Examples of such higher layers are applications that access the DNS with very short requests that can easily be retransmitted by the application. Another example is SNMP, which must avoid adding traffic when managing a congested network. Another reason for using UDP instead of TCP is that there is not enough time to retransmit any data that was either corrupted or discarded by the network. Voice over IP (VoIP) is just such a protocol.

The UDP header is shown in Figure 4–7 and has the following fields:

- **Source Port** (16 bits) – This is used in the same manner as the Source Port field of TCP; it simply specifies which higher layer protocol has provided the data. However, an application using UDP with a given port number and a second instance of the application using TCP with the same port number will not be confused by the protocols. They are assumed to be different applications.
- **Destination Port** (16 bits) – This field is used by the receiving UDP processor to deliver any data included to the appropriate higher layer protocol.
- **Length** (16 bits) – This is the length of the entire packet, including the header and the data.
- **Checksum** (16 bits) – As in TCP and IP, this is a simple sum of the header, the data, and a pseudo-header, which contains the source and destination IP addresses, the protocol field, and the UDP length. These are included when performing the checksum calculation but are not actually transmitted. This allows the receiver to detect packets that the IP layer has delivered to the wrong IP address or protocol.

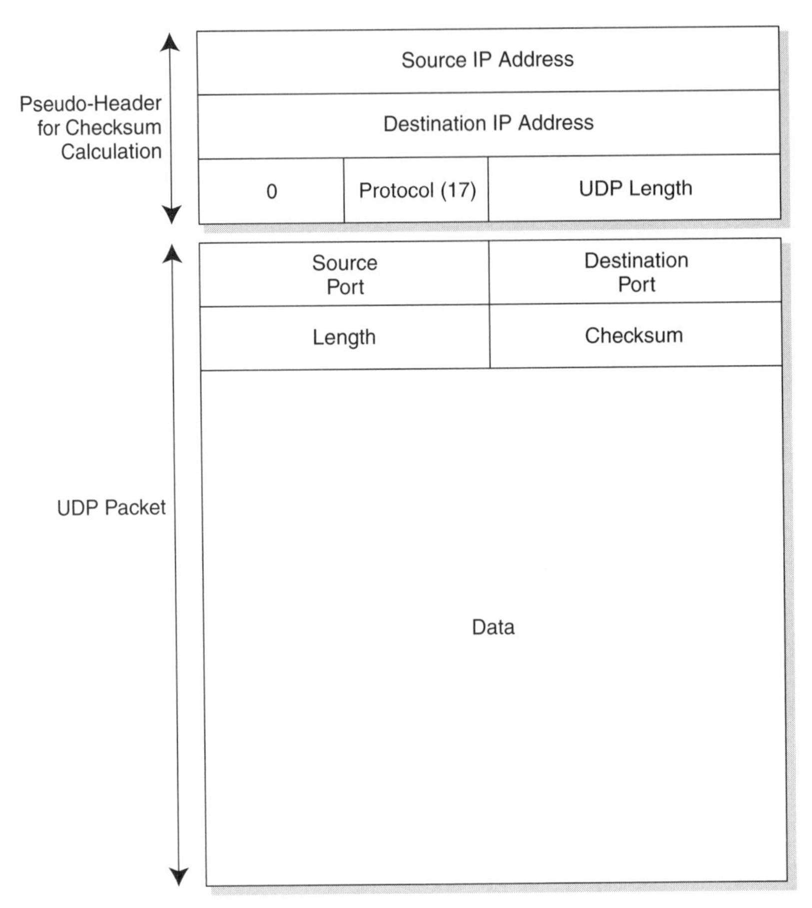

FIGURE 4–7 *UDP packet format.*

For applications like VoIP, UDP is not an ideal layer. However, the overheads and delays of TCP make UDP a better choice. Issues such as variable delay, loss of data, and out of sequence packets must be dealt with by higher layer protocols used by VoIP. These protocols will be described in the next chapter.

Address Resolution Protocol (ARP)

IP makes use of the underlying link layer that transports packets across a given physical media. Each item of equipment that is terminated on the physical media has a link

layer media address associated with its interface. This is different from the IP address for the same interface. This allows IP to use many different physical media such as Ethernet and ATM. ARP is the protocol that discovers the media address for an interface associated with an IP address inside a subnetwork.

Figure 4–8 shows a subnetwork, an Ethernet with five entities attached to it. Each interface has an assigned IP address and also a media address. Notice that one of the entities on the subnetwork has two interfaces and, consequently, two IP addresses and two media addresses. The IP addresses are administered locally by the network manager.

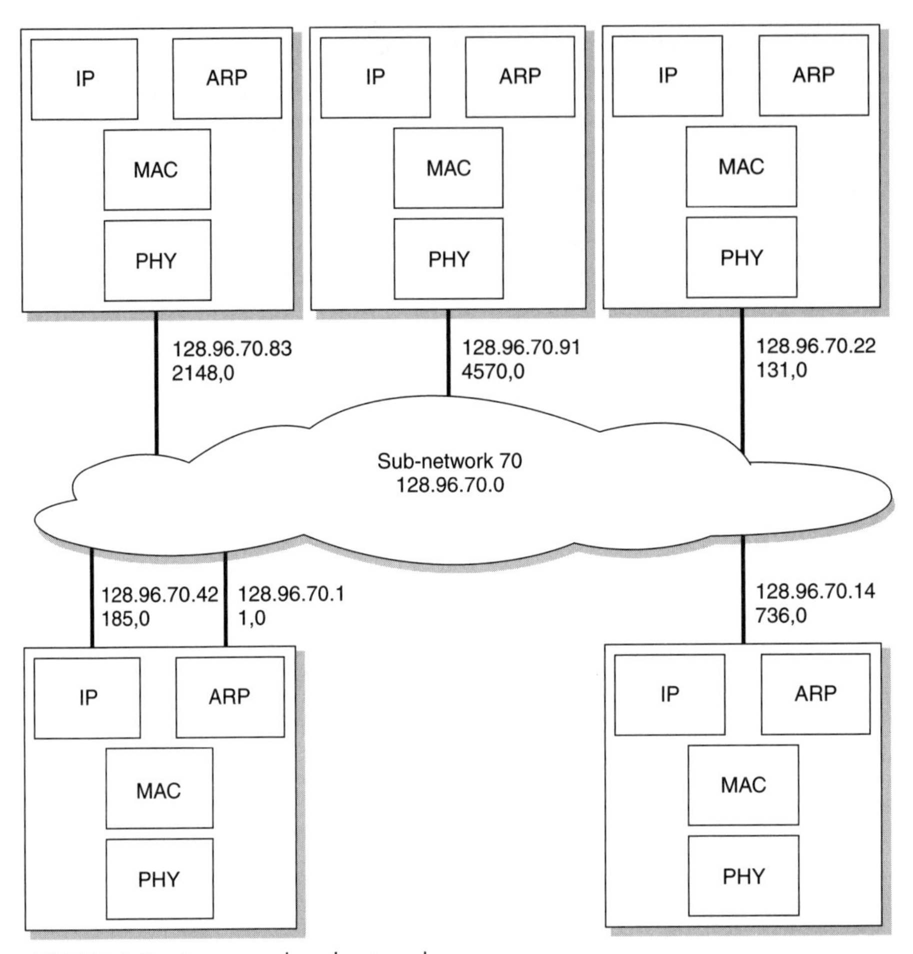

FIGURE 4–8 *An example subnetwork.*

The IP layer assumes that every interface connected to the subnetwork is addressable by the link layer and reachable using the media addresses. Figure 4–8 depicts a single subnetwork, which bears the subnetwork ID of 70. This subnetwork is part of network 128.96, and the various entities on the subnetwork have host IDs of 83, 91, 22, 42, 1, and 14. Thus, IP address 128.96.70.83 denotes host 83 on subnetwork 70 in network 128.96. This host can be reached within the subnetwork using media address 2148.

The IP layer also assumes there is a broadcast capability in the media or available through an ARP server for sending messages that will be delivered to all systems on the subnetwork. In the Figure 4–8, the second number denotes the media address used for broadcast and has the value 0. All stations in the subnetwork will accept messages addressed to media address 0.

These media addresses are found using ARP. ARP discovers media addresses by employing a simple procedure. When the media address of an IP address is needed for the first time, ARP transmits a request containing the IP address to be resolved over the media broadcast address. Because messages sent on the broadcast address are processed by all entities on the Ethernet, all subnetwork entities will receive this request and the request will be passed to the ARP protocol processor in that entity. The entity whose IP address matches the request will respond and give its media address. Continuing the previous example, if any entity on subnetwork 70 broadcasts a request on media address 0 to resolve IP address 128.96.70.83, my notebook computer will generate a response giving its media address of 2148. The requesting ARP entity will then update its table by pairing the IP address requested with the media address returned in the response. Should there be no responses, the address is deemed unreachable. ARP maintains these values with its procedures, and the most used addresses are kept in a cache so this query/response exchange need not be repeated every time a packet is sent.

In the case of link layers that are connection-oriented, such as ATM, a version of ARP must be defined in order to operate IP over the media. This is because each specific link layer will have its own unique means of addressing and reaching every entity connected to it. If the link layer is connection-oriented, there will be direct virtual circuits having specific connection ID values established between every entity in the subnetwork. Most connection-oriented link layers such as ATM do not directly provide a broadcast capability, so this must be simulated using a server. By providing a connection with a known connection ID value from every subnetwork entity to the server, broadcasts can be created by having the server repeat any message received on one broadcast interface to all other broadcast interfaces.

When a host computer wishes to send an IP packet to another IP address, it will first determine if the destination is on the same subnetwork as the sending host by applying the subnetwork mask and comparing the result to its own subnetwork address. If these match, the host will simply transmit it directly to the destination using the link layer media address that ARP has found for the particular IP address. But, if the destination is on a different network or subnetwork, the host will send the packet to the IP address of a router on the subnetwork, which will then forward it according to its routing tables.

The IP layer in a host discovers the IP address of the local router(s) using the ICMP protocol. This IP address, like any other, will be found using ARP and associated with the media address that reaches the router through the subnetwork. So, when the IP layer sends a packet, it is always "thinking" in IP addresses. But the actual transmission of the packet uses the media address associated with the IP address found by ARP, so a host will have an entry storing the media address for every IP address on its own subnetwork and one or more entries for routers on the subnetwork.

Ethernet and Switched Ethernet

If the media layer is Ethernet, then a unique 48-bit station ID is assigned at every interface. These IDs are assigned at the time the interface is manufactured, so they do not require local administration. Figure 4–9 shows the format of an Ethernet frame. The Ethernet frame[5] consists of six elements. First, there is an 8-octet preamble that allows the receiver to determine that a frame is being transmitted and to synchronize its circuitry with the transmitter. This is followed by a 6-octet destination address. Next is a 6-octet source address, and then a 2-octet type field that is unused and a data field carrying from 46 to 1500 octets. Finally, a frame check sequence is included to verify that the frame is correct.

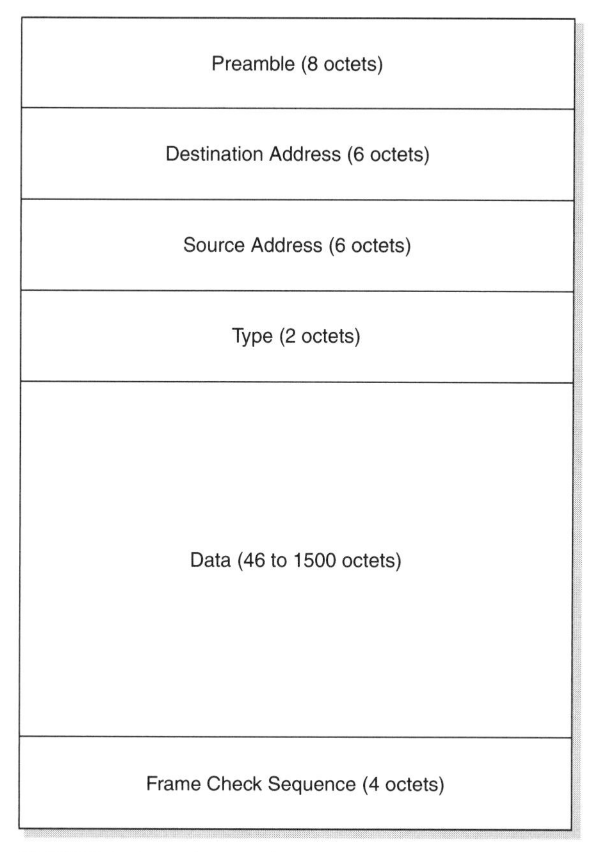

FIGURE 4–9 *Ethernet frame.*

Ethernet interfaces use Carrier Sense Multiple Access with Collision Detection (CSMA/CD). Because this type of Ethernet uses a bus concept whereby every station on the

5. Link layer nomenclature uses the term *frame* to distinguish its transport payload from *packet* at the network layer. This should not be confused with the other meaning of frame from SONET and other TDM structures.

bus must share a single media for both transmitting and receiving, it is necessary for each station to listen before it starts transmitting so as to be sure no other station is using the media. This is shown in Figure 4–10, a continuation of the previous subnetwork example. When a frame is transmitted, every station receives it. This keeps the electronics in all stations synchronized, because the Ethernet receivers at every station are constantly monitoring the media, receiving frames bit by bit. When there is data to transmit, the interface will wait until the media is idle, and then it will immediately commence transmitting. But if the media is busy, it will wait until the frame being sent is finished before it starts sending. Thus, transmitting involves receiving at the same time.

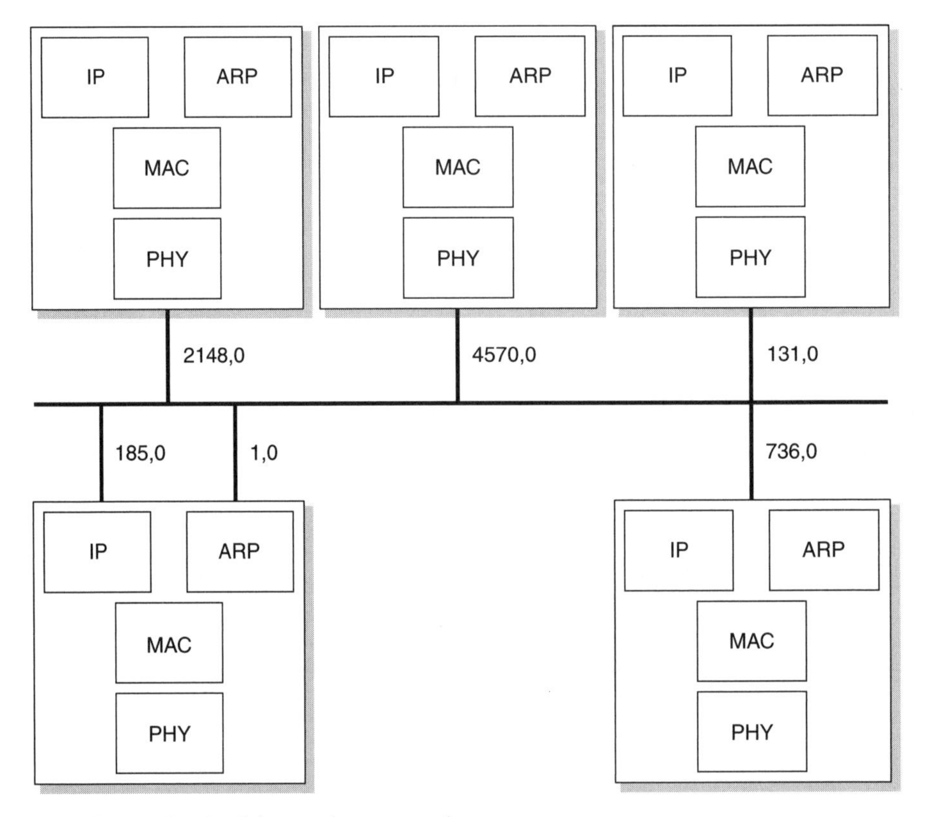

FIGURE 4–10 *An Ethernet bus example.*

It may be that two or more interfaces attempt to transmit at the same time. This will cause a collision that is detectable because the interface's transmitter is sending one value while the receiver receives a different value. When this occurs, the station will transmit a jamming signal to ensure that all stations notice the collision. This will prevent the possible reception of corrupted frames. Then, all stations that were attempting to transmit will wait a random amount of time and start over again by checking the media to see if it is idle.

Ethernet operates by using selective listening. This means that each station interface receives all frames traveling across the Ethernet but only acts on frames carrying its media address. If the destination address of the frame matches the station's media address, then that frame is delivered to the IP layer. If the address does not match, the frame is discarded. There is a special media address in Ethernet, all ones, which is the broadcast address. Frames sent with this address are received by all stations and are delivered to the IP layer. As can be seen in Figure 4–10, each host on the Ethernet bus has a unique media address and a broadcast address. These are identified next to the interface.

There is a binding of IP addresses within the subnetwork to the Ethernet media addresses. When the IP entity wants to send a packet to another system within the subnetwork, it will consult a table that stores the associated Ethernet media address for every IP address known within the subnetwork. The IP entity then simply passes the packet to be sent and its associated media address to the Ethernet layer. The Ethernet layer then transmits the packet as a frame on the actual physical layer. This table should not be confused with a routing table; it is simply the physical address of interfaces associated with IP addresses within the subnetwork and has only local significance.

Modern networks now use switched Ethernet, as shown in Figure 4–11. All of the interfaces shown in the figure are normal Ethernet ports; however, there is only a single host at each end of the interface. This prevents the occurrence of collisions and other synchronization problems that limit capacity. In this way, every station can operate at the full bandwidth of the interface and transmission between systems can occur simultaneously. The switching element simply receives frames from the host computers and examines the media address to which they are addressed. If the address is the broadcast address, then the frame will be replicated and sent to all of its interfaces. However, if it is addressed to a normal media address, it is sent only on the interface that reaches the specific host. The switch learns the media addresses of the hosts by examining the frames it receives on each interface and extracting the source media address. Switched Ethernet is now widely deployed in LANs and has been propelled into very high-speed transmission rates ranging from 10 Mbps to over 10 Gbps.

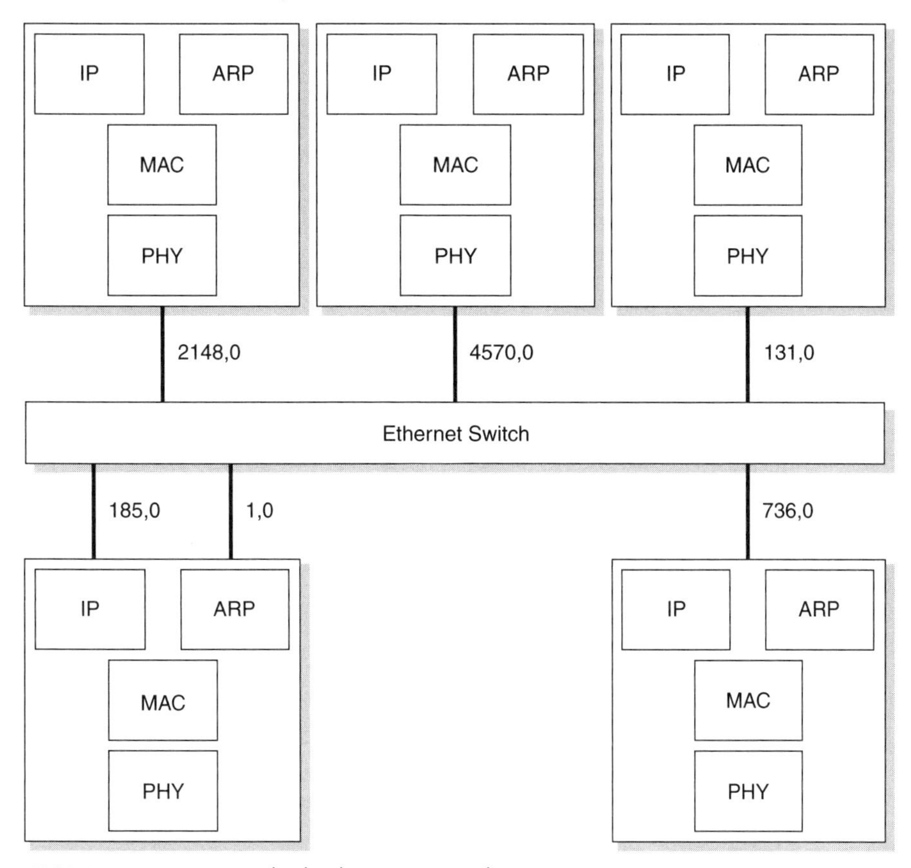

FIGURE 4–11 *A switched Ethernet example.*

Asynchronous Transfer Mode (ATM and AAL 5)

ATM is a protocol that utilizes small fixed-size packets called cells. ATM is connection-oriented, which means that each cell has a number within it that uniquely identifies it within a particular physical interface as belonging to a particular connection. Many standards and specifications for ATM have been created in both the ITU[6] and the ATM

6. ITU is the International Telecommunications Union. ITU includes the former CCITT as ITU-T. In this body, experts from interested nations meet to debate and create technical recommendations for worldwide application. This body generally restricts its work to interfaces between users and networks and interfaces between networks.

Forum,[7] including signaling procedures for setting up these connections. Unlike packets at an IP layer, ATM cells are assumed to arrive in the order that they are sent within a connection. Because ATM is connection-oriented and operates directly over simple physical layers, this will be the case, because every cell follows the same route within a network and neither ATM switches nor the underlying physical layers will reverse the order of cells within a connection. Because errors may occur in either the transmission or the switching systems, ATM procedures must deal with bit errors. Also, switches may become congested if too many cells are destined for an output. The queues within the switch may become saturated, and cells may have to be discarded. So, traffic management of bandwidth in an ATM network is an important issue.

Connections within an ATM network are of two possible types: virtual path and virtual circuit. Figure 4–12 shows these concepts. Within a given physical layer, there can be multiple virtual paths. Within each virtual path, there can be multiple virtual circuits. When a connection traverses several switches, each switch can relabel these fields to avoid merging traffic from other connections that are intended to be separate. In the figure, a connection is shown from a user through a virtual circuit switch, then through a virtual path switch, then through a second virtual circuit switch, and finally delivered to the destination user. The parenthesized label on each link is the virtual path and virtual circuit values found in the cells. Either signaling protocols or administrative systems can be used to assign these values so that the connection reaches the proper destination on an end-to-end basis.

7. The ATM Forum has created a number of ATM specifications, particularly in areas not addressed by ITU, such as within a user's network and inside a national network.

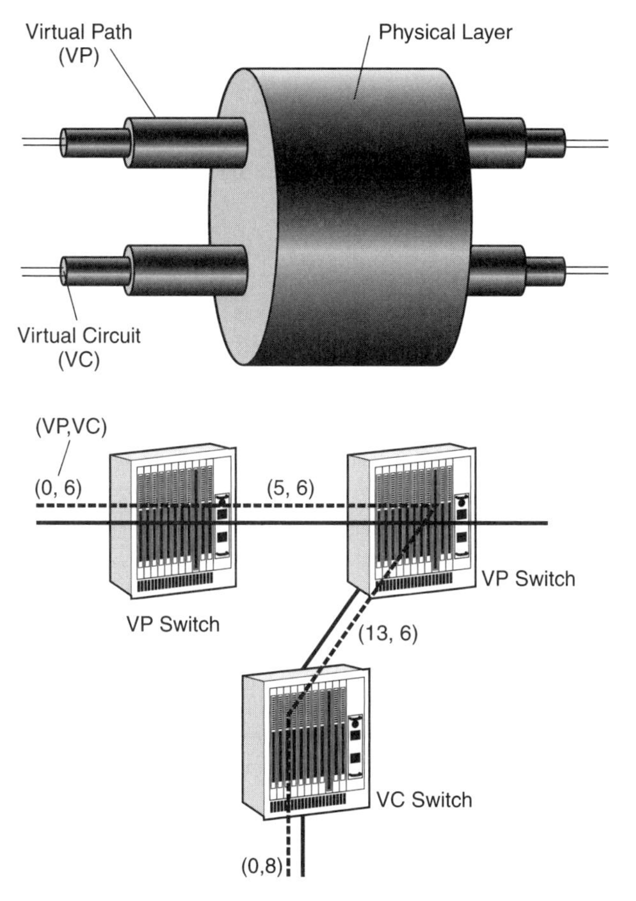

FIGURE 4–12 ATM concepts.

ATM also has a set of operations and administration capabilities for detecting quality in end-to-end or link-by-link flows. This is done using cells that are designated OAM (Operations Administration & Maintenance) cells. These cells carry special messages that OAM processors at either end of a connection can create and interpret. These processors are able to detect link failures, bit rate errors, and other problems present in any network. Using this information, higher layer operations systems may decide to take a link out of service or to dispatch repair personnel to fix a problem.

The format of the ATM cell is shown in Figure 4–13. There are six fields defined that control the transfer of information across a physical layer. In all, the cell consists of 53 octets,[8] including 48 octets of higher layer information.

- **GFC** (4 bits) – This is the Generic Flow Control field. This field was intended to provide indications specific to performing flow control algorithms, but neither its content nor any flow control algorithms have been standardized. Thus, it is left "For Further Study," the ITU nomenclature for work that was not completed.
- **VPI** (8 bits) – This is the Virtual Path Identifier field, and it allows two levels of switching to be performed within a network. A virtual path is a group of virtual circuits. If a switching system utilizes the VPI only when switching cells from one input to another, all virtual circuits within that virtual path will be switched to the same destination. This allows a network to be structured by bulk switching large "pipes" of information between endpoints. VPI numbers can either be assigned on a semipermanent basis by the carrier or selected dynamically by a signaling protocol. As a cell traverses a network of ATM switches, the VPI field may be overwritten by each successive switch.
- **VCI** (16 bits) – This is the Virtual Circuit Identifier field. The numerical value within this field denotes a particular connection along a link and within a virtual path. Like the VPI, these values can be statically or dynamically assigned. They also may be modified as the cells pass through switches within a network.
- **PTI** (3 bits) – This is the Payload Type Identifier field, and it is used to indicate if user information is present in the payload field, whether or not congestion has

8. There is an incorrect belief by many that the 48-octet payload was proposed because it is halfway between the European proposal for 32 octets and the 64-octet proposal from the United States. In truth, the United States proposed 48 octets because it was the smallest payload that could carry the header of a Switched Multimegabit Data Service (SMDS) packet. This was necessary so the packet route could be calculated without waiting for a second ATM cell to arrive. This is but one of many small "ITU insider" secrets.

been experienced along a route, and the presence of OAM information or resource management controls within the payload. When user information is present, it can be indicated as having payload type 0 or payload type 1. This indication is used by some of the higher layers using ATM, particularly AAL5 that is described later.

- **CLP** (1 bit) – This is the Cell Loss Priority bit. It indicates to the switching systems that this cell is either high or low priority with regard to loss. If the switching system's queues are filling, cells with CLP = 1 should be discarded first.
- **HEC** (8 bits) – This is the Header Error Check field, and it is a cyclic redundancy check (CRC) calculated over the 5-octet header. This is a polynomial calculation, and not the simple checksums from the IP suite. The CRC chosen can be used to either detect multiple-bit errors or to correct single-bit errors. In its normal operation, errors are detected, but once a single-bit error has been found, it will be corrected. The receiver will continue correcting all single-bit errors until a header having no errors is received. Then, it resumes simply checking for new errors. The original intent of ATM was to operate mostly over fiber optic transmission systems. Most fiber systems tend to have either an occasional rare single-bit error during normal operation or errors in practically every bit when there is a failure. The HEC is also used to determine if synchronization with the physical media is lost and to regain it.
- **Payload** (48 octets) – This is a fixed-size block for carrying higher layer protocol information.

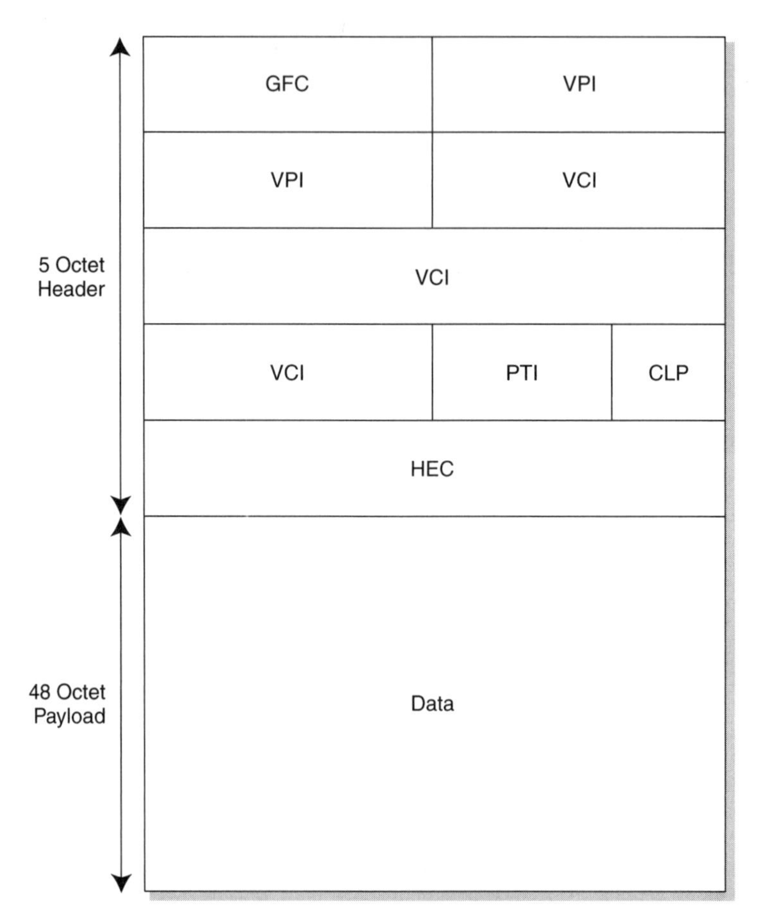

FIGURE 4–13 *ATM cell format.*

Because ATM cells are fixed size and because the address is short, it is possible to switch ATM at very high rates. This fast switching capability, coupled with its ability to provide a logical allocation of traffic within the transmission systems of a network, has kept ATM in use in many carrier networks. As will be discussed in the next chapter, this allows a carrier to control the quality of service for a given set of connections that in turn will allow voice to be carried simultaneously with data across a common network.

Because a 48-octet packet would not be of much use in data communications, ATM also defines an ATM Adapta-

tion Layer (AAL) that segments large packets into 48-octet blocks for transport across an ATM link and then reassembles them at the destination. The ITU defined several AAL protocols, but only one of them, AAL 5, is of use in the Internet for carrying IP and its family of protocols.

Figure 4–14 shows the structure of AAL 5. It consists of a payload passed to AAL 5 by a higher layer and a trailer that AAL 5 adds to the payload, which it uses for controlling the transfer. AAL 5 has no header.

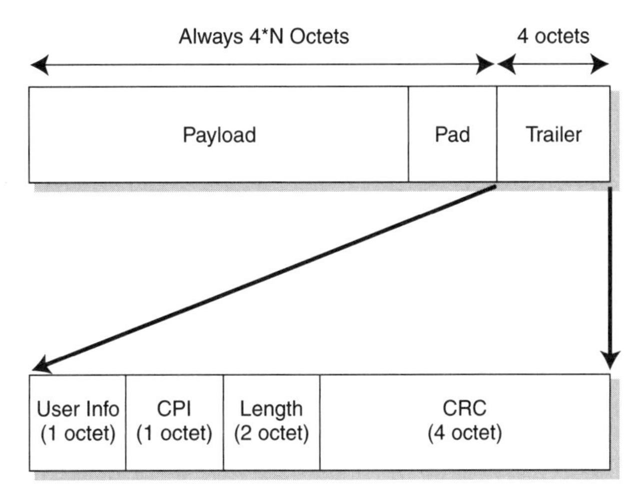

FIGURE 4–14 *AAL5 format.*

- **Payload** (as required) – This is the actual payload of the packet being transmitted.
- **Pad** (as required) – This is an unused field that simply ensures that the AAL 5 control information is at the very end of the last cell transmitted. This enables easy and quick access of the information in the trailer that is needed for processing the packet.
- **CPCS-UU** (8 bits) – This is user-to-user information and is passed transparently to the higher layer. This field could be used by a higher layer protocol for transporting control information.

- **CPI** (8 bits) – This is the Common Part Information, which other AALs utilize for controlling the transfer. AAL 5 specifies only a single coding for this field. As such, it is not used.
- **Length** (16 bits) – This is the length of the actual user data within the payload.
- **CRC** (16 bits) – This is a Cyclic Redundancy Check field for detecting errors within the entire packet, including both payload and trailer.

AAL 5 operates very simply. It receives ATM cells from a given virtual path/virtual circuit and examines the payload type. As long as the payload type is 0, AAL 5 places the cells in memory one after another. When payload type 1 is received, this indicates that this cell is the final cell of a packet. Since some cells may have been discarded along the route, AAL 5 will then check the length of the packet to see if it is correct and also calculate the CRC. If these checks are confirmed, the packet is passed to the higher layer, usually the IP layer.

Multiprotocol Label Switching (MPLS)

Even though IP routers treat each packet as though it were being seen for the first time and has no relationship to any other packet seen before, the actual probability of more than one packet traveling from a source to its destination is relatively high. Intuition, which can sometimes be dangerous, explains why this is so. Host computers do not arbitrarily send packets all around the Internet for no reason. If the set of IP addresses accessed by a host is considered, there are some obvious implications. For one, there will be a lot of very short transfers between a host and its DNS for translating URLs into IP addresses. These transactions are quite short, consisting of only a few packets. Routers will broadcast their location and transfer their routing tables, creating a few more packets. Most of these transfers are fairly small, usually a few dozen packets. But the first time the user browses a distant Web site, there will be large

HTTP transfers to set up the browser window that will usually contain several JPEG images that will fill many IP packets. Every click of the mouse will transfer masses of information, usually from the same place. These packets constitute the bulk of the traffic in the Internet today. And each packet will go through the same routing steps as any other; all the IP functions must be performed, including address translation, even though the exact parameters existed on most of the packets going through the router.

Because routing costs money and can be time consuming, it would be preferred if these packets could somehow all be identified and sent directly on without doing any of the routing functions. This could increase the capacity of a router, something that is always desirable. Besides, it might be possible to use this to control the level of service quality at the IP level by avoiding congestion. If the packets could be given the right priority and treatment, this mechanism can be used to achieve quality of service. This gives rise to the concept of a "flow," which is taken to mean any sustained traffic between two protocols. For example, HTTP is a busy generator of large flows, whereas DNS tends to generate small ones.

Flows are not permanent; they are transient relationships between endpoints. Once the transaction is completed between the endpoints, the flow is complete. After some indeterminate amount of time, the flow is over. Our problem is to somehow identify the large flows early in the life of the flow and bypass the router for the large ones. If this is done, time and money can be saved. To accomplish this, a media layer capable of "switching" packets (as opposed to routing them) is needed.

However, it must be remembered that having the connecting layer present and manipulating it in real-time to establish the bypass has both cost and complexity associated with it. Thus, a balance must be struck between the cost/performance of routing and the cost/performance of switching. If we measure traffic to determine a flow and use a low threshold, we will convert some flows into connections that don't have many more packets to send. This will be result in wasted effort to establish a flow that is not needed. If we use a higher threshold, we will allow more packets to be routed before making the decision to switch, but once switched, it is likely that the flow will continue. This will result in less than optimal treatment of the flows that do get switched and will waste router capacity. Other ways of identifying the flow can be considered, such as checking the IP Protocol field along with the TCP Port field and always establishing flows for certain protocols, such as HTTP or FTP.

Newman, Lyon, and Minshall explored this topic in a landmark 1996 paper in which they reported that a small number of flows accounted for a high percentage of the total packets traversing a router. Table 4–5 summarizes some of their findings. For example, HTTP is seen to generate 73.0 flows per second, with each flow lasting 57 seconds, and carrying 74 packets for a total of 6,717 packets per second. In contrast, DNS can be seen to generate a much larger number of flows per second, 216.0, but each flow averages only 4 packets and lasts only 15 seconds, for a total of 929 packets per second about 1/8 the rate of HTTP.

TABLE 4-5 *Packet statistics for various protocols*

Protocol	Flows per second	Flow Duration	Packets per Flow	Packets per second
HTTP over UDP	73.0	57 sec	74	6717
FTP over TCP	2.2	118 sec	525	2018
NNTP over TCP	0.7	177 sec	627	1096
DNS over UDP	216.6	15 sec	4	929
SMTP over TCP	49.5	18 sec	15	802

They considered different schemes for identifying large flows and concluded that during an interval of 60 seconds, a threshold of only 10 packets from the same IP source/destination/protocol was sufficient to identify large flows. If these flows are switched rather than routed, they would constitute 86 percent of all packets and 92 percent of bytes submitted to the router. When this scheme is applied, the combined switched/routed system would have nearly 3.5 times the capacity of a pure router. In making these calculations, they included the overhead of the control algorithm for setting up the connections to carry the flows.

They proposed that when a router identifies a flow, the router's lower layer could bypass the IP layer for the remainder of that flow. In their particular scheme, they isolated the flow by moving it from the router to its own ATM virtual circuit and notifying the router upstream from it what circuit was used. This action would be taken by every router along the path and would result in a direct "tunnel" between the endpoints. Figure 4–15 illustrates this scheme. As can be seen, Router 1 and Router 3 are being used but the switch beneath Router 2 has bypassed it. This saves one hop of routing.

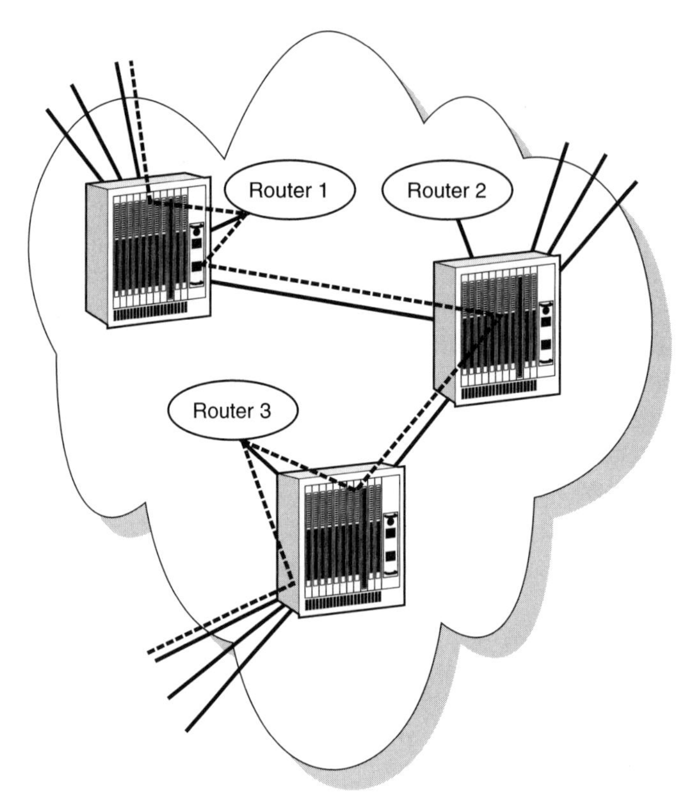

FIGURE 4–15 *IP switching example.*

Although Newman et al. devised their scheme for an ATM media layer, any lower layer can be used, but connectionless layers such as Ethernet require the addition of a label. Schemes for bypassing the routing function were quickly devised for Ethernet and Frame Relay. Some of these schemes depended on the application identifying the flow, while others measured traffic statistics. Eventually, IETF undertook the specification of what is now called Multiprotocol Label Switching (MPLS). MPLS has two parts, one for flow identification and a second for label distribution (Label Distribution Protocol, or LDP). In MPLS, it is assumed that there is an underlying media layer that is able to switch packets based on a short label. The labels can be considered as connections through the media layer to reach more distant routers in the network. These connections are established based on whatever criteria the operator wishes, and they can be dynamically established as the need arises by using signaling protocols to command the media layer to set up such connections. Routers within the network must be able to store labels within their routing tables to make use of the media layer. When a packet enters the network, the first router encountered makes a decision about labeling the packet. In doing so, it can use any criteria it wishes. Obviously, the IP address will be used to select a route, but it can also use criteria such as quality of service indicators or the sending protocol in determining a route. Once the routing table is consulted, the router will attach a label to the packet and pass it to the media layer. In some cases, the label will simply carry the packet to the next router along a default route. But in others, intermediate routers will be bypassed. When a router determines that a new flow is starting and wishes to bypass intermediate routers, it will request a connection to the proper endpoint using the media layer's signaling protocol, and it will use the LDP to assign and notify the other routers of the new tunnel. ATM is one case of a switched media layer that is being used for this function in a number of networks.

With the advent of optical networking and Dense Wave Division Multiplexing (DWDM), an even greater emphasis has come to MPLS due to the possibility of achieving extraordinarily high throughputs for IP networks. By aggregating flows at the proper level, it is possible to reach terabit capacities. While this is still an item under intense study, it would appear feasible to establish a media layer using wave division optical switches that switch each wavelength to a different destination. Then, MPLS labels would be assigned to the various wavelengths available. This is known as Multiprotocol Lambda Switching (MPλS). Some would reach default routers along the network's path, while others would reach more distant routers perhaps all the way at the edge of the network. This and other architectures are under consideration, including GMPLS, Generalized Multiprotocol Label Switching.

Reservation Protocol (RSVP)

In an effort to allow some level of resource reservation to ensure quality of service, IETF has created RSVP, the Reservation Protocol. RSVP operation involves both the source and destination of packet flows, but it is receiver-initiated. This allows applications at the ends of connections to request and receive the quality demanded by their users without providing a single ultra-high quality to all users. This policy does not waste network resources.

In RSVP, sources transmit a special Path message that carries a template that can be applied to the source's packets so as to delineate them from all other flows and a specification that indicates what resources are necessary to ensure quality of service for that flow. These Path messages follow the same route as the session's data from the source to the destination (or destinations, in the case of a multicast session). The flow template is normally the combination of the source's IP address, the Protocol field (usually TCP or UDP), and the Port number. Along the route, each router's RSVP process intercepts these packets and saves the flow template and quality specification. Included in the Path message is the IP address of the previous router handling the message; this establishes a "bread crumb" trail along the path that can be used for sending messages backwards along the route to reach all the routers in the path. The Path messages ultimately arrive at the receiver, where the IP address of the last RSVP processor in the route, the flow template, and the resource specification are saved for future use. These messages simply provide the information necessary for the routers to identify the flow and what type of treatment it should receive in order to provide the proper quality of service.

When a receiver wishes to make a reservation, it simply transmits an RSVP Reservation Request message to the last router in the route. This router will then note that subsequent messages to that destination be given the appropriate quality of service treatment as specified by the source. It then forwards the message on to the previous router in the route that also notes the requirement. This is repeated until the initial router in the route has received and processed the reservation request. Once all the routers along the path have been notified, quality of service will be assured, provided sufficient resources are available. Remember that there is no magic or free lunch in RSVP; it cannot get blood from a stone. If there is insufficient capacity in the network to honor the reservation request, it will not be honored. RSVP provides messages to the receiver to inform it should this be the case.

Reservations are temporary and must be repeated periodically. This is necessary in case the network routing protocols shift the flow's path to a different route. This could happen in case of a failure in the network equipment or because the routers simply found a better route for the session due to traffic or other requirements. If this should happen, a new set of routers with no information about the flow, its requirements, or the receivers may be suddenly thrust into the path. By periodically repeating both the path message and the reservation message, this problem can be solved.

Since the Path messages are emitted by the sources periodically, any new routers involved in a path will become informed of the flow specification and its requirements. Since the Reservation requests from the receivers are repeated periodically, these new routers will begin to give the needed service, once the request is received. This allows RSVP to be independent of routing protocol, an important feature that allows it to operate in any network regardless of what routing protocol is being used as well as allowing new future routing protocols to be developed independently. It also prevents resources from being reserved for long periods when they are not being used.

RSVP also has messages for immediately canceling resource reservations by either the source of the destination processes.

A major problem with RSVP that seems to have no imminent solution is that it does not scale well. In order to utilize RSVP, it must be implemented all across the network before any significant use can take place. This has slowed the adoption of RSVP. Also, it is arguable whether or not RSVP, which is quite complex, is capable of handling large amounts of traffic and reservations. Because each receiver must repeat its request periodically, RSVP will be quite busy receiving, processing, and responding to these requests. For these reasons, many do not consider RSVP a good long-term mechanism for achieving quality of service on a broad scale.

Differentiated Services (DiffServ)

DiffServ is another method for achieving quality of service in IP networking. This concept makes no attempt to identify flows within a network, but instead relies on the packets being marked appropriately, using the IPv4 Type of Service field. Using this field, DiffServ classifies packets as receiving Expedited Forwarding (EF), Assured Forwarding (AF), or best effort treatment. The marking of packets is done at the edge of the network so the network operator can control the allocation of bandwidth that will result from these markings. Packets are classified and marked based on requirements for a particular type of traffic at the edge of the network. A DiffServ edge processor will mark the packets based on a flow identifier such as the source/destination IP address, Protocol field, and Port ID. This would allow the identification of a flow that needs a specific type of resource treatment. The DiffServ processor will know the availability of resources through the network and will mark the packet accordingly if sufficient resources are available. If they are not available, the packet's treatment will be given best effort service. Note that the word

"Assured" does not imply an absolute guarantee; rather, it means that if the source submits traffic according to the predetermined traffic profile, then under normal operation, the needed grade of service will be provided. Using this scheme, routers inside the network are not involved in the classification of the packets or the marking of packets. This allows DiffServ to scale well to large networks. However, the routers must have transport media resources that can meet the EF and AF criteria (as well as a best effort media resource) and must be programmed to direct packets marked to the appropriate transport resource. ATM is one means for creating these differentiated transport media.

DiffServ is a promising mechanism for achieving quality of service in large networks. However, RFCs have only recently been released describing DiffServ, so it is too soon to reach a definite conclusion in this regard. As research continues in optical networking, DiffServ combined with dense wave-division optical MPλS switches may prove to be an excellent high–capacity, long-term solution as well as a means to reach extraordinary throughputs.

Point-to-Point Protocol (PPP)

Many IP devices use direct point-to-point links, such as dial-up modems, ISDN, and other networking arrangements, that unlike Ethernet, where systems are directly wired together, dynamically establish and disestablish connections. These interfaces create special problems for IP and ARP, since the link must first be established and then authenticated. Also, there are many different types of these interfaces, and each has different protocols and requirements for establishing and using link layer connections. PPP is designed to smooth over these differences and present a uniform link layer to the IP layer.

PPP works in conjunction with ARP to establish links to remote systems. Some media addresses may direct IP to use the PPP for utilizing the link. PPP will establish the link as appropriate for the particular networking interface by a member of the Network Control Protocol (NCP) family. For dial-up modem connections, NCP will control the modem and make the phone call to the remote destination. For other devices, it will perform whatever equivalent control is necessary to establish the link.

Next, PPP will invoke an authentication protocol to satisfy the remote PPP layer that it is a valid user of that interface. This will normally involve a user ID and password that is uniquely known by the remote system and the initiating PPP layer. Once the authentication protocol has completed its task, PPP will indicate to the IP layer that the link is established. IP can then transfer packets across the link. When transfers are completed, PPP will be ordered to disconnect the link. This is normally performed when the application is terminated.

Routing (RIP, OSPF, BGP)

In order to introduce routing protocols, it is necessary to introduce the concept of an Autonomous System (AS) because there are routing protocols that operate within an AS and others that operate between AS. The definition of an AS is simple and a bit ambiguous. It has three basic properties:

1. It is managed by a single organization.
2. It uses a common routing protocol.
3. It is *fully interconnected* when operating normally.

So an AS might be a backbone IP network operated by a commercial carrier, or it might be a corporate network for a major business. Even though it may be managed by a single organization, it may not be owned entirely by that organization. An AS may consist of multiple network ID numbers. This may be needed to accommodate the number of hosts or interfaces within the network. An example would be a large corporate network spread all across North America that has leased private line connections between its presence in various cities. Figure 4–16 shows such a network with three parts interconnected by private lines. Several network ID numbers as well as subnetworks are involved. There are two connections to the Internet, which allow traffic to enter or leave the corporate network at points near the users.

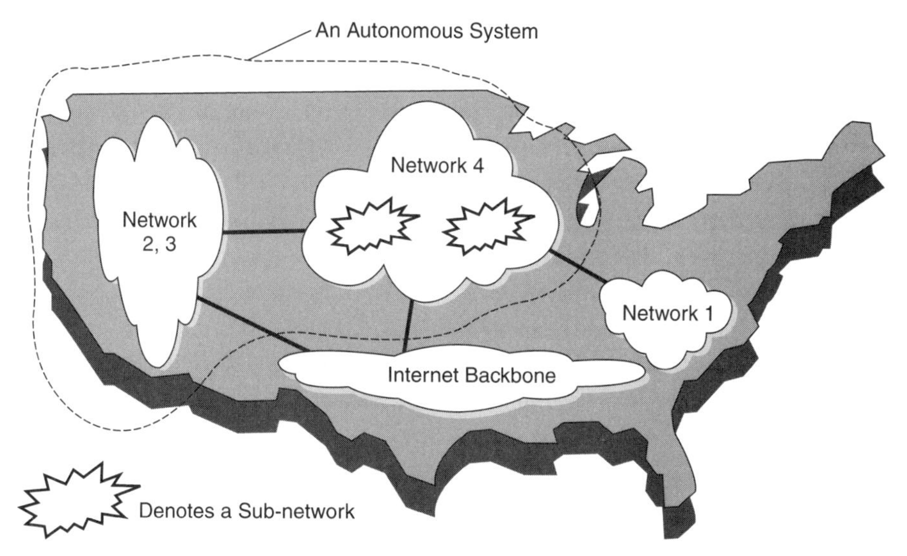

FIGURE 4–16 *Autonomous systems.*

Because an AS is fully interconnected, it is expected that any host or router within the AS is reachable using the common routing protocol. That is, the AS is responsible for routing packets to any of its constituent parts. Naturally, a failure might occur that breaks the AS into pieces, leaving one part or another unreachable. But this is not to be the case during normal operation, and in general terms, this should be avoided even during failures by having sufficient connectivity within the network. One implication of this is that a packet destined for some point inside the AS can enter the AS at any permitted entry point and still be delivered. "Permitted" is a keyword here, since the network operator may not wish to allow the transfer of traffic into the network at certain points, and the routing protocols are designed to allow this flexibility by the manager. Also, the manager may choose to prohibit traffic that is not destined for the network from entering it, because then he would be carrying someone else's traffic through the network. For some operators, such as a backbone network company, this is their bread and butter. But for others, such as a corporate enterprise, this would be an undesirable waste of resources. Fortunately, the routing protocols will give the operator of the network control over exactly these factors.

Each AS takes responsibility for its own operation and well being. Key to this is the routing of packets to elements within the AS, because routers outside the AS will not know how to reach addresses within it. This is because routers within an AS do not pass on information to outside routers about the internal addresses within their network. This means that routers within a network that are part of an AS will know the subnetwork mask to apply for routing to the proper subnetwork. Routers external to the AS will not know these values and will be able to route only to the proper network number ID.

For these reasons, routing is clearly divided into two different problems with two different solutions: interior routing and exterior routing. These designations refer to the router's position with regard to an AS. Those that are interior will be able to deliver packets to hosts and will know the subnetwork masks to use. Those that are exterior will be able to route only to the network number ID in the packet, since they will be unaware of the correct subnetwork mask to use. There are many interior routing protocols, but the most commonplace today are RIP and OSPF. One of the most used exterior routing protocols is BGP. Figure 4–17 shows this relationship. You may consult the references given at the end of this chapter for an exhaustive treatment of these and other routing protocols, as only a basic introduction is provided here.

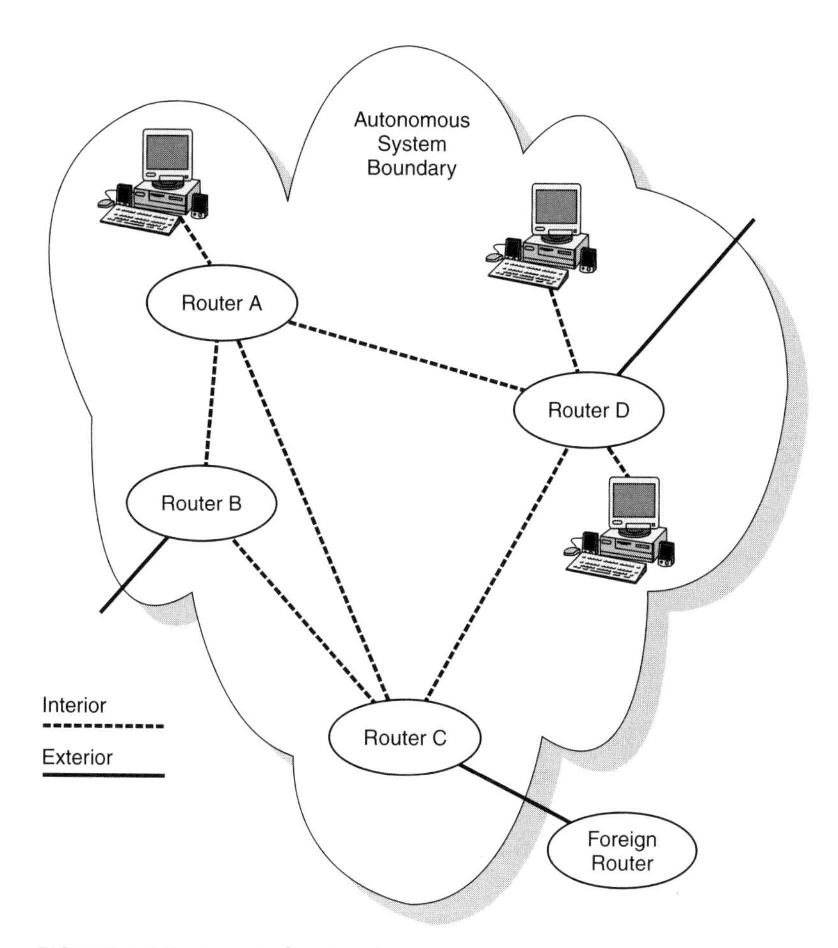

FIGURE 4–17 *A routed network.*

Remember that all routers, irrespective of protocol or location, do the same basic function. They receive IP packets, verify that the packet header is correct by computing the checksum, extract the destination IP address from within the packet, and examine the upper bits of the destination IP address to determine the address format (A, B, or C). The router then looks up the destination IP address in its routing table, which tells it the "next hop" IP address that will reach the next router along the way. Since routers normally have multiple physical interface ports, this look-up will also provide the physical port to use and the media address on that port that will reach the next router. A cache is used to store the most frequent values seen by the router.

Every IP address has three parts, the network ID, the subnetwork ID, and the host ID, but the routers outside a network are only interested in the network ID. Routers inside a network will know the subnetwork masks to apply so they can route to the proper subnetwork, but they will not know about hosts outside their own subnetwork. Then, it queues and sends the packet, using the physical interface port and media address found in the table. These actions get the packet closer to its destination. The destination address within the packet is left intact so the next router can determine the next hop for it. This continues at every routing node until the packet reaches the specified destination. All routers perform this function in the same way. The only differences are the content of the routing table and how the routing table's content was decided. This will depend on the router's position, interior or exterior, and the routing protocol that produces the tables. Each router maintains a routing table that specifies the address to use for any given network ID. This table has been filled out by one of several routing protocols the router may use.

RIP is one of the earliest routing protocols created for the Internet and is still in widespread use. It operates by exchanging information with its nearest routers. Because the information includes a "distance" that is associated with each of its links; it is called a *distance-vector protocol*. Ordinarily, the distance provided is the hop count, but different measures can be used. Also, the distances can be increased or decreased by a system administrator to make a link more or less attractive to the routers.

Since an IP address represents an interface, then a router with several interfaces will have a group of IP addresses, one for each interface. These are the networks and/or subnetworks it can reach directly. If they are all subnetworks, the router can easily forward packets received on one

interface to any of the others. But when the interfaces are network IP addresses, the router must forward them in the proper direction by using other routers. RIP allows routers to discover each other's presence in a network and to create a routing table for subnetwork destinations to which it is not directly connected.

RIP discovers its peer routers by broadcasting a message containing its list of interface IP addresses and associated distance vectors on all of its local interfaces. Thus, a router on one of the interfaces receiving this broadcast will know that the sending router can forward packets to those interfaces and their associated distances. It also knows which interface the message came from, so it also knows how to send packets to that router. It and any other routers present on the interfaces will use this information to update their routing tables. First, they will increment the distance vectors in the message by one, since an additional forwarding step will be added. They will then check each interface addresses in the list against their routing table. If this is a new address, an entry will be created for it and the associated distance vector set. If it is an existing entry, the distance vector will be replaced by the new value. Timers are maintained for each entry so the router will know that it has been recently updated.

By exchanging information with its neighbors, a routing table can be constructed by each router that will eventually contain the addresses reachable by all the other routers within the AS and the distance to them. This may take some time to create, because more distant points will require several iterations for their presence to propagate to all nodes. Because RIP repeats these exchanges every 30 seconds, the existence of all points in the network and a route to reach them will become available to the routers. If there is more than one path to reach an interface, these will also be known, but one route or another may have a smaller distance vector and be preferred. Routers will learn about failed equipment, such as links and routers, which they can bypass if the network has alternate paths. Failures are indicated in the protocol as having an infinite distance vector.

The algorithm by which RIP creates its routing table does not ascertain the network topology; it only finds the next hop for forwarding the packets and any alternate routes. This, along with the nature of its flooding, leads to various problems. It is possible, depending on the timing of the messages, for loops to appear in the routing tables whereby a packet will travel back and forth until its Time-to-Live indication exhausts. Eventually, RIP will resolve these into proper routes, but they may persist for some time in the network, causing congestion. The congestion, in turn, makes the routing messages themselves less likely to arrive, leading to even greater confusion. Since RIP uses UDP, a protocol discussed later that does not assure the delivery of the packets, some will surely be lost in the presence of congestion. As the network becomes larger, these problems become more and more difficult to resolve. There have been various improvements to RIP to minimize these and other problems. However, there are even better ways to create the routing tables.

OSPF does not transmit its information only to neighbors; it floods the network with messages so as to reach every router. In doing so, it can be assured that every possible route between itself and every other router is discovered and that at least one of the routes will be the shortest. Since every router does this, all routers are able to derive the entire topology of the network and have everything needed to create a routing table that gives not only the current shortest path, but the shortest alternatives as well. Unlike RIP, OSPF uses TCP to transmit information, a protocol that provides reliable delivery of the information. Furthermore, when the routes are advertised, more than just the distance vector can be exchanged. Various parameters, such as monetary cost, reliability, throughput, and delay, can be considered when routing packets based on the packet's Type of Service field (see IPv4). OSPF may maintain multiple routing tables, one for each Type of Service indicator. OSPF continually updates its information through these communications and quickly discovers broken links and routers. When this occurs, it marks the routing table accordingly, and subsequent routing will use an alternate path. Overall, this method is called link-state routing.

OSPF allows a network to be organized as "areas," which are connected by a backbone, a capability that limits the broadcasting to manageable traffic volumes. It also allows easier administration of the routing. Routers will only know the topology and be able to route within their area; they rely on the backbone for delivering packets destined for points outside their area. Because each router knows the entire topology of the area and all the Type of Service parameters for each link, traffic is handled with greater efficiency. OSPF is the best interior routing protocol available today and has been widely deployed in the Internet.

When routing between Autonomous Systems, different rules must be applied, which preclude the use of either distance-vector or link-state protocols. There are many reasons for this. Perhaps the network is a private network and does not wish to carry traffic through it for other parties, they only wish to accept traffic destined for a host within their network. The links in the network may be of an unusual nature having a wide range of parameters to consider when routing. The network may be experiencing congestion and does not wish to accept traffic for a time. For these and other reasons, the BGP follows a different set of procedures for establishing routing with its peers in other networks. BGP is found in operation between every private network and carrier, between ISPs and backbone providers, and between backbones and MAEs.

Gateways are simply routers that are located at the edge of an AS that exchange traffic with the outside world. These are normal routers but with a few extra functions. Specifically, they must be careful that the traffic they accept is allowed for the network. BGP is the protocol they use to establish a relationship with the outside world. As the name implies, these gateways are at the "border" of the AS to which they belong. For traffic inside the AS, an interior routing protocol is used, such as RIP or OSPF. So, gateways will have two protocols cooperating to create their routing tables.

The first step performed by BGP is neighbor acquisition. In this step, BGP sends an Open message to determine if the neighbor wishes to participate in routing. If it does, it will respond with a Keepalive message. Subsequently, on a periodic basis, the neighbors will send Keepalive message to each other to maintain the relationship. The addresses of these neighbors are established not by the protocol but by information supplied by a system administrator. Once routers have established a relationship, they will exchange routing information giving the networks and subnetworks for which they can accept traffic. These are provided in Update messages. All BGP messages are exchanged using TCP that provides reliable delivery of the information. This makes BGP operation reliable.

Once the gateways have shared routing information, they can begin exchanging packets for routing. At each gateway, packets arriving from the outside world will be discarded if their address was not part of the routing information exchange. This prevents the AS from being inundated with traffic that it is unwilling to accept. Also, gateways within the same AS can exchange information to determine if there are multiple entries to the AS from the outside. If so, they can organize their exchange of information with the outside gateways so as to properly focus the traffic on the best entrance. This is done by adjusting the metrics provided to the outside gateways in the updates sent to them.

Domain Name Server (DNS)

Because IP addresses are these cryptic, lengthy numerical codes,[9] a scheme was created to allow the use of names to

be associated with them. These domain names are what most of us remember from browsing the World Wide Web and from sending email. Besides being easier to remember, DNS isolates users from changes in IP addresses that might be needed for various networking reasons, such as moving hosts around within a network or creating new subnetworks. While DNS greatly facilitates the use of IP, it has no direct role in routing of IP packets. The routing function is performed solely by the IP layer and depends only on the IP address.

DNS is a large distributed database that stores and retrieves the IP addresses associated with a domain name. DNS can also perform reverse look-ups to translate from an IP address into a domain name. Like any large distributed database, it must maintain itself, and the DNS protocol does this function by updating all the other DNS servers occasionally.

Most readers will be familiar with the term "URL" which stands for Uniform Resource Locator. URLs give the location of an object such as a webpage. Two other terms which are less well known are URN, Uniform Resource Name, and URI, Uniform Resource Indicator. URN is simply a unique name given to an object. That object might be found at several locations within the Internet, each having a unique URL. URI is a generic reference to the combined terms URN and URL.

DNS names have two parts: a top-level domain, such as *org, com,* or *net,* and a subdomain name, such as *telcordia*. So, *telcordia.com* is a valid DNS name that corresponds to IP address 128.96. Actually, there could be several IP addresses associated with telcordia.com, and DNS will retrieve and provide all of them to a requesting party. It is up to the IP layer to decide which one to use based on other requirements given by the higher layer. Some appli-

9. Hmmm, this seems a bit like those 10-digit phone numbers. Which is more memorable: (732) 758-2994 or 128.96.70.83?

cations add their own naming structures with the DNS name, such as such as *swalters@telcordia.com* or *http://Astro-photo.home.att.net.* These are the basis for higher level applications to refer to users and systems associated with the application without knowing those nitty-gritty binary IP addresses (TFIC[10]). However, DNS is not responsible for these extensions. DNS uses UDP for transport of its queries and responses.

When an application wishes to translate a DNS name into an IP address, it queries a DNS server at an IP address that must be known to it. This is commonly placed in the IP profile of the system as the DNS address. The server may not directly store the domain name and its associated IP address, but it will provide the address of additional name servers. For example, it you try to access an application at *science.research.telcordia.net* and your local DNS does not know the associated IP address, it will return the address of the *.net* server, which, when queried, will return the address of the *telcordia.net* server, and so on. Eventually, the associated IP address will be found, and the requesting application will then cache it for future use.

Besides translating names, DNS can translate E.164 telephone numbers. The representation for the numbers is that each digit is separated by a decimal point, they are written down in reverse order, and the suffix *e164.arpa* is appended. The E.164 number must include the country code. For example, my office telephone number is +1-732-758-2994, which would be written as 4.9.9.2.8.5.7.2.3.7.1. e164.arpa. The application processor performs this step, so the user need not do this burdensome processing. DNS will return the URI stored for this entry, if there is one, as well as an application such as SIP or SMTP, depending on the user's preference for connecting with them. This capability of DNS, known as ENUM, is a precursor to providing

10. TFIC = Tongue Firmly In Cheek

telephony service over the Internet and is described in Chapter 5.

Reaching the Internet

In the next few sections, access of the Internet is discussed. Today, there are four main methods for residential users to access the Internet. These include dial-up modems, Digital Subscriber Loop (DSL), cable modems, and wireless. Each scheme has its advantages and disadvantages. Evolution to the new telephony will be affected greatly by what happens in the access portion of the Internet.

Access Using Dial-Up Modems

Today, dial-up modems are the most common means of accessing the Internet. By using the PSTN, customers can reach their ISP from any point where a telephone jack is available. Figure 4–18 shows a host computer using a modem to reach its ISP. Because the telephone network is so widely deployed, modems have become the mainstream method of transporting digital data. Early modems operated at rates around 110 bps, but they quickly improved to 300, 1200, 9600, and now 56,000 bps. The great flexibility of modems and the lack of any other type of network access made modems the primary Internet access technology.

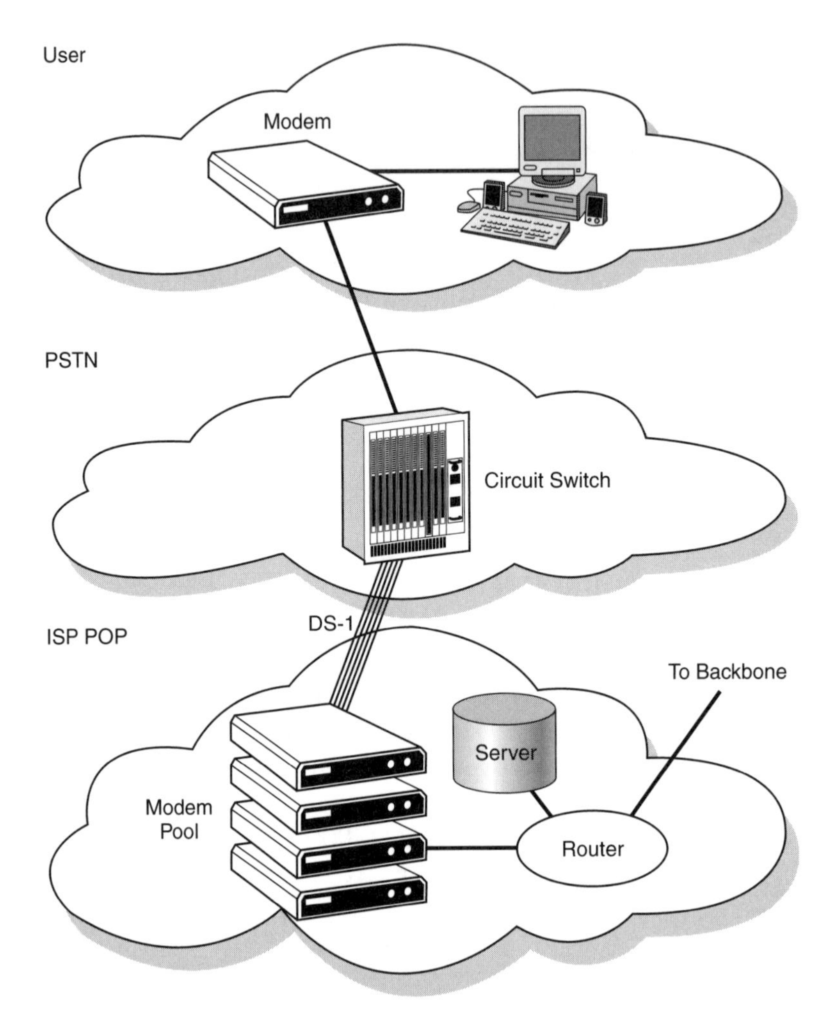

FIGURE 4–18 *Dial-up access.*

Because modems use the voice network, they are limited in the range of frequencies that can be utilized. This in turn greatly limits the data rates that can be carried. Early modems used a pair of tones with one frequency carrying information in one direction and a different frequency carrying information in the opposite direction. Today's modems use complex modulation schemes to transport the digital bits through the telephone network. These modems use sophisticated digital signal processing tech-

niques and adapt during a training period at the beginning of each call to achieve the maximum operating data rate possible. This will vary according to characteristics of the network connection, including bandwidth, attenuation, echoes, and so forth. Because of these bandwidth limitations and other impairments, it is only possible to transmit with reasonable reliability at rates approaching 56 Kbps over a single telephone connection.

Besides the ability to send and receive digital data across the telephone network, it is also necessary for the modem to be able to signal to the network to make the connection. This is most often done using a Touch-Tone generator that can be controlled by software in the computer to dial the telephone number that reaches the user's ISP. The modem is able to make more sophisticated calls by programming it to wait various amounts of time or until a certain signal, such as dial tone, is received. It can detect most of the various call control tone signals, such as ringing, busy, and so forth.

The computer connected to the modem must contain a suite of IP software as well as the user's applications. When an application is initiated, it will invoke the IP protocol stack, usually through TCP. TCP will then generate a connection request to its peer. This packet will pass to the IP layer, which will then ask the lower layer to make a connection to the ISP. PPP will start the modem and cause it to dial the phone number of the ISP. Once connected, PPP will use its authentication procedures to provide user ID and password information to the ISP, which will then validate the user. Once validated, the IP stack will be informed that a connection is ready. Acknowledgment of this will pass upwards through the IP stack, and TCP will then begin its transfers. All the time, the IP layer will perform its normal services of mapping IP addresses into media addresses and, if required, segmentation and reassembly of large data blocks.

At the distant end of the phone call is the ISP. Because the ISP serves many users simultaneously, it is necessary that they have multiple phone lines and modems available to receive calls. Typically, the ISP will have several T-1 connections from the central office to its place of business, since each T-1 transmission facility can carry 24 simultaneous phone calls. The T-1 lines terminate on modems so that when a customer calls the ISP and the telephone network connects her to the ISP, the modem will activate and handshake with the customer's modem. Behind the modem is a router, which, once the customer is validated, will allow her access to services such as email and Web browsing. Often, the ISP simply provides IP capability; the services are located in a different network, and the ISP is just one link in a chain of networks that reaches them.

This configuration has proven to be problematic to the telephone network. Because of the popularity of the Internet, a great many ISPs have appeared and ordered T-1 services. This demand has proven hard to fill. Further, the high number of calls concentrated into a single termination module of a switch will normally create higher blocking probability for all calls within the switch, because this was not expected when the switch was configured. The switches can be reconfigured to avoid much of this problem, but it takes time and resources for the telephone companies to do this. Lastly, there has been an increased demand for second-line telephone service by end users who want to have a dedicated phone line to their computers so the computer will not interfere with their telephone service. This has led to the need for more telephone numbers within an area, which in dense metropolitan regions have been exhausted within an area code. In these regions, new area codes have been introduced, which has frustrated all telephone users.

The primary appeal of the voice band modem is that the user can rely on the availability of telephone service practically anywhere. Because of this, computer manufacturers include a modem in nearly every personal computer sold.

Once the computer is out of the box, it is immediately connected to the telephone network so the user can browse the Internet. Since virtually every home computer in operation today includes a modem and has a telephone connection available, this has served the Internet well. Because it is so ubiquitously deployed in home computers, it is not likely to disappear quickly, even though there are much faster access techniques now available. Later, when we discuss an evolution away from the PSTN, this will be an important consideration. There is a lot of inertia behind the PSTN from both the voice telephone business and the Internet access business.

Access Using DSL Systems

During the 1970s, the telephone industry noticed that it had converted all its switching base to digital switching and nearly all of its backbone transmission systems to digital with many of these being fiber optic based. The next logical step was to convert the loop to digital. As might be expected, this step was attempted and the Integrated Services Digital Network (ISDN) was born. ISDN extended two 64-Kbps digital channels and a new 16-Kbps signaling channel to the user's premise. By sticking with a 64-Kbps channel rate, existing digital switches could continue to be utilized for telephony, and the new signaling channel was expected to usher in a new group of services. When multiplexed together, these channels add up to 144 Kbps.

One key problem for ISDN was how to transport this 144-Kbps digital circuit over the old analog loops. A solution was found by using high frequencies over the analog loop, even though they are severely attenuated. Figure 4–19 shows the attenuation for various loop lengths versus frequency. As can be seen, the loop characteristics in the frequency band from 0 Hz to around 4 kHz is relatively flat. For frequencies higher than 4 kHz, the loop attenuates the signal at a rate of about 20 dB per decade. This means that at 40 kHz, the signal will experience about 20 dB of attenuation, and at 400 kHz, attenuation will be up to 40 dB. Such high degrees of attenuation would be unacceptable for speech, but for digital receivers, it is possible to reconstruct the signal even after such dramatic attenuation. After a great deal of research, several schemes for transporting ISDN across the copper loop were standardized. This was the beginning of high-speed digital transport using the local copper loop and led to the present day DSL technologies.

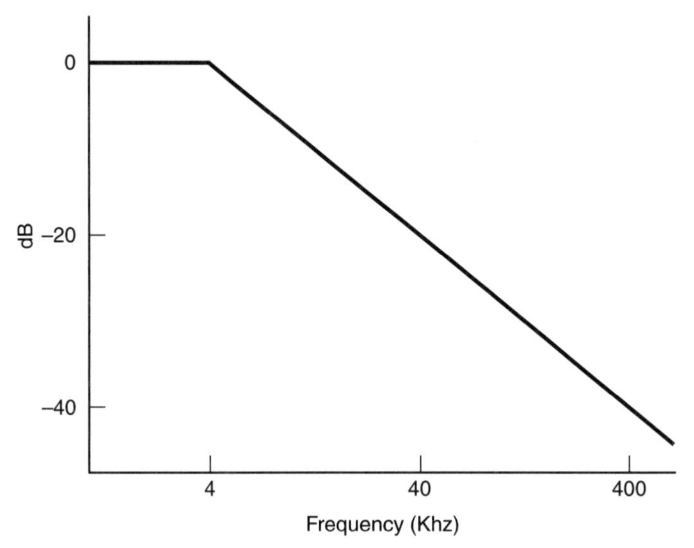

FIGURE 4–19 *Loop attenuation.*

Several variants of DSL have been defined, each with slightly different characteristics. In addition, standards do not force manufacturers to use particular techniques. As a result, there is considerable variation in implementations and performance. For the purpose of this book, only ADSL will be described, as standardized by ANSI,[11] since it is by far the most popular of the DSL family.

ADSL is intended to operate over loops up to 12 kilo-feet in length. The upstream direction from the user to the net-

11. American National Standards Institute—this organization has primary responsibility for carrier network standards within the United States.

work uses the frequency band from 25 kHz to 138 kHz, while the downstream direction from network to user uses 138 kHz to 1100 kHz. Because the downstream direction has a bandwidth of 962 kHz while the upstream direction is only 113 kHz wide, the two directions do not support the same digital bit rate. Hence, the name *Asymmetric* Digital Subscriber Loop. This allocation of bandwidth between the two directions allows the network to support 640 kbps upstream and up to 8 Mbps downstream, although lower speeds will be found in actual operation. This is a reasonable match to residential applications, since most tend to have far more information sent to the user's computer than is generated by it. Two modulation schemes are defined: Frequency Division Multiplexing (FDM) and Echo Cancellation (EC). Most systems in use today utilize FDM because it is cheaper to implement, although EC can achieve slightly higher bit rate.

DSL will not work with every loop encountered in the telephone network. Sometimes, as discussed in Chapter 3, there are loading coils and bridge taps on the loop. In the case of loading coils, these must be removed entirely, which requires a technician to locate and remove it. DSL can compensate for bridge taps so long as there are not too many of them. It is also necessary that the bridge taps not be in a configuration that causes extreme power reflections or attenuation in the loop. There are other impairments that create cross-talk in the cable that can be so severe that DSL will not operate, and certain other kinds of transmission systems, such as T1, cannot be present in the same cable. To determine the suitability of a loop for DSL service, it is necessary to test it and qualify it for the service. Fortunately, this can be done using a special test apparatus.

Figure 4–20 shows the overall architecture for ADSL as it is implemented today. The host computer at the user's location connects to a DSL modem that in turn connects through a splitter to the telephone loop. The splitter serves to isolate the telephone service from the data service, although there are now versions of DSL that no longer require the splitter. Although the splitter-less operation will have lower data rates, it requires less sophistication when installing the equipment. Normally, the user leases the DSL modem from the carrier. The computer software includes the normal IP stack and PPP for session initiation and user authentication identical to the dial-up modem architecture. However, the IP packets are carried over an ATM circuit that rides over the digital DSL bit stream.

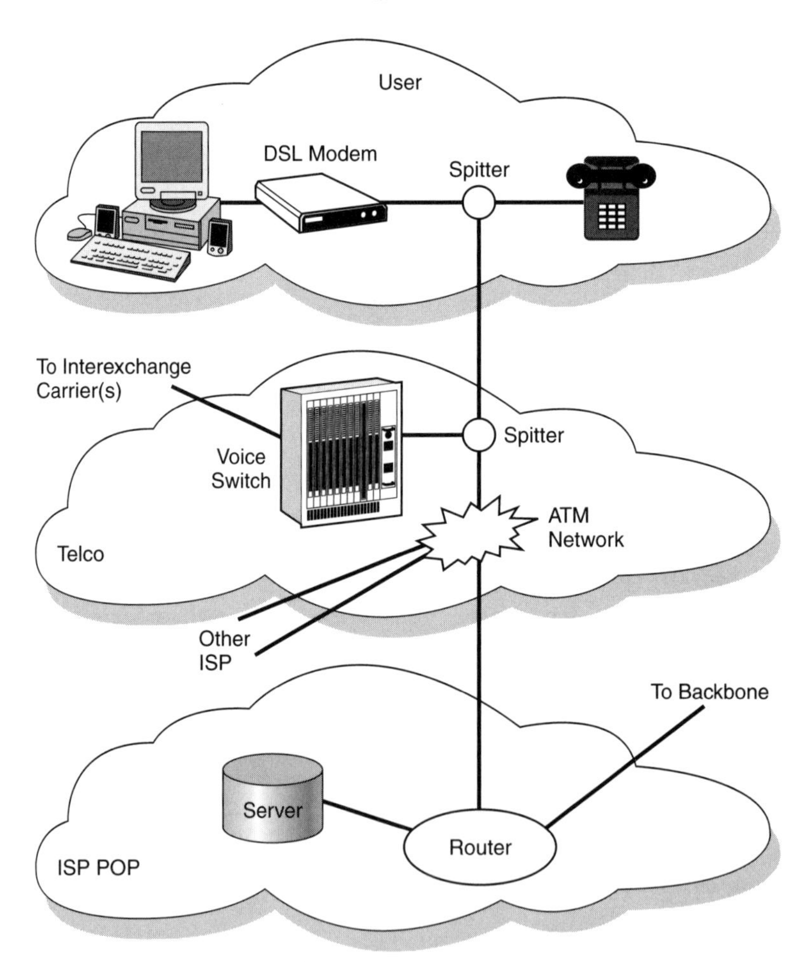

FIGURE 4–20 *ADSL architecture.*

At the carrier's wire center, a splitter again isolates the telephone service from the data service, with the telephony portion being passed directly to a voice switch. The data service connects to a Digital Subscriber Loop Access Module (DSLAM), which contains the companion to the ADSL modem. The DSLAM extracts the user's ATM cells and places them on an ATM network that reaches all the ISPs active at this wire center. There is a semipermanent ATM connection from the user to the ISP that carries all the user's data to the selected ISP. Notice that in this architecture, there is no use of the voice switch for the data service; consequently, there is no telephone call required for the host computer to connect with the ISP. The computer is always online, a significant benefit to the user but one that must be carefully guarded to avoid theft of information, viruses, and other problems.

The chief disadvantages of DSL are its very slow upstream channel from the user to the network and the uncertainty of whether it will work on a particular loop. When initial tests discover loading coils or other impairments, it will be necessary for a technician to remove them. This will cost money. And then, there may be other remaining impairments that require further work. In the end, the loop may still not be able to qualify for service. Even though this is a rare scenario, it can be a costly one. While technology improvements will probably be forthcoming in future years to provide slightly higher rates, the near-term prospects for improvement are not likely to show any dramatic improvement in speeds. For many users, the current rates of 6 Mbps down and 640 Kbps up are quite useful and represent a tremendous improvement over dial-up modem speeds. But for an increasing group of users, these speeds are limiting, especially the upstream channel. DSL will have a difficult time satisfying bandwidth demands from users in the future. One possible solution is to employ two copper wire loops to serve a customer, but this would add cost to the solution and a greater administrative burden to the operator.

The primary advantages of DSL are twofold. It utilizes an existing capital asset, the copper wire loop, and it can be deployed on a customer-by-customer basis. This means that the operator does not have to make a large capital investment just to enable the service. If, for example, the operator wanted to place fiber to get closer to the customer, trenches would have to be dug and fiber and electronics purchased and installed. This would require a large capital outlay and would take years to accomplish. While there have been many architectures for doing this, such as fiber-to-the-home and fiber-to-the-curb, today's competitive environment does not allow the time nor the capital outlay needed to deploy these architectures. But DSL allows the operator to target the service by adding DSLAMs at wire centers serving customers that are likely to buy the DSL service. Then, when a customer subscribes to the service, a DSL modem will be added at the customer's location. This minimizes capital outlays to offer the service.

As DSL becomes more commonplace, VoIP becomes more practical due to the higher speed IP service available and the fact that the interface is continuously available. The notion of VoIP over dial-up modems, while possible, is not a good candidate for replacing normal telephony service due to the lengthy boot and dial-up call connection times. But using DSL or cable modems, which are described next, a telephony service can be deployed that has the potential of competing with normal telephone service.

Access Using Cable Modems

Cable television systems (CATV) are widely deployed within the United States. These systems utilize coaxial cable for carrying VHF and UHF television signals. The overall architecture of the cable system is shown in Figure 4–21. The cable head-end is where signals from the various television sources are combined to create the cable's menu of channels. At the head-end there are various Radio Frequency (RF) systems for shifting the frequencies of the signals and amplifiers to boost their level for transmission down the coaxial network. The cable composite signal is then carried over a trunk network that distributes the signal to a set of nodes near the customers being served. When these systems were first built, coax was used for the trunk cable network, but this required many amplifiers spaced along the cable to compensate for loss in the coax. Modern systems utilize fiber optic cables between the head-end and the fiber nodes to avoid the loss and poor reliability of these amplifiers. At the fiber node, the signal is converted from optical to electrical and placed into coaxial feeder cables. These feeder cables wind through a serving area where pedestals are installed to serve several homes. In all, a single feeder cable may reach 600 homes. At the pedestal, the signal is adjusted to deliver the correct power level to each customer. Inside the customer's location, there is a set-top box that terminates the coaxial cable and allows the customer to select the channel he wishes to view.

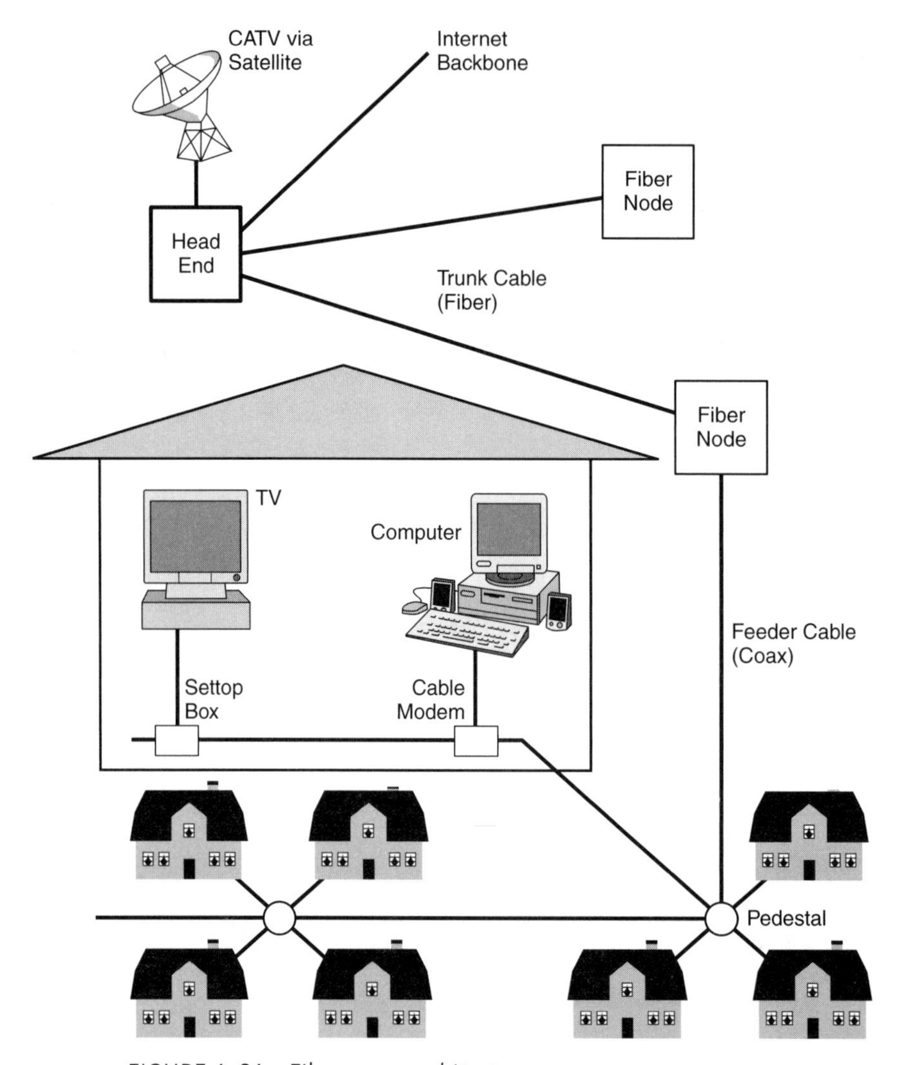

FIGURE 4–21 *Fiber coax architecture.*

Figure 4–22 shows the RF spectrum for a cable system as defined in DOCSIS,[12] the Data Over Cable Service Interface Specifications. The lowest frequencies, from 5 to 42 MHz, are reserved for upstream transmission from the user to the network. Next, there is a set of 6 MHz-wide RF chan-

12. Cable Television Laboratories, Inc. issues specifications for the CATV industry including DOCSIS.

nels that occupy the region from 50 MHz to 860 MHz or greater. The upper most of these channels can be digitally encoded to carry either digital television or digital data to the user's premises. A special termination unit called a cable modem is used to extract the data and interface it to a host computer, usually using an Ethernet interface, and to generate data in the lower frequency upstream band. All the digital data is encoded into the 6 MHz-wide RF channels. Back at the cable head-end there is a complementary system, the Cable Modem Termination System (CMTS), which interfaces to the Internet and allows the two-way delivery of packets to the cable modems. This architecture has been successfully implemented and deployed to millions of homes in North America.

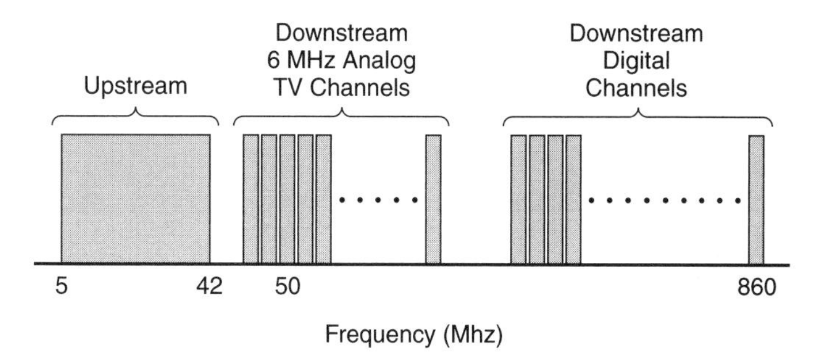

FIGURE 4–22 *DOCSIS RF spectrum.*

The chief advantage of the cable modem is that very high bit rates can be achieved over the system. Deployed systems typically reach 10 Mbps, but prototype systems operating at 100 Mbps have been built. These high speeds are due to the use of fiber for reaching equipment in the close proximity of the customer and the high bandwidth available in the 6 MHz RF channels of the cable. Because these channels are so much greater than the bandwidth of the copper wire telephone loop, they can operate much faster. The upstream link from the customers to the network operates at a similar rate. Speed is the cable system's great advantage.

Because the cable distribution network serves so many homes, these channels must be shared, at least in the current architectures. Since many of the 500 to 600 users sharing a single data link may be active simultaneously, there are three issues that arise in the use of the cable network.

The first issue is the sharing of bandwidth. When there are many active users accessing the Internet, the available bandwidth must be distributed among them. At times when there is not much activity, the performance will be excellent. But when many users are "surfing" the Web, capacity becomes an issue and throughput suffers greatly. This problem can be overcome by using more data links in the cable network or splitting the cable into multiple segments, but this will drive up cost of both equipment and administration for the cable operator.

A second issue that comes from the sharing of channels is security. Because the cable terminates in all the user locations, all the traffic to all users is available for monitoring at any of the locations. This means that any user can monitor the traffic of another user by manipulating the protocols. Fortunately, this is not a simple matter, and the average user who is not technically inclined would not be able to perform the necessary changes to monitor another user's traffic. But software for eavesdropping can be obtained for those inclined to do so. Encryption of the channel could solve this problem, but this would lead to greater complexity and more administrative burdens for the operator.

Lastly, reliability considerations can become important when such a large group of customers are served by a single link. In the DOCSIS architecture there are many single points of failure that would disrupt service for all 500 to 600 users. As long as Internet access is not a life-critical service, and customers do not complain too loudly when a failure does occur, a modest level of reliability can be tolerated. Today's fiber-based cable networks have far better reliability than the earlier all-analog networks, and failures are much less common. But if cable networks are to carry "lifeline" services needing high reliability and availability, the architecture will have to be modified to improve its reliability.

With regard to investment, not all cable networks today use fiber in the trunk facility. This is an expensive capital upgrade and requires time to accomplish. Electronic upgrades in the distribution facility are also needed to offer digital capabilities. But these expenditures will enable a large group of customers to receive the service, so once they are accomplished, a larger market will exist for the service. Then, as customers subscribe, cable modems will be placed at their locations.

Wireless Access

The Internet is now being accessed using several different wireless schemes. Many of these are point-to-point radio channels that simply provide digital connectivity. These can be quite useful in dense metropolitan areas for reaching large corporate customers, and they provide very high bandwidths. Such systems create no new issues for the Internet. However, mobile hosts using wireless connectivity are a different story. In order to connect these hosts, both radio connectivity and a change in routing schemes must be provided. Radio connectivity using packet mode is provided using the RF methods described in Chapter 3.

In order to route packets to a mobile host, a system of agents must be established, as shown in Figure 4–23. There are three key elements to the scheme. There is the mobile host whose device is in radio contact with a base station; a foreign agent that manages packet forwarding from the base to the mobile host; and a home agent that acts as a surrogate for packets inbound for the mobile host. The mobile host has a fixed IP address that it normally uses from its home location. It also knows the IP address of a router in its home area, known as the home agent with which it has registered its IP address. The home agent is normally on the same subnetwork as the home location of the mobile host so it can intercept packets destined for it. As we shall see, the home agent will know how to deliver them to the mobile host when it is remotely located.

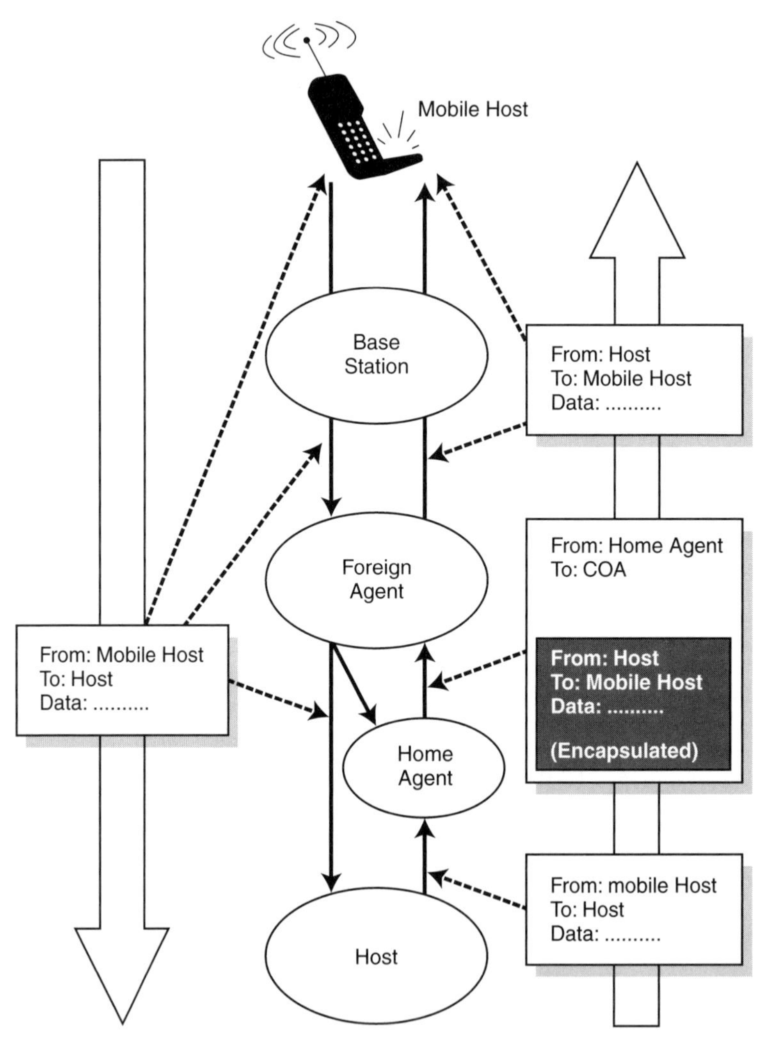

FIGURE 4–23 *Mobile IP.*

When the mobile host first attaches to a foreign network, there is an authentication procedure performed between the foreign agent and the mobile host in which the foreign

agent will learn both the mobile device's home IP address and the address of the home agent. Once the foreign agent has performed a handshake with the home agent to authenticate the mobile host, the mobile host will be able to transmit packets. During this handshake, the home agent will learn the IP address of the foreign agent. This is referred to as the Care-Of Address. All control messages use UDP; hence the authentication application must allow for nondelivery of packets.

In the figure, the mobile host is in contact with another host running an application. Packets sent by the mobile host to the host are simply addressed to the host's IP address and carry the IP address of the mobile host as the source address. The foreign agent receives these packets and simply routes them directly to the host. However, the network will forward any packets sent by the host to the home location of the mobile host where the home agent will intercept them. When the home agent intercepts a packet intended for the mobile host, it encapsulates it as IP-in-IP (known as *tunneling*) and forwards it to the foreign agent whose address (the Care-Of Address) is known to it from the authentication handshake. The foreign agent will receive the packet, de-encapsulate it, and forward it on to the mobile host through the base station.

If the user, being mobile, moves from one radio cell to another, the handshaking authentication will be repeated with a new foreign agent. This will update the home agent with a new Care-Of Address. Then, the mobile host will send a message to the original foreign agent, giving it the device's new Care-Of Address so the original agent can forward any subsequent packets to the new agent for delivery. This will allow packets already in transit through the network to be forwarded to the mobile host. This handoff attempts to minimize retransmission of packets.

In addition to problem of routing packets to the mobile host, there are also bandwidth considerations due to the limited capacity of the radio channel. As discussed earlier,

Web browsing can transfer rather large volumes of data, making the radio link a bottleneck for effective Internet access. Although there are efforts to create faster radio channels, such as 3G, the third generation of wireless, a more direct attack on this problem can be made by introducing a protocol that trims down the information being transmitted. The Wireless Application Protocol (WAP) is just such a scheme.

In WAP, there is a "microbrowser" that behaves much as a normal Web browser but makes more efficient use of bandwidth by knowing in advance that the mobile host display will have limited capability. With this knowledge, it can trim the size and resolution of images, a large consumer of bandwidth, to values that will fit the display that in turn will consume less bandwidth. There is a special language, Wireless Markup Language (WML), that is similar to HTML. WML allows Web page developers to create content that is easily viewed and used from a mobile device. It is also possible to place a proxy in the network that converts between HTML and WML so regular Web sites can be displayed. But, because WAP and WML affect the content displayed at the user's device, they may not find widespread use. In some cases, the wireless links do not use IP; instead, they use a variant known as WDP, Wireless Datagram Protocol, which is similar to UDP but is simpler and wastes less bandwidth. Likewise, there is the Wireless Session Protocol (WSP) that can initiate sessions over either connection-oriented services or connectionless services and Wireless Transaction Protocol (WTP) that provides TCP-like service.

Because of the limits in transmission rates, all these schemes make some compromises to the content being displayed to the user and have had limited success. In the future, as higher speed wireless rates become available, this problem will dissipate. In the meantime, applications such as Instant Messaging and Short Messaging Service (SMS), which transfer short blocks of information to users, are becoming very popular and driving the application for wireless data.

Internet Protocol Version 6 (Ipv6)

There is a more recent version of Internet Protocol known as IPv6. This new version addresses several issues in IPv4, namely, an increased addressing space, quality of service control, and IP switching. In addition, IPv6 simplifies or eliminates various features in IPv4 that are not being used or have evolved into a slightly modified use.

Figure 4–24 shows the header of Ipv6. The various fields, size, and their use are as follows:

- **Version** (4 bits) – The version of IP for this packet. Naturally, the value for version 6 is 0110.
- **Traffic Class** (8 bits) – The field can specify a requirement for quality of service for this and other packets associated with a flow (or otherwise). This can be used to reserve resources along routes to ensure that quality of service is met.
- **Flow Label** (20 bits) – This, in conjunction with the source address, fully uniquely specifies a flow. The source is expected to assign this label for the particular destination involved. This can be used in conjunction with either MPLS or RSVP style algorithms to meet quality requirements and to bypass routers so as to increase effective capacity.
- **Payload Length** (16 bits) – This indicates the length of the payload, which may include one or more header extensions.
- **Next Header** (8 bits) – This field is equivalent to the Protocol field of IPv4 and specifies what higher layer protocol is to receive the packet at the destination. Also, this field supports the introduction of a complex set of header extensions for various functions, such as routing extensions, hop-by-hop extensions, and destination extensions.

- **Hop Limit** (8 bits) – Routers use this field just like the Time-to-Live field of IPv4, but instead of measuring time, the routers count hops. At the source, the Hop Limit is set to a value, and each router decrements it. If it reaches zero, the router processing the message will not route it.
- **Source Address** (128 bits) – Unlike the IPv4 addresses that are specified as four decimal values separated by decimal points, IPv6 addresses consist of eight groups of four hexadecimal values separated by colons. Since each hexadecimal word specifies four bits, each group specifies 32 bits. Eight such groups can encode 128 bits. For example, the following is a valid address:

AA23: FE19:0013:0FC3:2315:ABCD:14EC:2106

- **Destination Address** (128 bits) – This field is identical to the Source Address, but specifies the destination for the packet. IPv6 includes several special address codes for loop-back, unknown addresses, and embedded IPv4 address (two types are used, one for routers that can process IPv6 and another for those that cannot).

Version	Priority	Flow Label	
Payload Length		Next Header	Hop Limit
Source IP Address			
Destination IP Address			
Payload			

FIGURE 4–24 *IPv6 packet format.*

Note that there is no checksum in the new header. IPv6 relies on the higher layer protocol's checksum for its check. This requires both TCP and UDP to be modified to include the complete IPv6 header in their pseudo-header calculation.

There are diverse views as to the importance of IPv6. This version was created in IETF RFC 2460 dated December 1998, and equipment using it has just started to appear. So, the deployments using IPv6 are quite limited at present. Because of the extremely large number of IP routers in the Internet today, it is likely that deployment of IPv6 will be slow, partly due to the cost of replacement and partly due to the sheer volume of routers. Also, interoperation with IPv4, while possible, is complex.

There are disagreements about how quickly the address space of IPv4 will exhaust. More conservative methods in assigning addresses can slow the consumption of addresses. Other architectural models, such as "IP in IP," allow the reuse of IP addresses when moving from one network to another. These and other concepts under consideration can greatly extend the life of the 32-bit address space and postpone the needed switch to IPv6.

In addition, IPv6 requires the modification of every protocol that manipulates or uses the larger IP address space. This is a very lengthy list of protocols including all the routing protocols, ICMP, RSVP, and so on. Any function that touches the address will have to expand its address storage field. Naturally, some tricks can be applied here as well to minimize the changes during a transition period. But this is a very difficult step to take due to the large number of procedures needing modification.

For these reasons, IPv6 may not see wide-scale deployment for some time. Certainly its features are quite useful and desirable, but as long as patches for IPv4 can be created and deployed, only the most aggressive networks will utilize IPv6.

Traffic

Traffic in the Internet is a topic receiving a tremendous amount of attention in the research community. Unfortunately, there are very few results that help carriers plan their networks; but this is not the fault of the researchers. The Internet has proven its ability to confound its builders by growing exponentially. Some experts estimate that it doubles every 12 months. Others believe even faster. This includes all aspects of growth, number of users, number of host computers, and the volume of traffic. Consider the following statistics[13] from AOL, the leading Internet Service Provider:

- 30 million users
- 2.2 million peak simultaneous users
- 194 million emails per day
- 245 million stock quotes per day
- 656 million instant messages per day
- 11 billion URL retrievals per day

Keeping up with this level of demand is an intense challenge. The difficulties an Internet carrier faces are three; these will be considered in turn:

- the unpredictable random nature of the traffic;
- the extremely fast growth in the number of users; and
- the unpredictable demand generated by applications.

Data traffic has proven to be an elusive creature to quantify and predict. It is, of course, a random quantity and can only be measured in a statistical sense. By comparison, traffic in the PSTN is very well understood. There are sophisticated tools for predicting demand and capacity. Telephony traffic also has random arrival of call requests and random call duration. But, by its very nature, telephony traffic is simpler to model; it has an average holding time of 3 minutes, and it consumes 64 Kbps for as long as a call lasts. There are more detailed models for call arrival rates for businesses, residences, and for different countries. Because telephony is so mature, its traffic is well understood. But data communications is a much more recent development and has a far more random nature. Data traffic has been shown to be "self-similar." This means that the statistics of the traffic is not dependent on the timeframe of the observation. For example, if we observe traffic for an hour and measure a particular set of characteristics such as mean and standard deviation of packet arrivals, we will

13. From AOL Website; retrieved August 9, 2001.

measure the same characteristics if we observe it for 1 minute or for 1 second. This means that our knowledge of the traffic's behavior cannot be improved by making longer measurements. This characteristic makes data networks quite difficult to engineer.

Consider the second challenge, the rate at which the Internet is adding users. The graph in Figure 4–25 shows AOL's growth in users since its first DOS-based offering in 1991.

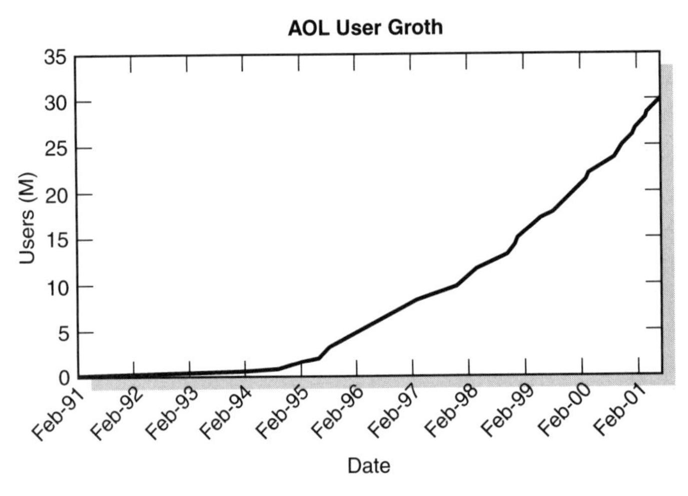

FIGURE 4–25 *AOL user growth.*

AOL is presently adding users at a tremendous rate, approximately 1 million users every month or two, and they doubled from 15 million to 30 million in only 2 1/2 years. This kind of growth rate is difficult to keep up with from the perspective of network planning and traffic engineering. ISPs such as AOL have steadily moved up the transmission hierarchy and are now installing 9.6 Gbps transmission equipment and Gigabit routers. As the world goes online, the pace at which network capacity must be expanded will continue unabated. This is in stark contrast to the PSTN. Because of its maturity, the PSTN has very slow growth and operates with a stable base of apparatus.

Internet network planners also face a third dilemma: They cannot predict the traffic demand generated by new applications or new ways of using old applications. When the World Wide Web was created, traffic began mushrooming on the Internet as users everywhere began to surf the Web. Because most Web sites include graphics and photos, the volume of traffic made a great surge upwards. Furthermore, the very nature of the Web browser, with its point-and-click capability, made it easy to request massive transfers of information using HTTP. This scenario will occur again and again as clever application developers add more and more capability to their products. There is no end in sight. Music is now a popular item to download, and video is lagging only a short distance behind. As more applications are deployed and more users access the information, the traffic will continue to grow unabated.

Because of all three of these problems, it is impossible to truly size and predict the needed capacity for any portion of the Internet. Traffic that is well behaved today may be a torrent tomorrow. The only solution carriers have today is to monitor their links and routers for congestion and to expand capacity where the problems are worst. This is like throwing water on whatever fire is burning brightest, but it's the only defense available. At some point, the Internet, like the PSTN, should reach a more stable equilibrium. After some critical mass is reached, each of these factors will have less of an impact on traffic. Then, carriers will be able to more carefully size their networks and plan for growth. This may not be for many years to come, but it will occur.

Security

When the Internet was first created, security was not a major item of concern. Thus, most of the Internet protocols that have been created made no provision for securing the system in any regard. Security is a complex matter and is difficult to achieve after the fact in these sophisticated protocols. Nevertheless, this is now a necessary issue for the IETF to tackle, and progress is being made on many fronts.

One example is the DNS. Because these servers routinely interchange information using the same network that users operate over, it is possible for a malicious user to trick a DNS server into updating the IP address entry for a URL. Once done, this will propagate all through the DNS. Remember that DNS is translating names into IP addresses, so once an entry is changed, all queries will direct requesting applications to the wrong place. This can create havoc in a business environment, so DNS has now had various modifications made to it to prevent this from happening. Changes include an authentication handshake using a password key that cannot easily be obtained. This, along with other modifications, has made DNS more bulletproof to hackers.

Denial-of-service-attacks have been widely publicized when they occur. In this scenario, an attacking party launches many simultaneous applications all around the Internet that continually bombard a site with seemingly legitimate requests. Typically, these involve dozens or hundreds of host computers. The Internet delivers these messages to the host system that the attacker wishes to render useless. The host becomes hopelessly entangled when processing these messages, all of which are intended to simply use up its processing capacity. Because these message come from a widely dispersed set of points, it is difficult to locate and isolate them to prevent the attack. After or during the attack, it is sometimes possible to trace the packets back to all their sources. However, because some networks deliver a pseudo-address that is not retained when the user's session is completed, this cannot always be done. Even if this is successful, it does not prevent the attack directly, but it may allow law enforcement officials to locate and prosecute the attacking party. Since IP packets carry both the source and destination address, it would seem possible to quickly identify the offending party. When this is coupled with the authentication procedures that occur when PPP attaches the host to the Internet, the source is clearly known. Unfortunately, the clever evildoers can "spoof" the network by simply changing their IP address once they have connected. Then, when they launch their attack or hack into a system, the network cannot always properly identify them. Reverse look-up of their IP address will provide erroneous information. However, since they are still connected and their system is using the IP address in the offending packets, it is possible under some conditions to locate them. Routers at ISPs can be programmed to check incoming packets for an authentic IP source address, but this consumes valuable router capacity, so it is rarely done.

Because many of the Internet interfaces can be passively monitored, an eavesdropper can learn much about the parties communicating through it. This is much like wiretapping a telephone, except it is more complex. An eavesdropper would need to assemble a somewhat special IP protocol stack that can intercept the data and reconstruct what a user is doing. In order to avoid eavesdroppers from seeing the content of packets, encryption algorithms can be utilized. Doing this requires a key distribution scheme so the sending and receiving parties can encode and decode the information. But this does not protect the IP header, since it must be processed all through the network in order to deliver the packet. For some criminal purposes, simply knowing the IP address with which a user is communicating is enough. Many of these issues are addressed in the various IP security (IPsec) documents created by the IETF.

Routing is another area where security must be considered. Early protocols, such as RIP-1, were not secure, and it was possible for a malicious user to build a system that would behave like a router but would deliberately provide incorrect routing information. This could lead the network into a state of chaos and an unusable condition or could provide the malicious users with a sort of wiretap inside the network. Since they could insert themselves in the route for a given IP address by issuing the correct messages to the routers, they could receive and copy all the packets destined for that address. If they continued to forward the packets back into the network, the destination device might never know of this interception. Newer protocols, such as RIP-2, OSPF and others, require authentication in each routing packet based on a password or other more sophisticated methods.

The Internet is the latest "frontier" of human society. Like any frontier, there will be a degree of lawlessness for a time. As commercial use of the Internet expands, there will be increased pressure to secure the Internet in ways that prevent lawlessness and allow perpetrators to be apprehended. Presently, this is the key problem area, and it is being addressed because corporations and users are demanding it in order to conduct commerce safely.

Operations

Just as the PSTN requires operations systems to monitor the network health, add and remove subscribers, and introduce and control new services, so must companies providing Internet services. Today, there is a cacophony of tools available that serve this purpose. Unfortunately, there are no comprehensive systems available today for operating a carrier service. Some traditional telephony network carriers that also provide Internet services are adapting their telephony operations systems to Internet requirements. Some steps that are unique to the Internet can be supplemented with manual operations. For example, they will use their existing order-entry system but will administer router configurations with technicians. Some systems built for managing IP networks, such as network monitoring systems, can be integrated into their current operations systems architecture.

Most Internet operations systems use object models for their operation and maintenance. This, in addition to SNMP, provides the basis for operations up to and including the Network Management Layer (NML). There is an object model for each system and for the elements that make up the system. For each element, there is a parent and usually a child. A parent may have many children. For example, a line card would be the child of a router. Thus, the router is a parent to the line card, of which it may have many, but the line card has no children. Lastly, there is a Management Information Base (MIB) that defines the attributes and parameters for each element. MIBs are written in a language called Abstract Syntax Notation One (ASN.1) that can be compiled from a graphical or textual representation. The Entity MIB includes names of objects and describes the object in detail sufficient to manage it. For example, the Entity MIB for a line card would specify items such as its maximum capacity, utilized capacity, error rate, and alarms that might occur. The Entity MIB for a router would include the number of interfaces it contains and their IP addresses. Each of these items may have further specifications included in the MIB. MIBs are negotiated and agreed upon in the IETF and issued as an RFC. Each MIB is assigned a registered number that uniquely identifies it. In this way, equipment can simply provide its identity to a management system that can then immediately understand its structure. Note that the structure of an MIB simply is the structure of the information describing a system, and not the value of the information. As stated, the MIB for a router will have a variable for the number of interfaces, but routers in the field may have different values in this position. SNMP is used to query the router as to the value of the variable in each particular system.

Figure 4–26 shows an example of a system. As can be seen, the NMS processor can access a database of MIBs. Stored in the database are all MIBs that have been standardized, including the definition of a router and an interface. In the figure, only a small portion of the information stored in an MIB is given. For the example, the router has only its number of interfaces, and the interface has a type, an IP address, and a status. In reality, the MIBs for these elements are far more complex. In the network, there are many routers, of which only one is shown. This particular router has three interfaces. When queried using SNMP, the router responds that it is "Router.5," meaning it is the fifth instance of "Router" in the network and it contains three interfaces. If further SNMP messages are used to query the IP address of Interface.1, it will respond with "128.19.4.3." If Interface.2 were queried as to its Status, it would respond "Out-Of-Service," because its transmission link has been cut.

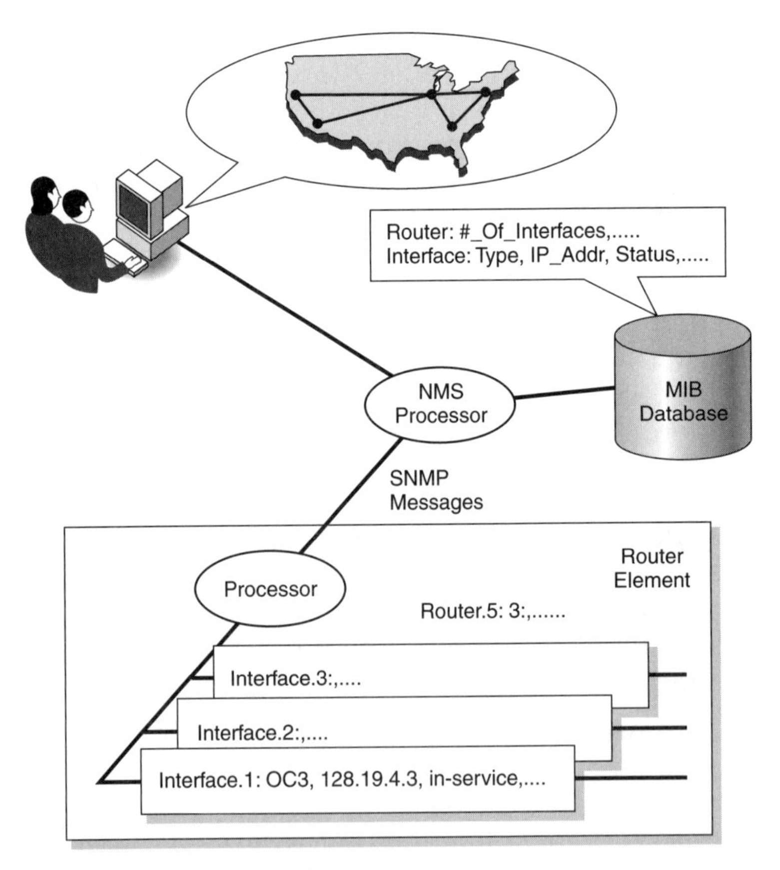

FIGURE 4–26 Network management.

The NMS uses auto-discovery to find network elements. It is able to send out broadcast messages and get responses back from systems receiving its query. Once the NMS knows of the other systems' existence, it is able to send SNMP messages to them to learn what kind of systems they are (MIB identity), what objects they contain, and what status the objects have. The naming convention is *x.y*, wherein *x* denotes the MIB standard name and *y* denotes the instance. Thus, the fourth line card in a router would be linecard.4. The NMS is able to display maps and status information either graphically or in tabulated form, depending on the user's needs and how the developer of the NMS chooses. Usually, the NMS is able to set filters on various alarm conditions and thresholds on parameters so as to control how quickly the NMS alerts the technicians. Since the network can usually survive an outage by using an alternate path, it is possible to defer the repair of a system. This, of course, depends on the operator having engineered sufficient redundancy into the basic network. Most of the new server systems used inside the network for various service functions such as DNS, email, and the like are highly survivable systems with multiple connections to the network to ensure their availability. The NMS is able to monitor and display all the equipment in the network to show how well the systems are working. Normally, status information is displayed as red, yellow, or green to visually inform the technical staff of the network's status. When an event occurs, such as a failure, it will be logged, and later the staff can browse through the log to unravel what occurred. Sometimes, one failure will trigger another type of alarm, and there will be fault propagation from child to parent further up the hierarchy of equipment. These fault trees can be quite complex to analyze, and today they are done manually.

SNMP has just a few basic commands. These are GET_REQUEST, GET_NEXT_REQUEST, GET_RESPONSE, SET_RESPONSE, and TRAP. Each command includes a number of parameters, especially an OBJECT_IDENTIFIER. This tells the receiving system which object within the system is being examined or manipulated. These allow the NMS to fetch the status of various objects within a system or to set a configuration variable. Like all IP messages, it is addressed to the SNMP processor at the IP address of an interface. SNMP uses UDP for message transfer.

Above the NML, there is little defined for Internet operations. These systems are the domain of the service provider, and many build their own systems. Many carriers who also have a telephony network utilize the same general form of operations systems as discussed at the end of Chapter 3, but these require modifications to be serviceable for Internet services. The types of services being provisioned, such as email, Web hosting, and IP addresses, require quite different parameters from telephony services. Nevertheless, the overall operation paradigm ranging from customer contact down through turning on the service can be approached with the same general structure. There are no standards for these systems or even guidelines for their functionality or interfaces. As an example, service level agreements (SLA) vary widely across the industry as to what items are provided under a contract and the level of support provided.

Over time, automated operations for the Internet will come to pass. But today, this is the biggest problem for all Internet carriers. The yawning chasm is the lack of fully integrated systems with complete flow-through for all major events. In order to have a truly high-quality and rapid response to customer requests and to network problems, such systems are required.

Summary

One factor that should be abundantly evident is that the Internet is founded entirely on software. Every one of the protocols discussed in this chapter is fundamentally an algorithm implemented in software. Here and there, there are portions of the functionality that can be transferred to hardware systems to increase the speed of the system. So, the actual implementation of these protocols is sometimes a mixture of hardware elements with software assisting and/or performing parts of the function that are either too complex for hardware or too infrequently utilized to justify the expense of a specialized hardware processor. Routing is one such example in which the basic routing table look-up is usually performed in hardware whereas the calculation of the routing table content is invariably performed by software operating in a processor inside the router.

A second factor that should be plain is that the Internet is not simple. It is a vast complex of interacting systems. The fundamental function of the Internet is routing, which on the surface appears to be simple. After all, a router simply receives a packet, checks its address, looks up the next place to send it, and forwards it out that physical interface to the next router. This action is repeated over and over until the packet reaches its destination. This is indeed a simple concept, but the protocols used for determining routes are quite sophisticated and complex.

By keeping the Internet core as simple as possible and by requiring only best effort delivery of packets, some complexity must be added to the systems using the network with its inherent unreliable delivery. But in considering the end-to-end nature of hosts communicating over the Internet, it should be realized that the intelligence lies at the ends of the connections. This is where most of the software, such as browsers, SMTP, HTTP, and TCP, is operating. If excellent real-time performance is to be achieved, this is the place to put it—as far from the core and distributed over as many processors as possible. Otherwise, this processing would creep into the core elements, driving up the cost of the network and lowering its performance.

The importance of the Internet in the future of telecommunications cannot be overestimated. It is not a fad that will pass in time—it is here to stay and it will only grow larger, more robust, and more sophisticated over time.

Eventually, it will absorb every media of telecommunications, including telephony and video. The Internet is just now past its infancy; perhaps it is a teenager at the moment, but already it has inserted itself into humankind's everyday life and society's commerce.

There are surely areas where the Internet is not mature. These would include operations, security, and providing multiple qualities of service. But these are solvable problems, and there is an army of brilliant technical experts producing solutions. In just a few years, all these issues will have well-understood technical solutions with proven field experience. Eventually, the "Inter-net" will be the "Only-net."

References

Banerjee, A., et al. "Generalized Multiprotocol Label Switching: An Overview of Routing and Management Enhancements," *IEEE Communications Magazine,* Jan. 2000.

Bernet, Y., et al. "A Framework for Integrated Services Operation over DiffServ Networks," RFC-2998, Nov. 2000.

Black, D., et al. "Per Hop Behavior Identification Codes", RFC-3140, Jun. 2001.

Boardwatch, *Directory of Internet Service Providers,* 13th ed., Spring 2001.

Braden, R., et al. "Resource Reservation Protocol," RFC-2205, Sept. 1997.

Cable Television Laboratories, Inc. "Data Over Cable Service Interface Specifications Radio Frequency Interface Specification," SP-RFIv1.1-104-000407.

Cable Television Laboratories, Inc. PacketCable™ 1.0 Architecture Framework Technical Report, PKT-TR-ARCH-V01-991201.

Case, J., et al. "A Simple Network Management Protocol," RFC-1157, May 1990.

Deering, S., et al. "Internet Protocol, Version 6," RFC-2460, Dec. 1998.

Dobrowski, G., and D. Grise. *ATM and SONET Basics*, ADGP Publishing, 2001.

Falstrom, P. "E.164 Number and DNS," RFC-2916, Sept. 2000.

Fielding, R., et al. "Hypertext Transfer Protocol (HTTP/1.1)," RFC-2616, June 1999.

Halabi, Bassam. *Internet Routing Architectures,* Cisco Press, 1997.

Heinanen, J., et al. "Assured Forwarding PHB Group," RFC-2597, June 1999.

Huitema, C. *Routing in the Internet,* Prentice Hall, 1995.

Jacobson, V., et al. "An Expedited Forwarding PHB," RFC-2598, June 1999.

Kwok, T. *ATM: The New Paradigm for Internet, Intranet, and Residential Broadband Services and Applications,* Prentice Hall PTR, 1998.

Malkin, G. "Routing Internet Protocol Version 2," RFC-2453, Nov. 1998.

Mockapetris, P. "Domain Names—Implementation and Specification," RFC-1035, Nov. 1997.

Moy, J. "OSPF Version 2," RFC-2328, Apr. 1998.

Newman, P., T. Lyon, and G. Minshall. "IP Switching: ATM under IP," *IEEE/ACM Transactions on Networking,* Apr. 1998.

Nichols, K., et al. "Definition of the Differentiated Services Field (DS Field) in the IPv4 and IPv6 Headers", RFC-2474, Dec. 1998.

Partridge, C. *Gigabit Networking,* Addison-Wesley, 1994.

Perkins, C. "IP Mobility Support," RFC-2002, Oct. 1996.

Plummer, D. "Address Resolution Protocol," RFC-826, Nov. 1982.

Postel, J. "Internet Control Message Protocol," RFC-792, Sept. 1981.

——. "Internet Protocol," RFC-791, Sept. 1981.

——. "Simple Mail Transfer Protocol," RFC-821, Aug. 1982.

——. "Transmission Control Protocol (TCP)," RFC-793, Sept. 1981.

——. "User Datagram Protocol (UDP)," RFC-768, Aug. 1980.

Postel, J., et al. "File Transfer Protocol," RFC-959, Oct. 1985.

Rekhter, Y., et al. "A Border Gateway Protocol 4," RFC-1771, Mar. 1995.

Rose, M. T., *The Open Book*, Prentice Hall, 1990.

Rosen, E., et al. "Multi-Protocol Label Switching," RFC-3031, Jan. 2001.

Simpson, W. "The Point-to-Point Protocol," RFC-1661, July 1994.

Stallings, W. *High-Speed Networks & Internets*, Prentice-Hall, 2001.

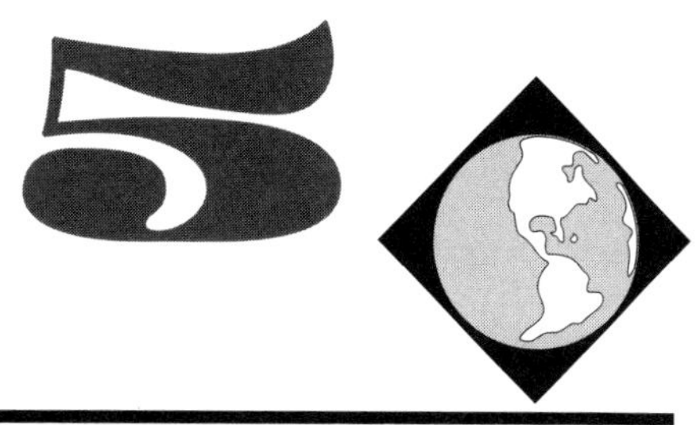

5 The New Telephony

To provide telephony service over any IP-based network, two things are necessary. First, there must be a means for actually carrying speech across the IP network that can provide an acceptable level of quality for users. Second, there must be a scheme for signaling to the network the endpoint with which the caller wishes to communicate. These are quite different problems. Providing a bearer channel over which the user can talk has one set of conditions and problems for IP-based networks, while signaling to launch the call and notify the endpoints has yet another set of issues. In both cases, the ability to interoperate with the existing PSTN is essential. At the outset, most, if not all, telephone calls launched on the IP network will be destined for a user on the PSTN. For the bearer channel, new regimes of quality, both improved and degraded, can be contemplated. For the signaling, entirely different schemes from today's telephone network are possible. Indeed, making choices in this domain is difficult because the more exciting methods of controlling the call are not necessarily easy to interwork with the PSTN.

For the bearer channel, there is a reasonably clear-cut scheme of protocols for carrying the speech. The key issues here are achieving a quality of service acceptable to the users. Today's Voice over IP (VoIP) methods have not been very successful in the quality arena. Users have become accustomed to "toll quality" voice connections in today's PSTN. Many users complain about speech quality for wireless networks, and the experience through 2000 with VoIP has been less than stellar. In some cases, carriers who installed VoIP networks have discontinued or curtailed their use. Nevertheless, it is possible to achieve toll quality in VoIP networks, and this will be discussed within this chapter.

Signaling for connections is not such a clear-cut issue. There are at least two architectures for call control that are significantly different. There is a case for a fully distributed model in which the network has very limited intelligence. In this model, all the intelligence is placed in the host computer at the user's location. The network serves only to carry the speech between the endpoints once there is an agreement to communicate and possibly some databases. Session Initiation Protocol (SIP) comes closest to this model. In SIP, host end systems communicate directly regarding connection requests, while the network mostly provides only a directory capability. A second architecture places much more intelligence inside the network in a manner similar to today's PSTN. The host end systems rely on the network for nearly all functions. There are two protocols that have been developed that are more or less in line with this model. The first is H.323, a protocol developed in the ITU that was originally intended for multimedia conferencing over LANs. H.323 aligns very closely with ISDN and SS7 signaling protocols used in the PSTN. The second is MEGACO (Media Gateway Control Protocol), which was developed in the IETF in collaboration with the ITU where it is Recommendation H.248. SIP, H.323, and MEGACO/H.248 are all quite different from each other.

It is difficult to say which of these three protocols will emerge as the winner for telephony, since each has its advantages and disadvantages, its supporters and detractors. Sadly, it is most likely that all three will coexist for quite a long time. This will make interoperability more complex for VoIP users and will slow deployment. Nevertheless, this seems inevitable.

In this chapter, the protocols for carrying the speech channel will be explained first. Then, the complex subject of signaling and control for telephony will be considered.

Transporting Voice

The basic method of carrying speech over IP makes use of several protocols that are used to transport the speech information as packets and to provide end-to-end timing for dispensing the sounds to the listener. This stack is generalized for any real-time media, such as video or audio, and it introduces the concept of a session in which there may be many media present at once. No assumption is made about the particular type of media or the manner in which it is represented. The protocols are:

- Real-time Transport Protocol (RTP)
- RTP Control Protocol (RTCP)
- Network Time Protocol 3 (NTP-3)
- User Datagram Protocol (UDP)
- Internet Protocol (IP)

As will be seen, RTP provides sufficient information about packet delivery to detect loss and incorrect ordering of packets, but it leaves the decision about managing these problems to the application. Likewise, RTP collects abundant information regarding the session, including round-trip delays and jitter, but makes no specific use of this data. The application can choose to use this data as it wishes. In this regard, RTP and RTCP are not completely specified. Details of what actions to take are left to the application. For example, a video application may choose to react differently to missing packets than an audio application might react. RTP/RTCP provides a framework for supporting real-time applications but leaves flexibility for applications to meet the requirements of different media. As a result, there is no "standard" RTP protocol implementation. Each application builds its own implementation based on the needs of its media.

NTP provides a synchronized clock source for timing the sampling of signals at the transmitter and for reconstructing them at the receiver. Its timestamps are carried inside RTP packets and it can be used to synchronize events at the endpoints using the IP network.

Figure 5–1 shows these protocols configured in two end systems on an IP network. Both RTP and RTCP are carried over UDP, which in turn is transported by IP. Specific UDP port values in the range from 1025 to 65535 identify the RTP and RTCP sessions where the even value is assigned to RTP and the next higher value (odd) is assigned to RTCP. Ports 5004 and 5005 have been allocated as default ports. There is always an RTCP session for every RTP session.

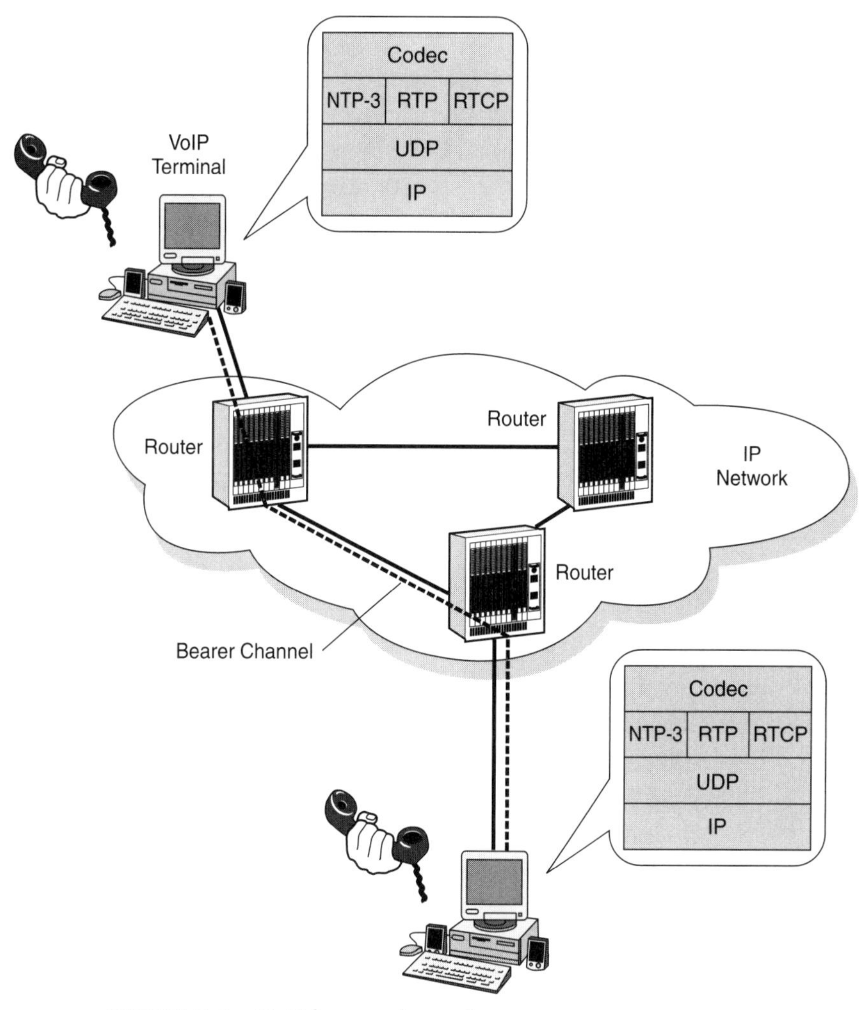

FIGURE 5–1 *VoIP bearer channel.*

Once these protocols are discussed, the various approaches to achieving an acceptable quality of service for the end-to-end connection will be considered.

Real-Time Transport Protocol (RTP)

This protocol is designed to supplement UDP for providing real-time services. RTP specifically carries real-time media, sometimes called the bearer channel. This is the data stream that represents the speech or video part of a session. Because there are many different encoding schemes for different media, RTP must be very flexible and somewhat complex to accommodate them all. Besides transporting the bearer channel, there is a companion protocol, RTCP, that is used to transport information between the transmitter and the receiver regarding lost packets, jitter, delay, and other impairments affecting the quality of the real-time session. RTP provides the means for collecting data and measuring these impairments, but it is RTCP that passes the reports between the endpoints. As was already mentioned, there are several schemes for signaling call connections to the network. RTP and RTCP have no role in this aspect of call control. Their purpose focuses on the actual voice or video channel being transported end to end. RTP packets are carried over UDP, which in turn is sent using IP.

The RTP header is shown in Figure 5–2 and contains the following fields:

- **Version** (2 bits) – The version of RTP protocol being used, the current version being 2.
- **Padding** (1 bit) – This field indicates whether any padding octets are present at the end of the payload.
- **Extension** (1 bit) – If there is a header extension present, this field is set to the value 1; otherwise it is set to 0.
- **Contributing Source Count** (4 bits) – This field indicates how many contributing sources (CSRC) are included in the header. There can be from 0 to 15 CSRCs. A CSRC is the generator of the real-time information, and several can be mixed together to create a single media stream.
- **Marker** (1 bit) – This field is used for some audio/video media streams and indicates whether silent intervals are suppressed or not.
- **Payload Type** (7 bits) – This indicates the encoding system used to generate the RTP payload and its format. Various real-time media utilize differing payloads due

to their inherent characteristics and the specific encoding scheme utilized. For instance, JPEG coded video requires a different formatting scheme than G.723 audio coding. This field also allows the correct decoding device to be assigned at the receiver. As examples, a few payload types are 0 = PCM audio at 8 KHz; 4 = G.723 audio at 8 KHz; 9 = G.722 audio at 8 KHz; 34 = H.263 video at 90 KHz; and 26 = JPEG video at 90 KHz.

- **Sequence Number** (16 bits) – This is the value of a counter that is incremented for each packet sent. Since UDP does not assure sequential delivery, this field can be used by the RTP application to reorder the packets if desired. The sequence number also allows the detection of missing packets that have been discarded by routers or other apparatus due to the presence of errors or congestion. RTP itself does not specify taking any of these actions; it is up to the application to decide an appropriate strategy for dealing with these and other problems. But RTP includes the mechanisms that enable such actions.
- **Timestamp** (32 bits) – This field is the value of a clock that was sampled at the moment the packet was generated at the source. The clock source, usually NTP-3, must be sufficiently accurate for the media being transported. Since the packet will contain many samples, the timestamp value will change from packet to packet according to the number of samples within each packet and the sampling rate. Since different packets may contain differing numbers of samples, the timestamp will move forward by non-uniform steps. The timestamp is used at the receiver to properly arrange for playback to the user. It is used to ensure that the samples are played back with the same relative time between them so no synchronization between the endpoints is necessary.
- **Synchronization Source ID** (32 bits) – The SSRC is a random value chosen at the transmitting end that identifies the source that is setting the sequence number

and timestamp values for the real-time media. Normally, this source is sending the packets. This should be a unique value across all media streams being handled by the sender so each can be identified.

- **Contributing Source** (32 bits) – This field identifies the CSRC for the media. Up to 15 CSRCs may be mixed together to create the media stream. There can be from 0 to 15 CSRC values present in the header. Thus, there may be multiple copies of this field, each identifying a source. The number is given in the CSRC count previously mentioned.
- **Data** (*n*-bits) – This is the actual information payload that represents the data generated by an encoder as specified by the Payload Type field. For example, it could be a block of data from a G.723 speech compression device. When decoded by the proper system, the original signal will be reconstructed for the user.

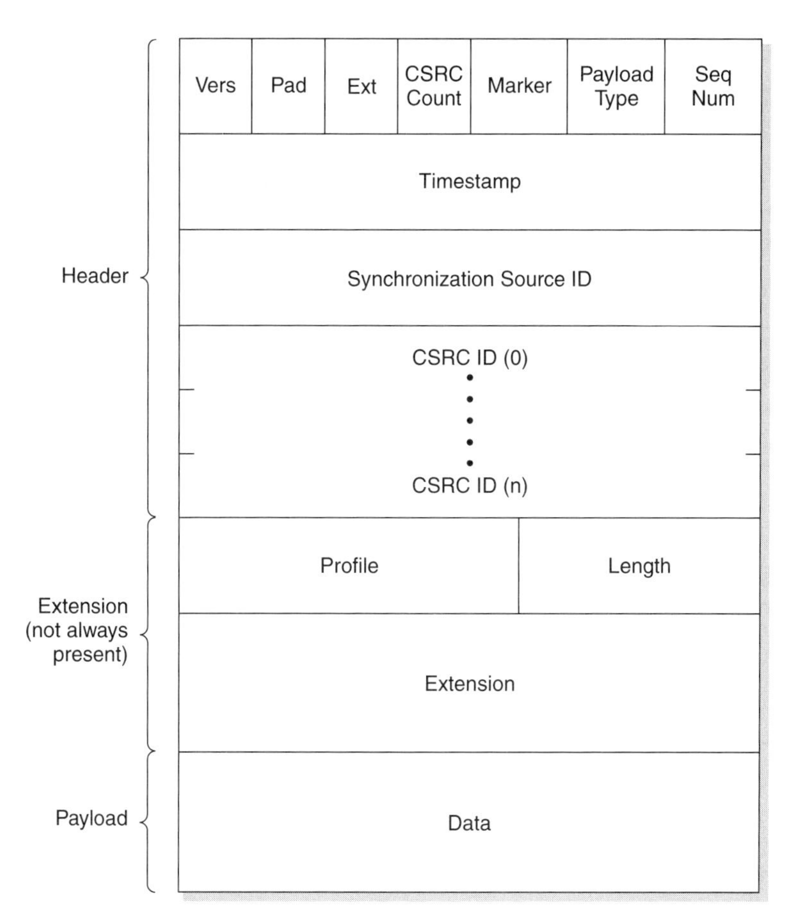

FIGURE 5–2 *RTP packet format.*

The header extension shown in Figure 5–2 contains three fields. The extension is not always present, but if it is, the Extension field must be set so the receiver can properly decode the header. The extension size is variable and can be created differently according to the media being transported and its associated encoding scheme. The extension fields are:

- **Profile** (16 bits) – This field can be used to indicate the type of extension present. The RTP specification does not place any specific requirements on this field, so it can be programmed as desired by the developer.

- **Length** (16 bits) – This indicates the length in octets of the header extension. This is a required field so that the packet can be correctly subdivided at an RTP receiver.
- **Extension** (*n* bits) – This field can be any length and can contain whatever control information may be needed to pass from transmitter to receiver for the specific protocol being used.

RTP is the meat and potatoes of VoIP. It can take the output of a speech encoding device and transport it across the network. Since UDP is used, there is no assurance that RTP packets will reach their destination at all or in the submitted order. But, through the use of sequence numbers, these losses can be detected and dealt with. For example, values can be substituted for missing packets during playback. By using time-stamps, RTP can manage the playback of the signal even though the network may provide variable delays. This also means that bursts of speech can be transmitted as one or more RTP packets. Since each RTP packet specifies its encoding method, sophisticated schemes can be used to lower bit rates in the presence of congestion or other network impairments.

Real-time Transport Control Protocol (RTCP)

As mentioned, RTP has a companion protocol, RTCP, which provides information between the transmitting and receiving systems regarding the various parameters important to its transmission. It does not establish or route network connections, Instead, it enables control by the endpoints through an exchange of information about the quality of the connection between the endpoints based on data collected by RTP. Using the information from the RTP header, such as timestamp and sequence number as well as its local clock, RTCP is able to calculate the frequency of lost packets, the average round-trip delay, and the inter-arrival jitter for the session. This allows the media protocols to adapt, if possible, to changes in network performance. It also allows a network operator, which can monitor the exchange, to determine whether or not the required quality of service is being provided for a connection.

RTCP can manage multiple simultaneous media transfers. Each media is referred to as a CSRS. Each CSRC is numbered so the endpoints can differentiate between them. RTCP messages allow for multiple CRSC parameters to be included in a single message.

There are five different types of RTCP packets:

- **Sender Report (SR)** – This is used by participating endpoints to inform receivers of key information about the session. It may also include reports relating to media it is receiving from other senders.
- **Receiver Report (RR)** – This is used by receive-only endpoints that are not transmitting media to pass reports about their reception to the sender of that media.
- **Source Description (SDES)** – This packet is used to describe the nature of the media source. Among other items, it contains a name (CNAME) by which the source can be referenced. In some instances, multiple media streams may be generated by the source, as in an audio/video conference. All media streams present are mapped to this source name. The description can also include other useful information, such as a participant's personal name, email address, or telephone number. These items can be used as part of the session in various ways.
- **Application Defined (APP)** – Application-specific functions. These packets are not specified by the RTCP protocol, so they can be anything the application requires for managing the media layer.
- **Goodbye (BYE)** – This packet indicates that the end of participation in a session has been reached and terminates the media transfer.

Although there are five different packet formats, they are not sent as individual packets. RTCP allows these packet types to be concatenated into a single larger compound packet to reduce overhead. This is important, since many control packets may be exchanged to manage the quality of a session, and sending them individually would be an unnecessary waste of resources. The compound packets will normally start with a Sender Report packet followed by a Source Description packet. If the endpoint is not sending media data, the Sender Report is replaced with a Receiver Report. In either case, a set of Report Blocks can be appended, which indicate how well the transmission is being received. If the session is terminating, a BYE packet may also be present. In some cases, an Application Defined packet may be present to carry information to the endpoints that is needed by the application. The compound packet has no header; it is simply the concatenation of the individual RTCP packets being sent. Figure 5–3 shows the format of the RTCP compound packet. Each RTCP compound packet is sent using UDP over IP.

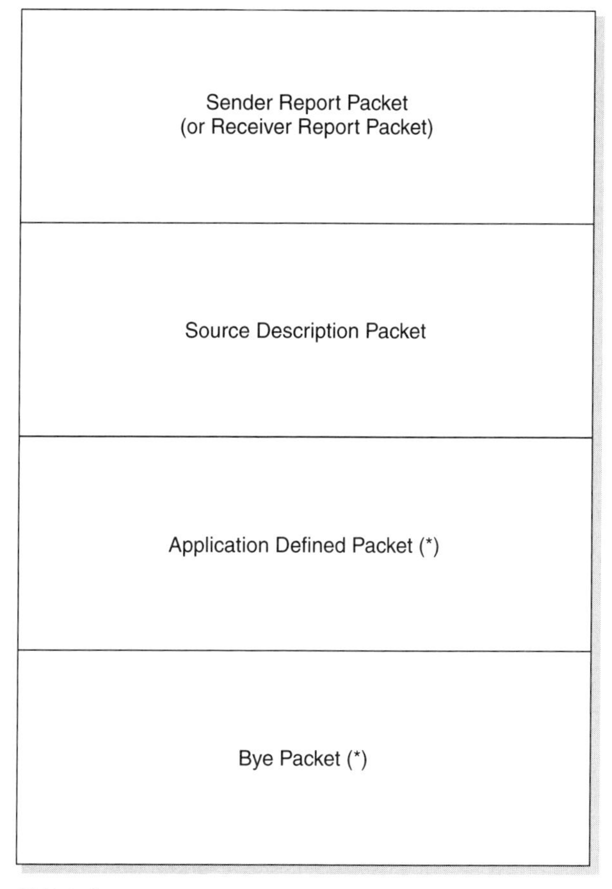

FIGURE 5–3 *RTCP compound packet.*

Next, each of the different packet types is discussed. Every RTCP packet has its own header, but each begins with a common part carried in a single 32-bit word with the following fields:

- **Version** (2 bits) – The version of RTCP packet being carried, the current version being 2.
- **Padding** (1 bit) – This field indicates whether any padding octets are present at the end of the payload.
- **Report Count** (5 bits) – This field gives the number of receiver Report Blocks present in the packet.

- **Packet Type** (8 bits) – This field specifies the packet type, where the value 200 = Sender Report (SR) Packet, 201 = Receiver Report (RR) Packet, 202 = Source Description (SDES) Packet, 203 = Goodbye (BYE) packet, and 204 = Application-Defined (APP) Packet. Each of the five packet types has a different format.
- **Length** (16 bits) – This is the length of the packet in octets. Note that this is not the length of the compound packet; it is only the length of the specific packet following this header. Each packet within the compound packet will have its own header.

The RTCP Sender Report packet format is shown in Figure 5–4. Sender Report packets begin with the common part followed by Sender Information. This can then be followed by up to 31 Report Blocks. The Sender Information is as follows:

- **Sender SSRC** (32 bits) – This is the Synchronization Source number of the sender.
- **NTP Timestamp** (64 bits) –This field carries the NTP Time when the Sender Report was originated. NTP is discussed later in this chapter. This field is organized into the number of seconds elapsed since 0:00 GMT on January 1, 1900 (the upper 32 bits) and fractions of a second (the lower 32 bits).
- **RTP Timestamp** (32 bits) – As described previously, RTP has its own timestamps that change based on the number of samples within an RTP packet and the sampling rate. This must be coordinated with the NTP Timestamp.
- **Sender's Packet Count** (32 bits) – This is the total number of packets transmitted since the session began up to the point in time when this Sender Report was issued. This value is reset to zero if the sender's SSRC value changes during the session.

- **Sender's Octet Count** (32 bits) – The total number of octets sent by the source since the start of the session. Like the Packet Count, this value is reset to zero only if the Sender's SSRC changes.

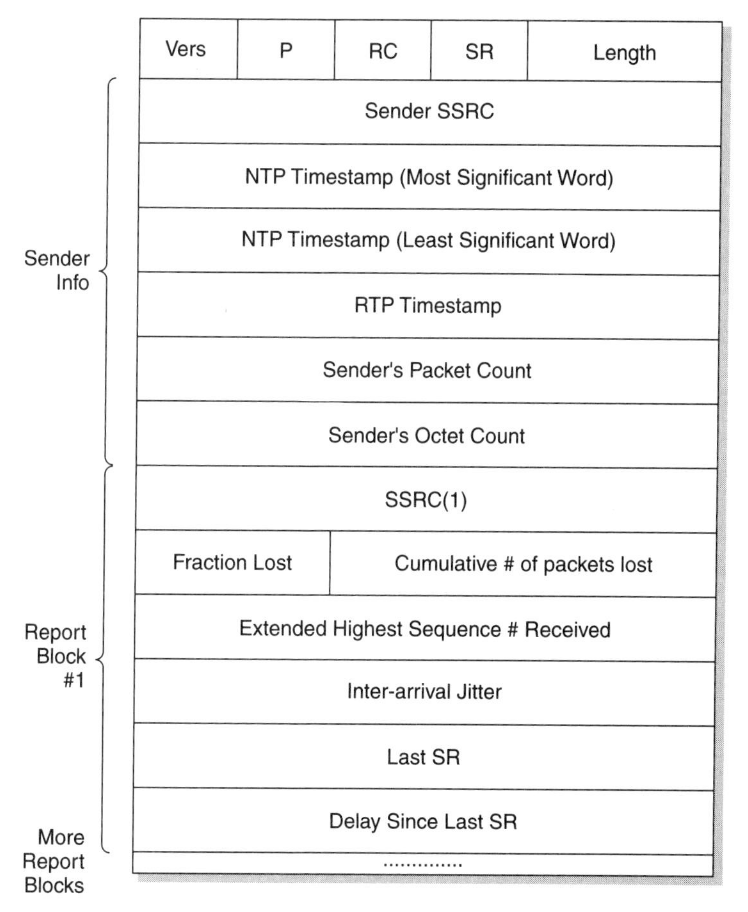

FIGURE 5–4 *RTCP sender report.*

The Sender Information Block may be followed by up to 31 receiver Report Blocks, where there is a Report Block for each media being managed. The receiver Report Block gives information as collected by the receiver of an RTP media stream and is used to inform the transmitter how well the network is treating its session. The field specification of each Report Block present, if any, is as follows:

- **SSRC** (32 bits) – The SSRC of the media source being reported on.
- **Fraction Lost** (8 bits) – This value is the number of packets lost divided by the number of packets expected. From examining the RTP sequence numbers, it is possible to know how many packets were sent.
- **Cumulative Packets Lost** (24 bits) – This is simply the total number of packets lost since the start of the session.
- **Extended Highest Sequence Number Received** (32 bits) – The low-order 16 bits is the latest RTP sequence number received from the source. Each time the sequence number "wraps around," a cycle counter is incremented. The cycle counter is carried as the upper 16 bits.
- **Inter-arrival Jitter** (32 bits) – This is an estimate of the jitter in RTP packet arrivals. Since each RTP packet carries a timestamp that can be compared to the receiver's local clock, it is possible to calculate both the absolute delay and the variation in delay between packets. The delay variation is averaged to produce an estimate of the jitter.
- **Last SR Timestamp** (32 bits) – This is the middle 32 bits of the NTP timestamp present in the last Sender Report packet. This allows the source to determine if its Sender Reports are being received or not.
- **Delay since Last Sender Report** (32 bits) – This is the delay since the last Sender Report, expressed in units of 1/65536 seconds.

The compound packet can also begin with an RTCP Receiver Report. This report is used in the situation that a device is only listening to the media and is not transmitting, such as may occur in an audio or video broadcast. The format of the packet is shown in Figure 5–5 and is identical to the Sender Report except there is no Sender Info provided other than the Sender SSRC. As in the Sender Report, up to 31 Report Blocks can be attached with the same format and fields as described above.

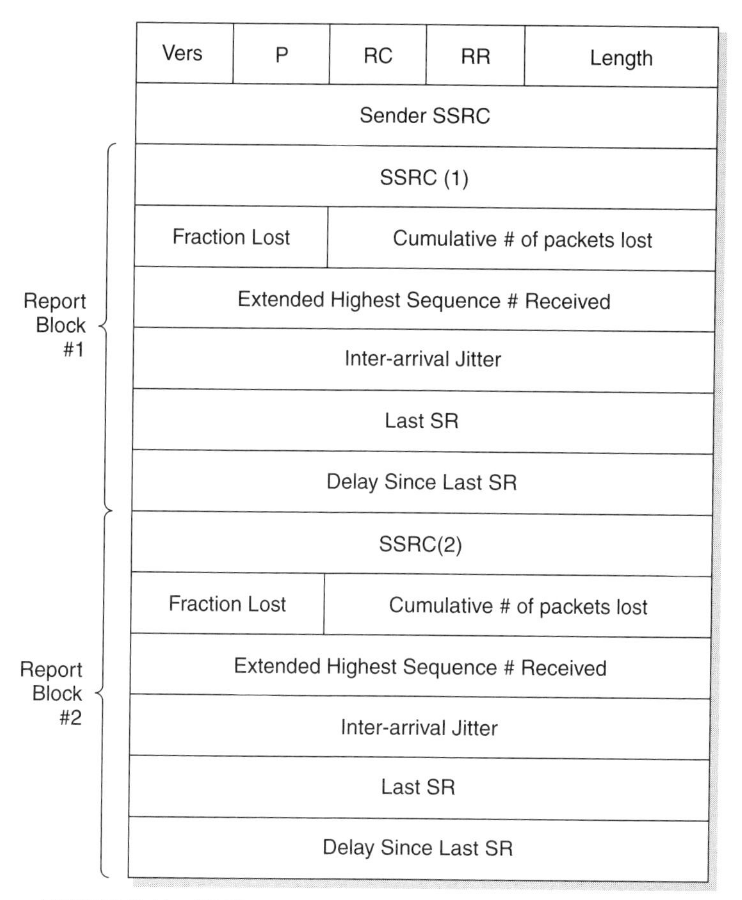

FIGURE 5–5 *RTCP receiver report.*

In a compound packet, an RTCP Source Description packet follows the Sender (or Receiver) Report packet. The RTCP Source Description packet format is shown in Figure 5–6 and contains the normal RTCP common part followed by up to 31 SDES items. The RC field in the common part specifies how many SDES items are attached. The format of each SDES item is:

- **SSRC/CSRC** (32 bits) – This is the Synchronization Source or the Contributing Source identification value for the media stream carried by the RTP protocol.

- **Type** (8 bits) – This value defines what type of SDES Item Data follows. Several values are specified, including 1 = CNAME, 2 = NAME, 3 = EMAIL, 4 = PHONE, 5 = LOCATION, 6 = TOOL, 7 = NOTE, and 8 = PRIVATE. Each of these items is a variable length string of ASCII characters. CNAME is the unique endpoint identifier given for this session that binds together all the media being used to support it. Normally, CNAME is in the form of "user@domain" and each endpoint has its own identifier. NAME can be a personal name, but it can also be a common name the users use to refer to such a session. EMAIL is the email address for the user, and PHONE is the user's phone number coded in international format (e.g., +1 for the United States). TOOL denotes the name and version number of the application being used during the session, while NOTE conveys useful information to the participants, such as notification of coffee breaks during a conference session. PRIVATE does not indicate secretive information but is used to convey experimental data between some users or applications that might not be useful to all users in a session.
- **Length** (8 bits) – This gives the length of the SDES Item Data in octets.
- **SDES Item Data** (*n* bits) – This is an ASCII text field with the given length and carries the particular information indicated by the Type field. For example, if Type = 3 (EMAIL), then *swalters@telcordia.net* would be valid. The field is padded at the end so the next SDES Item will start on a 32-bit word boundary.

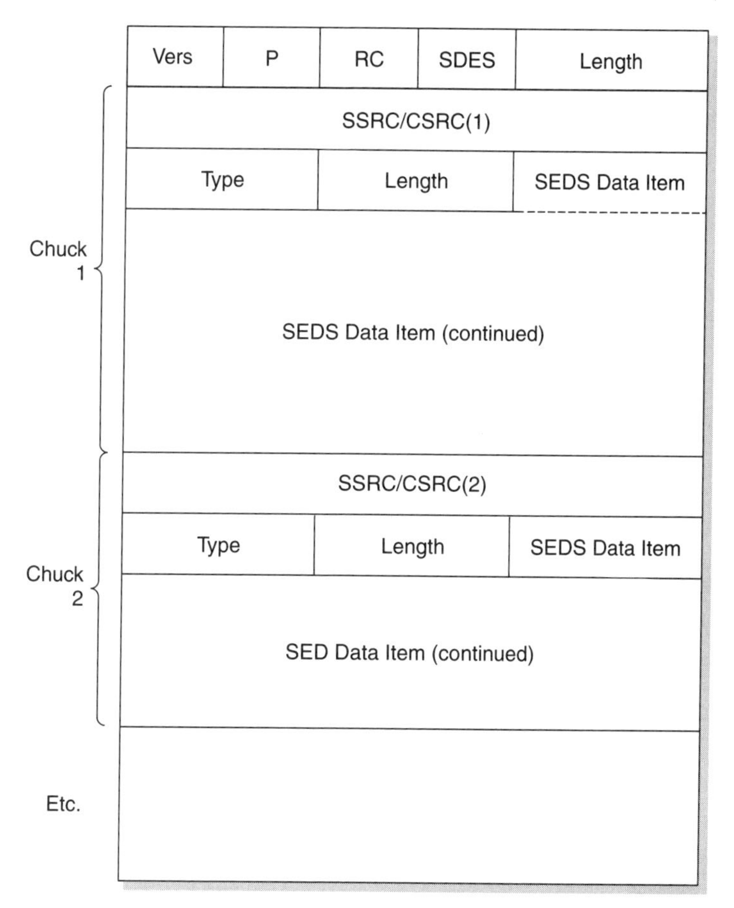

FIGURE 5–6 RTCP Source Description (SDES) packet format.

The BYE packet is shown in Figure 5–7. Whenever one or more media sources go inactive, the BYE packet is sent so all endpoints that were receiving the media will know it has ceased transmission. It includes an optional field for giving the reason for discontinuing transmission. The fields of the BYE packet are:

- **SSRC/CSRC** (32 bits) – This identifies the Synchronization Source or Contributing Source that has gone inactive. Up to 31 sources can be identified, each in a separate field. The RC field in the RTCP common part provides the number of such fields that are attached.

- **Length** (8 bits) – This is the length of the Reason field in octets. This field and the Reason field are optional and may not always be present.
- **Reason** (*n* bits) – This is an optional text message that gives the reason for ceasing transmission. Examples might include "Broken Camera" or "Time for Lunch." This field is variable length up to a maximum of 255 octets. It is padded at the end to reach a 32-bit word boundary.

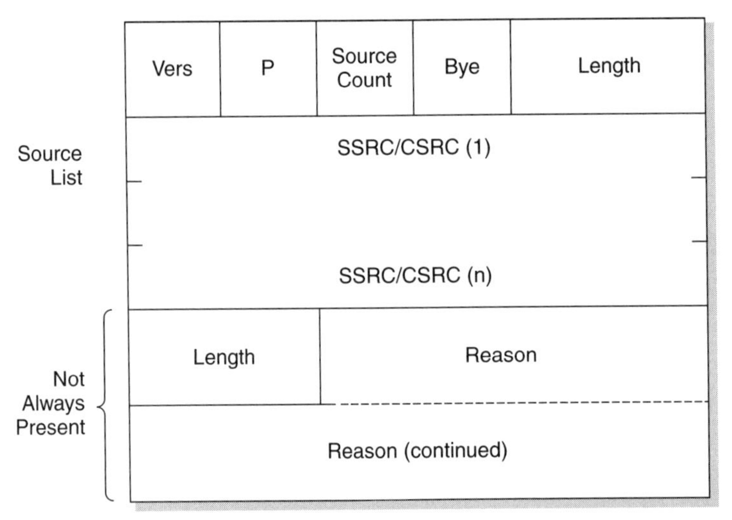

FIGURE 5–7 RTCP BYE *packet format.*

The application-defined RTCP packet is shown in Figure 5–8 and is quite simple. It contains the usual common part followed by the SSRC/CSRC field. This is then followed by an ASCII text string that is the name of the application, and then whatever data the application needs. The fields are not fixed in length. This message is intended to allow the support of proprietary mechanisms in applications. Example might include camera motion requests, volume changes, blocking of a media, or whatever the application developer wishes to do.

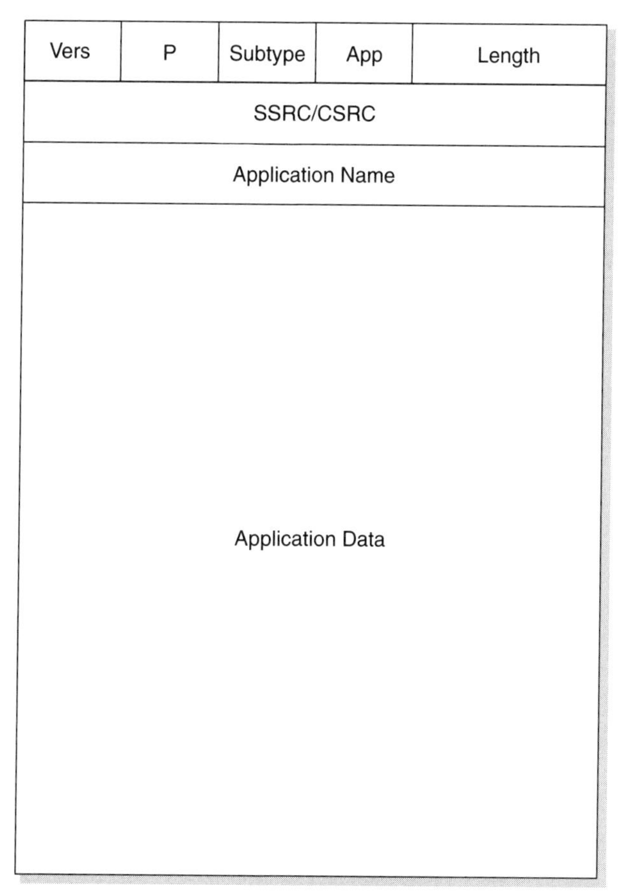

FIGURE 5–8 *Application-defined RTCP packet format.*

RTCP messages allow senders and receivers to determine how the network is handling their information, and they facilitate sessions. As network performance degrades, more packets will be lost. Such events will be detected by RTP using its sequence numbers, and RTCP will provide periodic summaries to the opposite end of the session regarding how well things are going. Delay and delay variation can be measured and reported. Sessions can be modified through the use of the BYE message by discontinuing sources. These features make RTP/RTCP a sophisticated means for carrying speech or other media over an IP network.

Network Time Protocol (NTP-3)

A key function in providing any real-time transport across any network is timing. In circuit-switched networks, the timing is distributed with the signal, since each bit and octet of the circuit is carefully synchronized to a reference standard. However, in a packet network such as the Internet, such timing may not exist on the interfaces or it may not be at the appropriate rate or have sufficient accuracy. For this reason, it is necessary to provide a timing source at the endpoints. NTP-3 is a protocol for providing a highly accurate local clock that can be used to timestamp RTP and RTCP packets and to generate local timing for collecting and playing back speech, audio, or video.

NTP generates a timestamp that represents the number of seconds and fractions of seconds that have expired since 00:00 UT on 1 January 1900. The timestamp is a 64-bit fixed-point number in which the upper 32-bit portion is the integer part and the lower 32-bit portion is the fractional part. This allows NTP to represent time values as small as 233 picoseconds. NTP can operate over either UDP or TCP. NTP clocks provide nominal accuracy in the low milliseconds in actual operation.

NTP functions by maintaining a local clock that can be adjusted to run faster or slower. Known sources of accurate time, such as the reference clock at Fort Collins, Colorado, are linked to servers placed within the network. NTP exchanges messages with one or more of these servers, which respond with their local time. NTP then makes adjustments to its local clock to improve its time. Because the time sources are at an unknown distance and because the network delivers messages with variable delays, it is necessary for NTP to estimate the average round-trip delay and compensate for the network delay when adjusting the clock. In order to do this, NTP places its own local time in its message and the responding clock source response includes the original timestamp and its own local time. See Figure 5–9 for the NTP message format. The requesting NTP system can then begin to estimate the round-trip delay, although this will not be very accurate until the local clock is near synchronization and has made good estimates of the delay from the reference source to the local NTP clock. NTP has very sophisticated algorithms to compensate for delay, dispersion, and other problems. It is also able to use multiple clock sources in its synchronization algorithm to average out deviations.

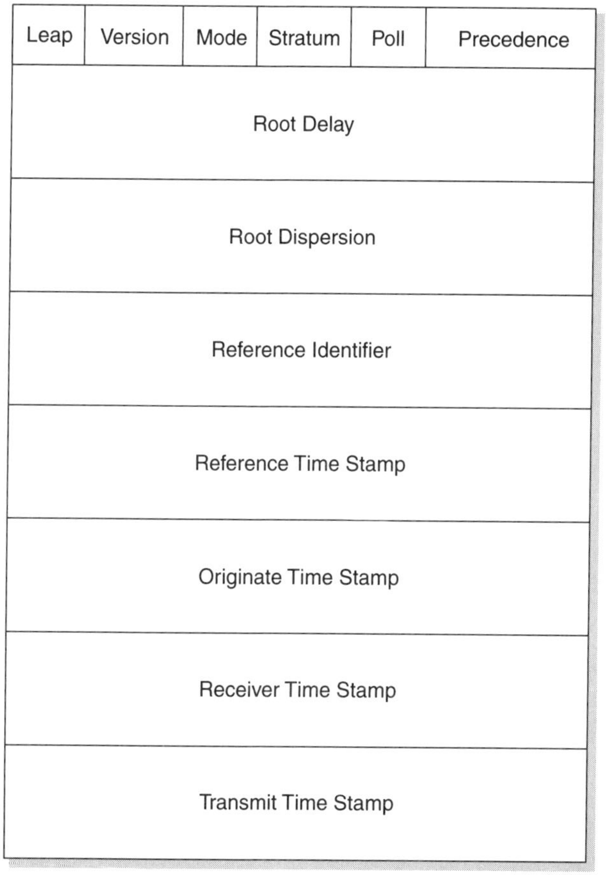

Leap	Version	Mode	Stratum	Poll	Precedence
Root Delay					
Root Dispersion					
Reference Identifier					
Reference Time Stamp					
Originate Time Stamp					
Receiver Time Stamp					
Transmit Time Stamp					

FIGURE 5–9 *NTP-3 packet format.*

In real-time applications, the NTP timestamp can be used as an accurate indication of time. Also, the local clock can be chosen to operate at a frequency that is useful for whatever the media streams require. For telephony service, this might be best chosen at a multiple of 8 KHz, perhaps 64 kHz.

Achieving Quality

When VoIP connections are carried across an IP network, the question of quality must be considered. There are three primary issues that affect quality. These are the codec chosen to compress and decompress the voice, the bit rate that the codec needs to function properly, and the network performance with regard to delivering the packets generated by the codec. These all interact to some degree, since a codec can reduce its bit rate, and thereby its performance, in the presence of congestion. However, the most desirable approach to achieving quality is to select an excellent codec, plan for the bit rate it requires to be provided, and engineer the network to avoid congestion. While this is the correct approach, other sources may cause the network to congest, and these may not be controllable by the network.

When routers congest or packets are discarded due to bit errors, information vital to achieving toll quality will not be delivered. The basic problem is simple to state. Consider first an IP network that is grossly over engineered. This means that at all times, there are more than enough resources in its routers and transmission links to carry all submitted traffic without ever discarding a packet. It also means that traffic delay is low and that router queues never overflow. In such a network, speech quality would be quite good.

Now imagine that traffic grows to a level where some fraction of submitted packets are not delivered due to congestion. As an example, consider the situation when 1 percent of the packets are lost. If this were the case, a 3-minute telephone call would have approximately 2 seconds missing. Whether or not this would disturb the user depends on which 2 seconds was lost and how the coding system dealt with the losses. If luck were on the user's side,[1] this would occur during silent periods or at times when the decoder could interpolate effectively. If it were distributed as 200 ten-millisecond lost bursts occurring at just the right times, perhaps a good interpolation might be possible and the user would not notice the losses. But in the worst case, there could be 200 significant impairments during the phone call. And this would be the case for every phone call. The operator of such a network would receive a lot of complaints from its customers. If you prefer a lower loss statistic, consider a value of 0.1 percent. Even at such a low level, there can be many dozens of events during a call.

It turns out that a lot of statistics are collected on the Internet's performance; the information is easy to obtain but difficult to interpret. For example, during August 2001, the North American Internet experienced a 136 ms average round trip time (RTT) and a 2 percent packet loss. However, during the same interval, some large individual carriers posted much better statistics, one as low as 0.1 percent loss and 41 ms RTT and another claiming 0.45 percent loss and 52.7 ms RTT within their networks. This means that if you subscribed to either of those carrier's service and most of your sessions were with systems directly connected to its network, your performance would be much better than the national average. As should be expected, there is a lot of variation in the delay and loss statistics for any real network. But for any of these carriers, it is likely that telephony would perform poorly if carried over even the best of networks.

This doomsday scenario assumes two network properties that lead to poor quality and many user complaints:

1. There are not enough resources.
2. Every packet is treated equally.

---

1 Is it ever?

There are some technologists who advocate only worrying about the first item. They argue that if enough resources are available, congestion will not occur and all the packets will be delivered. Unfortunately, this pits the operator's budget against the user's demand. Even if the operator had an unlimited budget, it is questionable to think it could deploy capacity in the network as fast as users can increase demand. Furthermore, even if the operator were successful, this approach would provide the same quality to every submitted packet whether or not it is needed. In many cases, such as email, Web browsing, and file retrieval, it is not necessary to provide such high quality. The occasional lost packet would readily be retransmitted and the extra delay would not be apparent to users, so this would be an unnecessary expenditure. Also, it must be remembered that many Internet services, such as Web browsing, demand very high peak rates for very short periods of time to satisfy users. A network that is engineered to the average rate of such services would constantly be driven to congestion with every click of the mouse. If it were engineered to the peak rate, it would be grossly underutilized. Since Internet traffic has been shown to be self-similar in nature, it is impossible to make predictions about its behavior.[2]

Ultimately, it is necessary to address the second item and stop treating every packet equally with best effort service. If we take a simplistic perspective and divide Internet traffic into two classes, telephony and everything else, a solution using MPLS and DiffServ emerges. Since traffic statistics for telephony are understood, the necessary transport capacity can be set aside and adjusted as demand

2. An important exception to this statement is an IP network that serves only telephony. In this case, network engineering is reasonably straightforward because there are understood patterns to telephony demand and traffic statistics. The operator need only apply these engineering methods while allowing for the overhead of the protocols for speech transport, signaling, and operations traffic. In fact a number of long distance voice networks have been built on exactly this principle. The abyss looms large only when mixing telephony with other types of traffic in the network.

increases or decreases. In this way, a network operator can allocate sufficient resources within its network to ensure that telephony traffic will have low packet loss. Using MPLS, telephony flows would be directed into paths sized and reserved for telephony service. Thus, telephony connections would experience low packet loss. Since MPLS bypasses many of the routers otherwise encountered in an end-to-end connection, lower delay would also be realized. For telephony, delay is a paramount issue, so use of the Expedited Forwarding class of DiffServ would be appropriate. Then, wherever a router is encountered by the traffic, delay will be further reduced.

It is necessary that some aspect of the call control system participate by informing the ingress router and MPLS switching devices of the new flow. This requires that an admission control system operate within the network to manage the reserved capacity. This could take the form of a dedicated resource manager accessed by MEGACO/H.248, H.323, or SIP. At the ingress to the network, packets belonging to the telephony class can be tagged for MPLS switching into a reserved path. Before a user's connection is placed in the reserved path, a request must be submitted to the resource manager. The resource manager can decide whether or not to honor a new connection request by examining the route it would take. If the allocated capacity for telephony has been exhausted, the resource manager would deny the request. But if there is still sufficient capacity along the route to the destination, the resource manager could then record the increased demand along the route and notify the network ingress point that this user flow is to be allocated to the reserved telephony path. Thereafter, the ingress router would tag all packets belonging to this flow and they would be switched by MPLS along the reserved path identified for the reserved traffic flow. Links along this route would not enter congestion, since their capacity has been considered when admitting connections to the route. When the user terminates a call, the resource manager would again be notified. The resource manager would then deallocate its portion of the reserved capacity, and the released capacity would be available for new connection requests.

Call Control

In any VoIP implementation, it is necessary to have a means for signaling to and from the endpoints so that calls can be originated and terminated. This requires some additional protocols and, in some cases, additional network elements to process them. The distribution of intelligence between the terminal and the network elements is an important consideration. At one extreme, the network can be made to have very limited intelligence or perhaps no intelligence at all. In this case, the terminals must have the complete ability to locate the distant terminal, including directory capability and conferencing bridges for multiparty calls. At the other extreme, the network is highly intelligent and takes full responsibility for establishing or denying connections.

There are three protocols that are in use for VoIP networks: SIP, MEGACO/H.248, and H.323. In general terms, SIP has the least dependence on network infrastructure, while MEGACO/H.248 and H.323 place greater intelligence in the network. The choice of protocol is important, for it can make interworking with the existing PSTN either difficult or easy, and it can either block or enable the creation of new terminal equipment and sophisticated capabilities. The *softswitch* architecture is simply the separation of the bearer channel and the call control for the connection. There are numerous vendors implementing this architecture, including Cisco,[3] Juniper,[4] Lucent,[5] Nortel,[6] Sonus,[7]

3. http://www.cisco.com
4. http://www.juniper.com
5. http://www.lucent.com
6. http://www.nortel.com
7. http://www.sonusnet.com

Telcordia,[8] and others. You may wish to explore these different suppliers and their architectures to understand the differences between them. Each supplier is creating one or more products using these various protocols.

H.323

This protocol is used to establish for multimedia and telephony connections. It was created by the ITU and has been deployed in a variety of networks for telephony and multimedia applications. The architecture is shown in Figure 5–10 and has four major components that are interconnected using a packet network:

- **H.323 Terminal Unit** – This is the end system host that is running the H.323 user application. This system will exchange messages with systems in the network to request a connection to another user and to control the call. Besides the signaling function, the terminal unit will also contain the A-to-D converters and the set of protocols needed to transport voice over the packet network (RTP, RTCP, NTP, UDP, IP, etc.). The fundamental call control protocol is specified in ITU Recommendation H.225. In fact, there are three protocols involved in call control: RAS (H.225), Call Control (Q.931), and Media Control (H.245).
- **Gatekeeper** – This unit is responsible for managing the connection requests coming from the terminal units. It behaves much like a call processor in a circuit switch in that it receives call requests that it can either approve or deny depending on the state of the network. It provides, either directly or through DNS services, a directory capability. There are various options in H.323 as to the functions of the gatekeeper. Here, only the most fundamental aspects will be presented.

8. http://www.telcordia.com

- **Gateway** – When connections are requested to reach a user that is not within the network, a gateway system is utilized. The gateway sits on the boundary between the H.323 network and the PSTN (or other network). It provides interworking capability between the two networks. On the H.323 side, the gateway appears to be a normal H.323 terminal unit. On the PSTN side, it appears as a node on the PSTN. The gateway interworks the H.323 signaling protocol with SS7 on the PSTN side. It also converts the media streams from RTP packets to TDM circuits.
- **Multipoint Controller Unit (MCU)** – The MCU manages multipoint conferences between three or more terminals by signaling to the gatekeeper to obtain all needed connections. It then assigns a multipoint processor that actually combines the individual channels into the appropriate conference signals. These are then sent to the terminal units in the conference. These units can provide three-way or *n*-way audio conferences.

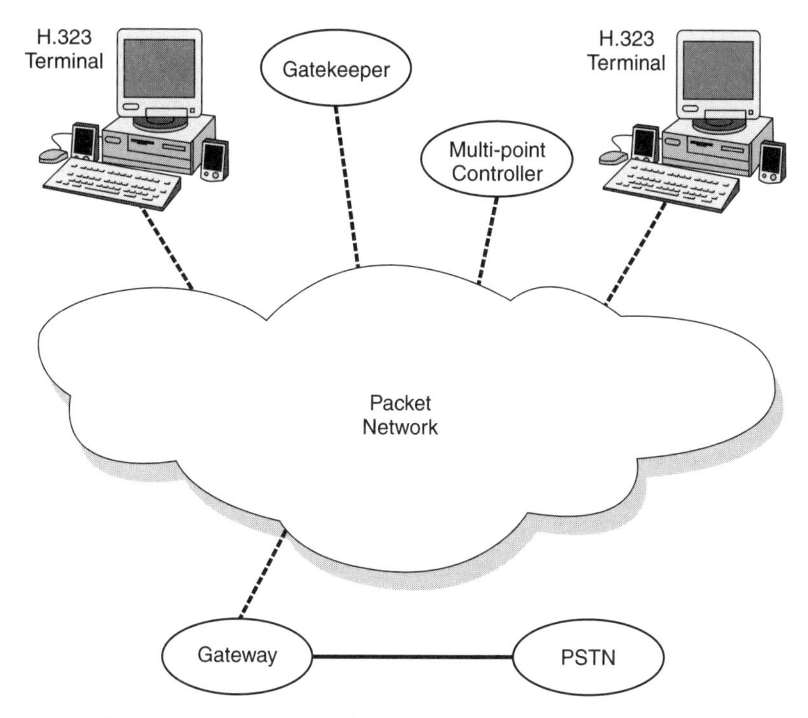

FIGURE 5–10 H.323 architecture.

The three signaling protocols provide different capabilities to the terminals. The first protocol performs Registration, Admission and Status (RAS). This protocol is used to locate a Gatekeeper, register the terminal with it, and exchange information relating to bandwidth availability and other resources. Once registered, the terminal can launch call requests to other terminals, using Q.931, a protocol created for ISDN that has been slightly modified in H.225. This protocol is where the calling terminal specifies the address of the terminal being called and the type of connection being requested. Terminals exchange messages with the gatekeeper to become connected, after which they can begin transmitting media using RTP/RTCP. The last protocol is used to control the media bearing the connection. The H.245 control protocol operates directly between the terminals to establish and control the media transmission. H.245 does not actually carry the media; that function is left to RTP/RTCP. Instead, H.245 is used to negotiate the type of connection to be created using RTP and selects the appropriate encoding/decoding system to convert the speech to data.

H.323 provides for several different signaling configurations, including direct terminal-to-terminal call requests. However, most implementations use the gatekeeper when establishing calls. Figure 5–11 shows the flow of messages between terminals and a gatekeeper to establish a call. First, each terminal uses RAS to locate a gatekeeper. To do this, the terminal sends a Gatekeeper Request (GRQ) message on a specially selected IP multicast address (port 1718 at IP address 224.0.1.41). If the gatekeeper accepts the terminal, it responds with a Gatekeeper Confirm (GCF) message. Next, each terminal must register with the gatekeeper. This involves sending a Registration Request (RRQ) packet and receiving a Registration Confirm (RCF) message. The RRQ/RCF exchange contains information, including the address of the terminal for call control. Once registered, the terminals can participate in sessions by sending Admission Request (ARQ) messages and receiving an Admission Confirm (ACF). An important element of the ARQ/ACF exchange is the selection of bandwidth for the connection. The ARQ/ACF messages also establish whether the subsequent signaling to the called terminal will be routed through the gatekeeper or not. There are other controls the terminal and gatekeeper can negotiate, including bandwidth changes during a call, status of resources, and terminal location for mobile users.

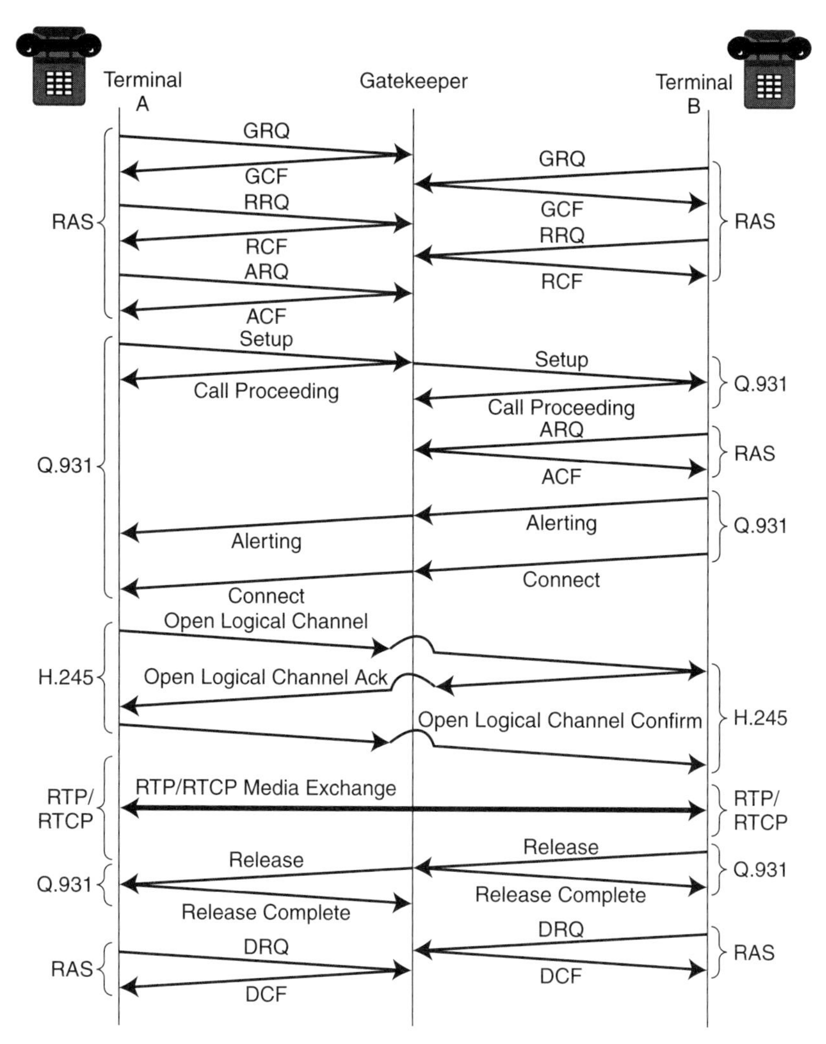

FIGURE 5–11 *H.323 call example.*

Next, Q.931 messages are launched from the calling terminal towards the gatekeeper. The first is a Setup message that contains the called party phone number. The gatekeeper acknowledges this message with Call Proceeding and then locates the address of the party being called. This could be done using the E.164 DNS service described in Chapter 4. Once the IP address of the called party is known, the gatekeeper sends a Setup message to the called terminal. The terminal will respond with a Call Proceeding message and then will use the RAS Admission Request to enable its participation. The terminal will then notify the user by some means and will transmit an Alerting message to the gatekeeper. This message is then forwarded to the calling terminal so it can indicate to its user that the distant party is being alerted. When the called party answers the call, the called terminal sends a Connect message to the gatekeeper that marks the call as active and passes the message on to the calling terminal. The calling terminal then uses an H.245 Control message to open a logical channel that the called terminal acknowledges. These messages establish the parameters to be used in the subsequent RTP/RTCP session, such as session ID, media type, and so forth. The calling terminal then sends a confirmation to the called terminal, after which RTP/RTCP packets are exchanged carrying the speech and the users can talk.

Once the conversation is ended, one party or the other will disconnect by sending the Q.931 Release message. The gatekeeper will acknowledge this with a Release Complete message and transmit a Release message to the other terminal. That terminal will then respond with Release Complete. Both terminals then use RAS Disconnect Request (DRQ) to clear the session at the gatekeeper and the gatekeeper responds with Disconnect Confirm (DCF) messages.

There are other scenarios possible within the H.323 framework; this example shows but one. The other illustrative case to consider is when one party or the other is not on the same network. In such cases, the gateway comes into play. The gateway will behave as though it were an H.323 terminal in its messages within the H.323 network, but it will act as though it were a network node on the PSTN, using SS7 messages there. Another case is that of a multipoint call involving three or more parties. In this instance, the gatekeeper will direct the media connections to and MCU that will create the conference connections.

An advantage of H.323 is its use of Q.931 signaling protocol; this makes interworking with SS7 very easy. Q.931 was initially created for the ISDN and was intended to extend circuit-switched telephony to digital user access. This signaling protocol was developed with careful consideration of SS7, the interoffice signaling protocol, so as to make it easy to complete calls in the circuit-switched network. This means that H.323 terminals can easily interwork with the existing PSTN, an important asset at the outset of deployment when there will be very few H.323 devices.

A disadvantage of H.323 is its complexity. As can be seen in Figure 5–11, there are many messages exchanged and most of them are of little value to the end user. This wastes transport capacity in the network and it complicates the software in the terminal. For example, the terminals must be prepared to receive unexpected messages when unusual events occur, such as the caller abandoning the call just as the called party answers it. These sorts of events make the software overly complicated due to the many recovery legs that must be included. An additional problem with H.323 arises when new features are desired. Because the call flow has an expected sequence and a corresponding state transition by the terminal, it requires modification of all the terminals to add a new feature. As a result, there will be many incompatible implementations in the terminals, and adding new features will be cumbersome.

SIP

SIP is another scheme for call control. It was created in the IETF and is documented in RFC 2543. SIP might also be called the Simple protocol, especially when compared to H.323 or MEGACO/H.248. There is a companion protocol, Session Description Protocol (SDP), which is normally used in conjunction with SIP, although other description methods are allowed. In short, SDP describes the session; the session might be a phone call with a single media or an audio/video conference with a complex multimedia stream. SIP informs the endpoint(s) of the session and requests their participation.

The SIP architecture identifies user agent servers, registrar servers, proxy servers, and redirect servers. Figure 5–12 shows these elements in the architecture. These are employed at various times in the course of a session as needed. The IP addresses of these various servers are found by querying a DNS server. Their purpose is as follows:

- **User Agent Server** – This is also known as a user agent client, since it is the element that has direct contact with the user. This would ordinarily be an application that has the ability to alert a user to requests by visual or audible means. The reason this device is both a client and a server is that it can both originate requests and respond to them. This is necessary since it is present at both endpoints of a session.
- **Registrar Server** – This device serves as a directory of SIP addresses for reaching users. The registrar records the SIP address, UDP port, and IP address so that the user can be contacted for future sessions. Users may register with multiple Registrars and may register multiple addresses. Registrations have a fixed lifetime and are discarded by the Registrar once it expires. The maximum lifetime is 136 years.
- **Proxy Server** – This server can act on behalf of a user or a group of users. There are many ways the proxy can be used. For example, it can act to redirect requests for incoming sessions to the user's actual location without ever divulging the address publicly, a feature that would be useful to highly mobile users. It can also screen incoming sessions from a user if desired. It can perform similar functions for sessions initiated by its users.
- **Redirect Server** – This server can be used to link a session to a different location. For example, if a user travels from office to home, he could inform the redirect server of his new address. As an example, if a session

were launched to *sip:swalters@telcordia.com,* the Redirect Server could return the new address *sip:swalters@home.att.net.* The Redirect Server can return a list of addresses to try for including phone numbers, pager numbers, and mobile notebook computer addresses.

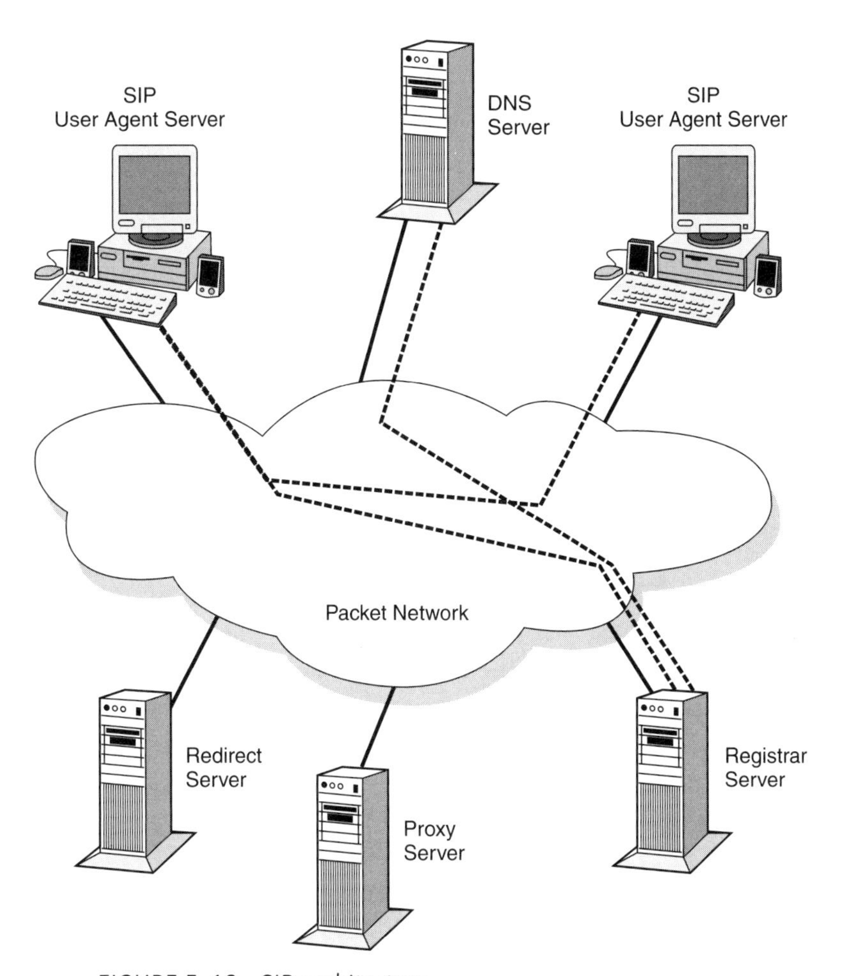

FIGURE 5–12 *SIP architecture.*

Each message is carried as a string of ASCII characters; however, some fields are ASCII numeric symbols. This allows easy formulation of the message. SIP has six message types:

- **INVITE** – This message announces the beginning of a session and includes a session description. The session could involve single or multiple parties and could involve many media. INVITE can also be used to bring additional users into an existing session.
- **ACK** – This message is used in SIP to indicate receipt of any other message. Since SIP uses UDP, there is no assurance of delivery of messages, so the SIP processor must be prepared to retransmit requests or to receive extra copies of earlier requests. Each SIP message includes a status code such as "OK" or "Ringing" and so forth. A partial list of SIP responses and their codes is:
    - 180 Ringing
    - 181 Forwarding
    - 200 OK
    - 400 Bad request
    - 403 Forbidden
    - 404 Not found
    - 486 Busy here[9]
    - 600 Busy everywhere[100]
    - 484 Address incomplete
    - 603 Decline
    - 482 Loop detected

  These parameters allow the processor to indicate the outcome of a request such as an INVITE.
- **BYE** – This request terminates participation in a session and can be sent by any party in the session. This does not mean the session is terminated, just the participation by the indicating party. In a multiparty conference call, the session would remain in operation as long as there is a participant or the source terminates it.

9. I don't want to talk to you.
10. I REALLY don't want to talk to you!

- **OPTIONS** – This can be used to query a server regarding its capabilities, for example, whether or not it can handle a particular media type or whether or not the user is available.
- **CANCEL** – This is used to terminate a pending request that has not yet been answered. For example, it can cancel an INVITE request that has not yet been accepted. If an application sends an INVITE request to a user at multiple locations (a "shotgun" approach to finding the user), it should send CANCEL messages to the locations that did not respond with an "OK" status.
- **REGISTER** – SIP devices must register with a SIP server so they can be located. Otherwise, it would be impossible to establish sessions with the device. SIP uses Uniform Resource Identifier (URI), such as *sip:swalters@telcordia.com,* for addressing devices. The REGISTER message informs the server of the user's URI, IP address, and type. For example, telephone numbers can also be supported, such as *sip:4.9.9.2.8.5.7.2.3.7.1@telcordia.com; user=phone.* After registration, users can be easily located using the SIP server. DNS is used to find the IP address of the URI.
- **COMET** (Condition Met) – This message and some yet to be approved extensions to SDP allow various requirements such as resource reservation, DiffServ admission or secure encryption needs to be met prior to accepting a session. When a session is initiated using the INVITE message, the SDP-encoded message body may contain various requirements that must be met for the session to be successful. These are usually associated with the media stream. Most of these requirements will require communication by the receiving host with various network entities such as RSVP or DiffServ systems. Once the host has met all these requirements, the COMET response should be sent. It is only then that the host will alert the user. This method is still in draft status within the IETF and you should obtain the latest information from the IETF Web page.[11]

Each message can carry a number of headers. Some headers are optional and others are mandatory. For example, the INVITE message requires the inclusion of a From, To, Via, Call ID, Content Length, and Command Sequence number (CSeq) headers. These messages are used to establish, control, and terminate sessions.

SDP messages are carried in the body of some SIP messages, particularly the INVITE message. SDP describes the session in great detail so the receiving system can configure itself properly for the media stream and the various control streams that may be required. SDP descriptions are carried as ASCII text and have a Session Level Information section followed by as many Media Description sections as are needed for the session. The Session Level Information includes a Protocol Version, the Originator and Session ID, the Session Name, and the Session Time. Each Media Description section includes a Media Name and Transport followed by Connection Information. The Session Level Information can also include a textual description of the session, such as "Department Planning Meeting for Managers," and a Web address for further information, such as an agenda. An email address and telephone number can be included, which could be the person responsible for calling the meeting. Connection information can include the type of network being used, the type of connection used, its bandwidth, and the connection address. A key can be included should the session be secretive and require encryption. The Media Description can include the media protocol being used, such as RTP/RTCP, the UDP port number, and the media's IP connection address. Other media attributes can be included as needed by various media types and protocols. Although not yet approved, some extensions to SDP allow for media requirements to be stated to ensure quality of service during the session. These requirements can be marked as a "precondition," meaning

11. http://www.ietf.org

that the receiving client must satisfy the conditions before even alerting the user. The client is expected to use whatever network mechanisms are available, such as RSVP or DiffServ, to satisfy the requirements. Once these are satisfied, the client informs the originating party with a COMET message.

Figure 5–13 shows a typical SIP session. There are two SIP phones belonging to Steve and Ray. Steve wants to call Ray, so he orders his user agent client to initiate a telephony session with Ray. The client sends an INVITE message addressed to Ray's SIP client giving the SIP version number (2.0), a Call ID that will be unique within Steve's client, a Command Sequence number that is the first INVITE command of this session, and a subject field that can be shown to Ray. Ray's IP address is found by querying a DNS server with Ray's SIP address, *sip:grritchie@telcordia.com*. The INVITE message also contains a SDP description of the session that would indicate telephony using RTP/RTCP and other parameters. Steve's client also indicates that it is using UDP for transfers. Since a port is not given, it is assumed to be the default SIP value of 5060. Ray's host will respond using these values and protocols. When the INVITE message arrives at Ray's client, some form of alerting will be applied to get Ray's attention, and a response will be created. The response gives a status of "180 Ringing," and the remaining fields are simply echoed from the INVITE message. Some fields, such as the session description, are omitted in the response. When this message arrives at Steve's client, an indication can be made by a visual or audible means that Ray's phone is ringing. When Ray answers his phone, a second response is generated with a status of "200 OK." This indicates that the session is accepted. When this arrives at Steve's client, an ACK message is returned.

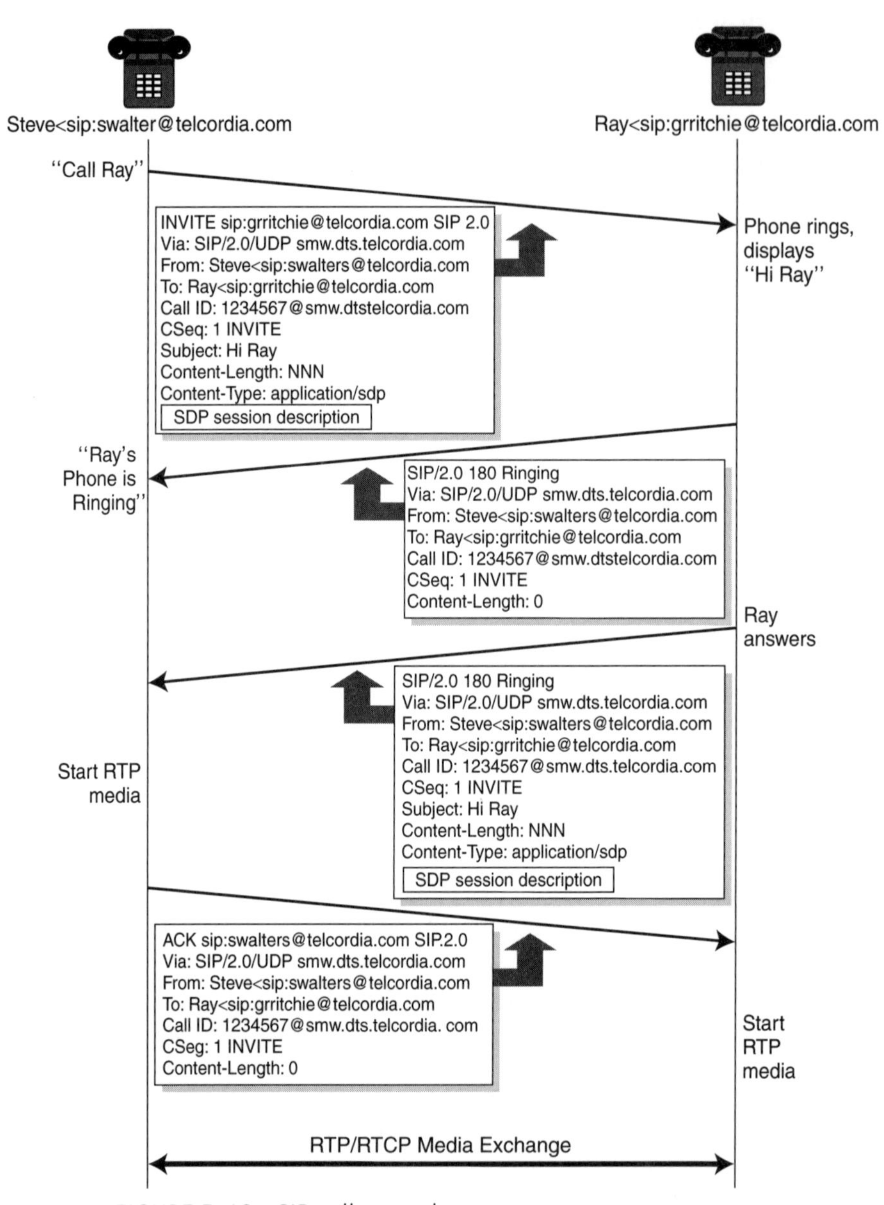
Steve<sip:swalter@telcordia.com
Ray<sip:grritchie@telcordia.com
"Call Ray"
INVITE sip:grritchie@telcordia.com SIP 2.0
Via: SIP/2.0/UDP smw.dts.telcordia.com
From: Steve<sip:swalters@telcordia.com
To: Ray<sip:grritchie@telcordia.com
Call ID: 1234567@smw.dtstelcordia.com
CSeq: 1 INVITE
Subject: Hi Ray
Content-Length: NNN
Content-Type: application/sdp
SDP session description
Phone rings, displays "Hi Ray"
"Ray's Phone is Ringing"
SIP/2.0 180 Ringing
Via: SIP/2.0/UDP smw.dts.telcordia.com
From: Steve<sip:swalters@telcordia.com
To: Ray<sip:grritchie@telcordia.com
Call ID: 1234567@smw.dtstelcordia.com
CSeq: 1 INVITE
Content-Length: 0
Ray answers
SIP/2.0 180 Ringing
Via: SIP/2.0/UDP smw.dts.telcordia.com
From: Steve<sip:swalters@telcordia.com
To: Ray<sip:grritchie@telcordia.com
Call ID: 1234567@smw.dts.telcordia.com
CSeq: 1 INVITE
Subject: Hi Ray
Content-Length: NNN
Content-Type: application/sdp
SDP session description
Start RTP media
ACK sip:swalters@telcordia.com SIP.2.0
Via: SIP/2.0/UDP smw.dts.telcordia.com
From: Steve<sip:swalters@telcordia.com
To: Ray<sip:grritchie@telcordia.com
Call ID: 1234567@smw.dts.telcordia. com
CSeg: 1 INVITE
Content-Length: 0
Start RTP media
RTP/RTCP Media Exchange

FIGURE 5–13 *SIP call example.*

Since these messages are sent over UDP, some of them may not arrive. The application will have timers running, and if a response is not made before it expires, the previ-

ous message will be repeated. Since it is possible that the response, not the command, was lost, the receiving application must be able to accept duplicate messages. By using the CSeq and Call ID values, duplicates can easily be detected.

SIP is a very powerful and simple protocol for session establishment. It can manage multiparty calls and multimedia connections. Its peer-to-peer methodology provides unlimited call completion capability, since there are no controls to limit admission to the network. The only thing that could slow SIP is DNS queries to obtain directory translations. It can easily interwork with the PSTN and allows new services to be conceived and implemented quickly. A difficulty with SIP arises when deployment of new services is considered. Since a new service will require all users to update their applications, rollouts could be slow to complete. However, SIP does allow the gradual update of applications; a capability which can also be an advantage during the early stages of a deployment. Many experts believe that SIP is likely to become the primary VoIP signaling method.

MEGACO

The MEGACO protocol is based on an earlier protocol, Media Gateway Control Protocol (MGCP); however, MEGACO has been standardized within the IETF as RFC 3015 and also in the ITU as H.248. A complete description of MEGACO/H.248 is beyond the scope of this book; you may refer to the RFC for details. Herewith, sufficient information will be given to provide a basis for understanding the basic concepts and operation of MEGACO/H.248.

The MEGACO/H.248 architecture is shown in Figure 5–14. Both MEGACO/H.248 and its predecessor, MGCP, represent quite a different approach to call control when compared to SIP or H.323. Within the architecture, there are four elements: end systems such as telephones and host computers; media gateways, which interface the end systems to the network; media gateway controllers, which control call establishment; and a packet network consisting of IP routers that carry both the bearer channel and the control channel. Henceforth the media gateway shall be referred to as a gateway and the media gateway controller will be referred to as a controller. Gateways have two functions: They convert the native media of the end system into packet representation, usually RTP/RTCP, and they participate in the call establishment by exchanging messages with a controller. Several different gateways are defined in MEGACO/H.248, including the residential gateway and PSTN gateways with either associated or disassociated signaling channels.

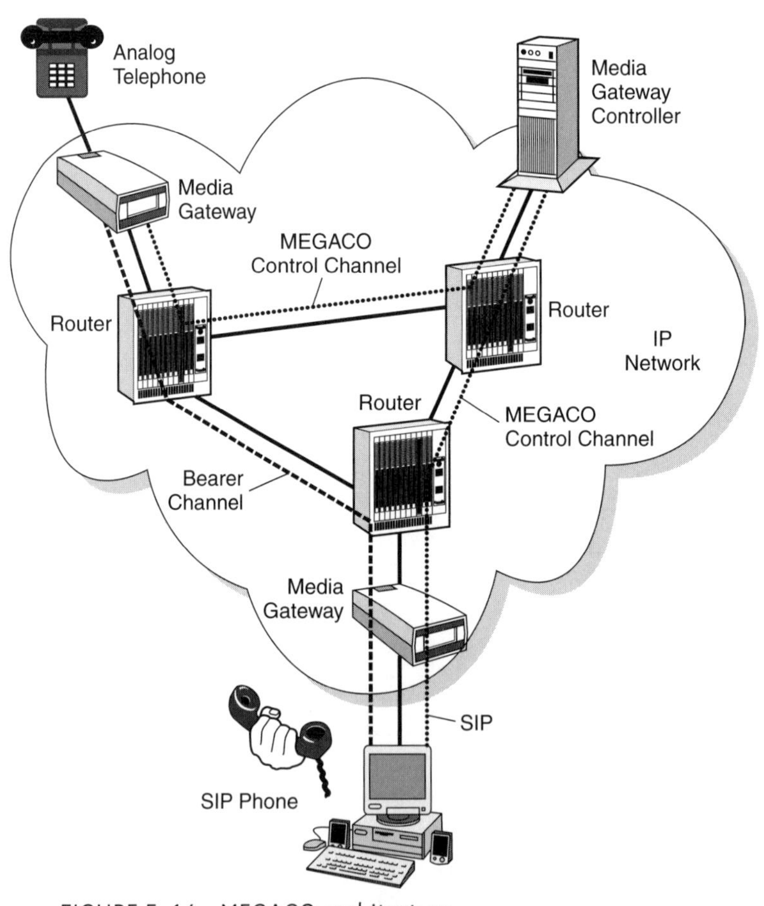

FIGURE 5–14 MEGACO architecture.

Terminations are either physical or a virtual interfaces that carry the RTP media stream. Terminations have a unique identification by which they are known so they can be manipulated. A *context* is an association of terminations in which the means of associating the terminations is defined and a topology description for the association between terminations is included. For example, this might be a multiport bridge between several terminations or a simple point-to-point RTP connection between two terminations. MEGACO/H.248 provides commands for creating, deleting, and modifying contexts as well as adding, subtracting, or modifying the properties of terminations within a context. Terminations can also be moved between contexts. As part of the context description, SDP can be used to describe sessions that are being controlled. The Notify command is used when an event occurs at a gateway that requires controller notification, and the Reply command is used to acknowledge receipt of a command as well as to provide whatever immediate response is required. The Reply command is also used to notify a controller of errors or invalid syntax in commands.

MEGACO/H.248 defines descriptors that are parameters to commands. These include:

- **Media Descriptor** – the media stream specification, which consists of two sub-descriptors: a Termination State Descriptor (in-service, out-of-service, test) and a Stream Descriptor (an identification code and the set of RTP parameters that specify the media stream).
- **Events Descriptor** – a possible event or group of events that can occur, such as on-hook, off-hook, and receipt of Touch-Tones.
- **Signals Descriptor** – messages and tones, such as dial tone, ringing tone, and touch-tones, that can be sent.
- **Audit Descriptor** – a list of items to check and report on.

- **Digit-Map Descriptor** – a dialing plan including syntax, procedure, completion, and timers as well as an event that activates its use.
- **Topology Descriptor** – a list of pairs of terminations and their association.

MEGACO/H.248 operates through instruction lists provided to gateways by a controller that, in essence, establishes the gateway's programming. The instruction lists can be quite complex and sophisticated. For example, a gateway can be told that when a customer goes off-hook, it is to provide dial tone, collect digits, analyze them against a digit-map, and when dialing is complete, to report the called party phone number to the controller. For each event, the gateway can be instructed to take one or more actions, including sending a signal such as a Touch-Tone, generating a SIP message, or whatever is appropriate. A key element in the instruction lists is a command to notify the controller when a certain event (or series of events or one of several possible events) has occurred at the gateway. The events can be any of a broad set of items, such as receiving a certain SIP message or an off-hook event by an analog telephone. When the event occurs, the controller will be notified and it can provide a new list of instructions to the gateway. In this way, there is virtually no constraint on how a call is established, and any scheme imaginable can be implemented. The only constraints are the set of events that the gateway can detect and the set of actions it can take. Fortunately, a very complete list of possible events and actions has been formulated as part of the protocol. MEGACO/H.248 also provides for timers that can be manipulated when various events occur and can serve as events themselves upon expiration. This allows for recovery from situations where an event is lost or corrupted.

This method allows the creation of a virtual state machine at a gateway that can be different for different terminations. A set of specifications can be defined as a *package* that can be reused for multiple terminations so as to avoid retransmission of identical specifications for every termination in a gateway using them. This would be the case for a residential gateway that terminates hundreds or thousands of analog telephones.

Figure 5–15 shows a simplified example of an exchange between two gateways and a controller for a simple telephone call. In the first pair of exchanges, the controller sends each gateway a digit-map that specifies the dialing plan for the user's region using a Modify command addressed to terminations 1 and 2 respectively. Each gateway responds with a Reply command that simply acknowledges the controller's command. Next, the controller orders the gateways to detect off-hook events so it will be notified whenever a user picks up her phone. This command is also acknowledged by the two gateways, using Reply messages. When the user at gateway 1 picks up the phone, her gateway immediately sends a Notify command indicating an off-hook, as it was instructed to do. The controller acknowledges this command and then issues a Modify command ordering the gateway to provide dial tone and to detect digits to be analyzed against the digit-map dialing plan. This is, of course, acknowledged by the gateway. When the user begins dialing, the gateway collects the digits and analyzes them for dialing completion using the digit-map. Once dialing is finished, the gateway notifies the controller and includes the dialed number. The controller acknowledges this indication, looks up the phone number to determine what user it represents, and then sends a Modify command to the indicated gateway: in this case, gateway #2, telling it to send ringing to the phone and to detect an off-hook condition. The controller could also exchange messages with a resource manager to determine if sufficient capacity was available between the two users and to reserve it. The receiving gateway acknowledges and begins ringing the user's phone. When the user answers, the gateway notifies the controller, which acknowledges and also sends a Modify to gateway #1, telling it to begin RTP/RTCP reception from gateway #2. Gateway #1 complies and acknowledges, causing the controller to repeat a similar command to gateway #2. Gateway #2 acknowledges and starts its RTP/RTCP session. At this point, the two users are connected and can have a conversation.

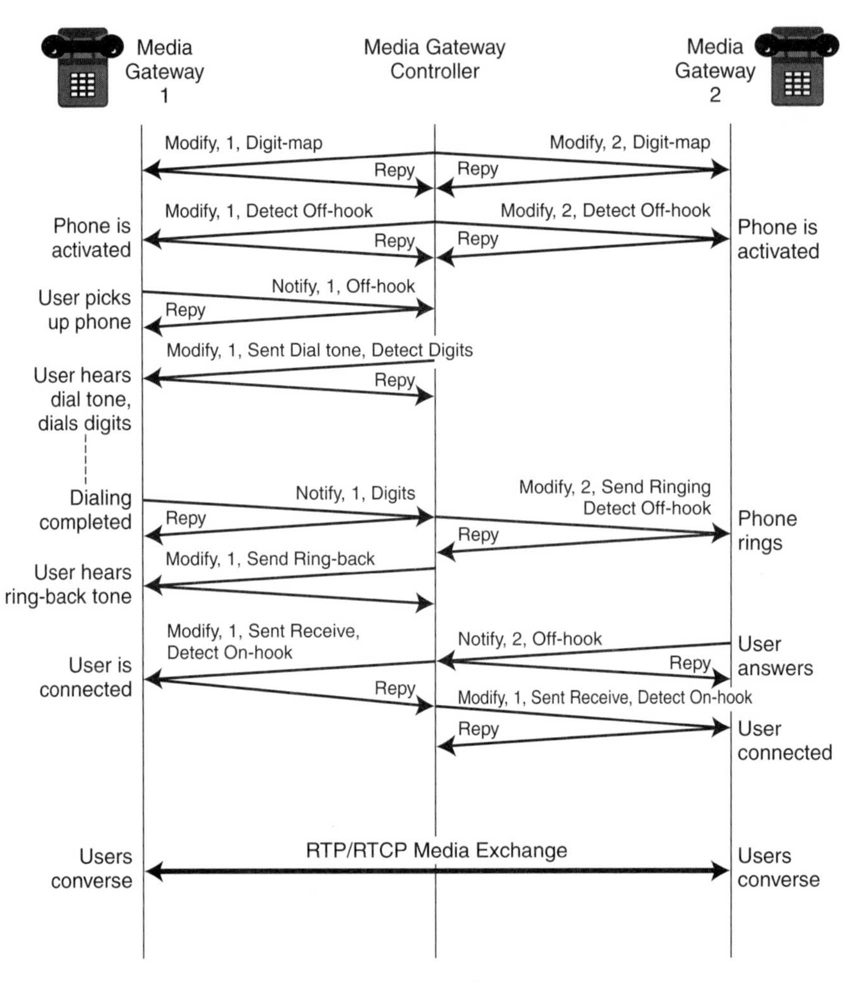

FIGURE 5–15 *MEGACO call example.*

As can be seen from even this simplified partial example, MEGACO/H.248 is a very sophisticated and complex protocol. The example could have been programmed to operate in many different ways. Using MEGACO/H.248, a programmer is able to define a set of actions based on any specified

event. Hence, it is possible to create any call flow imaginable. This is both a blessing and a curse. While any imaginable flow can be defined, it is also easy to make a mistake. Hence, there will be a significant investment in creating and debugging MEGACO/H.248 call scripts, especially when implementing supplemental services such as call forwarding, call waiting, and so forth. However, it must be remembered that any scheme for implementing these services can fall prey to problems; it is just that MEGACO/H.248 is not exempt from these issues. Nevertheless, MEGACO/H.248 represents a structured methodology for controlling gateways, and there is no doubt that accurately programmed MEGACO/H.248 scripts will be forthcoming. Graphical programming environments will become widely available, making it easy for operators and possibly customers to create new services.

MEGACO/H.248 is a centralized control strategy but one that can be easily modified by the operator or their developer. It is very easy to create new service concepts with MEGACO/H.248 that can interwork with the existing network. The flexibility of MEGACO/H.248 gives it powerful abilities, very unlike H.323, which will need new standards every time a new service is imagined. One disadvantage of MEGACO/H.248 is its greater complexity when compared to SIP. Also, having centralized processors for call control will require careful capacity allocation and processor sizing to ensure high call-completion rates. This, of course, is not a new problem and should be easily managed. However, the peer-to-peer model of SIP and its short, "to-the-point" exchanges will likely challenge MEGACO/H.248 for dominance in the VoIP arena.

Summary

VoIP has two important areas for development. First is the transport of the speech signal over the IP network. This utilizes the RTP/RTCP protocol and NTP-3. Together, these protocols in conjunction with UDP and IP provide a basis

for connections between users. In today's IP networks, these connections are likely to suffer from poor quality of service due to packet loss and delay. However, MPLS and DiffServ can mitigate these impairments and should allow the provisioning of high-quality voice transport. Second, there is the issue of signaling and control for the network to locate and alert users when calls are launched. SIP, MEGACO/H.248, and H.323 provide this capability. They are defined, and implementations are available for each. A key issue for signaling as well as for the transport of speech is interworking with the PSTN. In this area, there would appear to be no particular problem for telephony services as currently defined. However, as new SIP or MEGACO/H.248 services are created, interworking may become a greater issue due to the adoption of new call flow scenarios that are radically different from the PSTN call flow. The key issue to be resolved is the provision of quality speech connections, something that seems possible using MPLS and DiffServ.

References

Black, U. *Voice Over IP,* Prentice Hall, 2000.

Collins, D, *Carrier Grade Voice Over IP,* McGraw-Hill, 2001.

Crovella, M., and Bestavros, A. "Self-Similarity in World-Wide Web Traffic: Evidence and Possible Causes," Proceedings ACM Signetrics Conference on Measurement and Modeling of Computer Systems, May 1996.

Cuervo, F., et al. "MEGACO Protocol Version 1.0," RFC-3015, Nov. 2000.

Handley, M., et al. "SIP: Session Initiation Protocol," RFC-2543, Mar. 1999.

Hersent, O, D. Gurle, and J. Petit. *IP Telephony,* Addison Wesley, 2000.

ITU-T Recommendation H.245. "Control Protocol for Multimedia Communication," 1998.

ITU-T Recommendation H.225.0. "Call Signaling Protocols and Media Stream Packetization for Packet-based Multimedia Communications Systems," 1998.

ITU-T Recommendation H.323 "Packet-based Multimedia Communications Systems," 1998.

Leland, W., et al, "On the Self-Similar Nature of Ethernet Traffic (Extended Version)," *IEEE/ACM Transactions on Networking,* Feb. 1994.

Mills, D. "Network Time Protocol Version 3," RFC-1305, Mar. 1992.

Schulzrinne, H., et al. "RTP: A Transport Protocol for Real-Time Applications," RFC-1889, Jan. 1996.

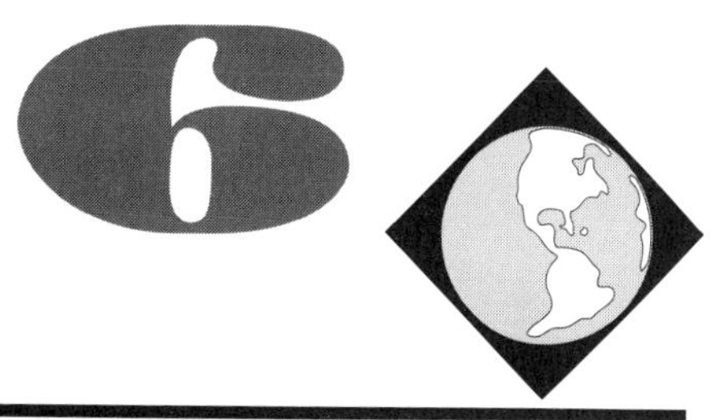

Growing Pains

As carriers begin to create new telephony networks, they must consider the issues that must be dealt with in order to provide a mature platform of services. At the time of this writing, the network systems and business concepts for the new telephony are still in their infancy and there are many areas where they need to "grow up." There is a lot for carriers to consider. For one, they should think about the overall target they hope to achieve in the long term from both a business perspective and network's technical capabilities. An established carrier must consider leveraging its assets and brand. It must consider the services, business arrangement, and architecture that it envisions as a "new telephony" carrier. It must plan its evolution to that target as a set of steps, using assets that it possesses today that fit the desired target and the cost of acquiring the needed additional assets. The carrier must know how it will get customers in the near term, retain them in the long term, operate under evolving regulatory rules and business standards, and how to move forward step by step to reach the long term target. This chapter outlines such issues and provides constructive ideas about how some can be resolved. Lest you think otherwise, there are many different views about where telecommunications should be headed and even more opinions about how to get there. A general understanding of the present direction and possible alternatives has emerged, but there is ample room for diverse opinions on this subject.

Goals for the New Telephony

What should be the goals for the new telephony? Should it be to simply emulate the current telephone service? Or, should it be to create a completely new alternative? These are difficult questions, depicted in Figure 6–1, especially given the rapid progress of technology and the dynamic business environment of today. Having an achievable goal is critical to near-term success.

FIGURE 6–1 Goals for the new telephony.

On the one hand, introducing a new service and its supporting technology can be very expensive even if existing assets are utilized, so there must be the clear possibility that customers will adopt the value proposition being offered. If the new telephony service requires its users to purchase new equipment or to make changes in their wiring, the service will be difficult to adopt or, at best, slow to expand to a large base of customers. So, for near-term business interests, it is important to support the use of existing telephones. But if all that is provided is pure emulation of today's existing telephony using today's telephones, then what is the point of introducing the service? Without something new and useful to the end user, the service will not be differentiated from today's PSTN.

Ideally, we desire a technical approach that allows the use of today's telephones at the same (or lower) cost as today's PSTN, but that also enables the use of new, radically different instruments with new capabilities. So, like a bride, we need something "old" and something "new." These demands appear to be mutually exclusive. To accomplish this, it is assumed that the new telephony carrier will provide IP-based data services such as Internet access and email. This means that the service should be based on IP. Overall, it must also be determined how to achieve the required quality of service for all services offered. Then, the questions of how to price the services and how to operate the network at low cost come into play. In considering the network itself, we must examine four key areas: customer premise, access network, core network, and operations.

Service Issues

Today's PSTN has numerous features that are offered and used by customers. These include the more familiar set, such as Call Forwarding, Call Waiting, Three-Way Calling, and other so-called "Class" services as well as 911, 411, and operator services. Besides these examples, there are hundreds of other features not widely known or used by customers, many of which are focused on the large business market. Some switch manufacturers have stated that their product has 2,000 or 3,000 such features.[1] Rebuilding all of these features over an IP platform using H.323, SIP, or MEGACO can take a lot of time. Due to regulatory requirements, some features that are now offered by carriers cannot be eliminated, and some carriers believe they must have all these features to be successful in retaining their existing customers.

On the surface, this would appear to be true, and most customers would confirm this statement; they would be unwilling to give up any of their current features and services. But once a new offering is made that provides some other benefit to the customer, such as lower cost, greater convenience, or a business advantage, users will work out a way to utilize it. This may disadvantage them in other aspects, but they will find a way to adopt the new technology if it sufficiently advantages them in some way. The mobile phone is a good example of such a tradeoff. It has lower quality and higher price, but its convenience outweighs these disadvantages. The carrier that insists on having all the t's crossed and all the i's dotted runs the risk of being left in the dust when the new technology is rolled out. And they may have wasted a lot of energy and time in re-creating services that the customer really does not need.

This is a difficult problem for incumbents. On the one hand, their desire to have service parity is rational and easily understood, and for some of their customers, it is a valid requirement. Incumbent carriers should look carefully at how much revenue is derived from the various services and discard those that are not real revenue producers. Otherwise, they risk being overcome by competitors when the new disruptive technology makes its debut.

1. Not all these features are used by any particular carrier. This is the complete set as built by the supplier for all of its customers.

New operators who have no existing investment have less difficulty resolving this issue. They can simply create new services that advantage the customer in some way and leave it to the customer to work around "holes" in their service portfolio. In this way, they can attract the customer base of an incumbent carrier by providing an alternative set of capabilities that they believe will appeal to a significant market segment of the users.

In any case, customer requirements are critical to success. But any customer will be willing to compromise some requirements for favorable advantages in other aspects. The wise carrier will not forget this fact and will plan carefully. A related factor is shown in Figure 6–2. As can easily be seen, the projected potential revenues from new services greatly overshadow those from existing services. The provision of these new services is clearly desirable for all carriers; however, it is not completely certain how accurate forecasts such as the one shown will prove over time. Carriers are naturally skeptical of enormous new revenue opportunities, and it is proper for them to be cautious.

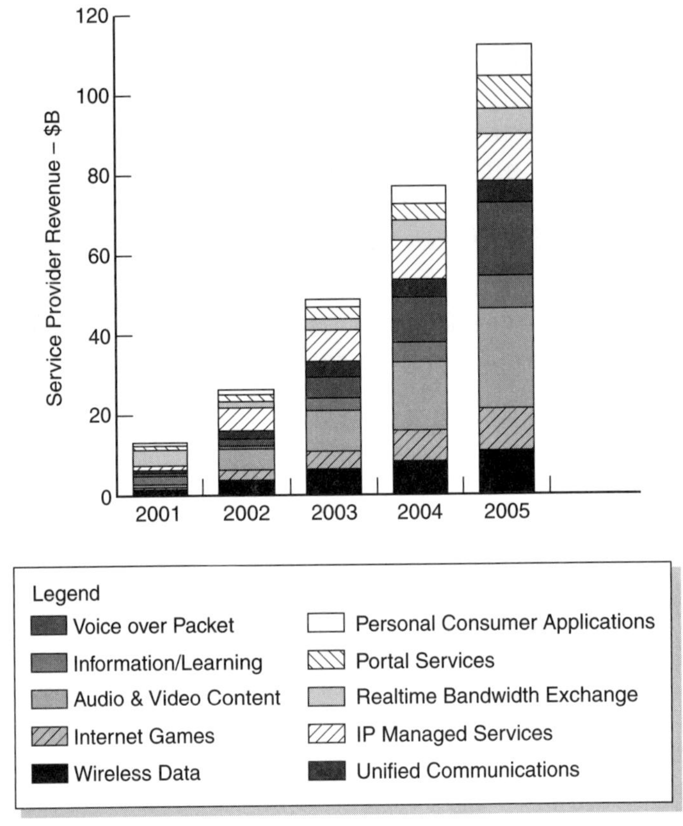

FIGURE 6–2 *Revenues for U.S. services.*

Billing Issues

In the telephone industry, there is a legacy of complex billing arrangements. Initially, telephone service generally consisted of a flat rate for monthly service, supplemented with long-distance charges based on the distance, time-of-day, and duration of calls. Today, there are various billing plans ranging from completely flat rate, unlimited duration long-distance calling to plans that give reduced calling rates provided that the destination called is a customer of the carrier and has joined a calling plan.

Data networks have generally been billed based on the speed of the customer access line, since this serves to indicate how much information can be transferred. There are some data services that bill customers based on the packet and byte count of delivered information, but these have not been as popular. The complexity of tracking this information drives up the carrier's costs and, at the same time, customers would prefer a flat-rate bill so their budgets can easily be projected.

In recent years, U.S. carriers have instituted the practice of "bundling," and today nearly all carriers and operators provide some selection of bundles for customers to buy. Examples include providing "free" long distance with wireless telephone service and selling Internet access combined with a long distance plan. The concept of bundling is based on two ideas. First, by providing two or more services to a customer, the carrier can benefit from economy of scale and can give a lower price to the user. Second, by purchasing more services that are linked together from one carrier, customer loyalty will increase because it is disruptive for the customer to move to a different carrier. For example, customers who have an email address and a Web page URL bundled with their telephony service are less likely to switch carriers due to the inconvenience it will cause them. "Churn," the act of customers switching carriers, is a significant problem, since the operational cost of customers starting and ending service is expensive.

Table 6–1 shows an example of bundled services. In the example, a customer who purchases all six of these services separately will spend $195 per month. But if the customer buys all of these services from a single carrier, a discount is applied, perhaps as much as 25 percent. If all of these services are provided over a single network, the cost to the carrier is less, and the carrier can afford to discount the price to the customer. Because the customer is buying all of his or her services from the carrier, it is more difficult for the customer to switch carriers. This too saves the carrier money.

TABLE 6-1 Bundled Service Pricing

Individual Service	Price per Month
First line telephony	$20
Second line telephony	$15
Long distance	$40
High-speed Internet	$40
CATV w/premium channel	$50
Mobile phone service	$30
Total "a la carte"	$195
Bundled service	$150

Technologists sometimes mention that these services are provided at widely differing bit rates and that, in their view, the prices are not too closely aligned with the network requirements. This is a point that deserves deeper consideration when planning to offer all these services using a single integrated network. For example, if high-speed Internet access costs only $40 per month and operates at 10 Mbps, then $20 per month for a 64-kbps single-line telephony service seems high. Of course, the telephony service is much more complex than the high-speed Internet service and today has a larger infrastructure and operations scope. But since we can provide telephony service using the Internet, will this infrastructure be needed in the future?

This leads us to the most significant issue lurking in billing. If telephony is merely another application running in the user's computer and all it does is make a few DNS queries and send a few thousand packets to the destination, what is to be charged for other than normal Internet usage? Indeed, this is the billion dollar question. On the surface, the answer is simple—sell the application and charge a flat rate for network use. If this approach is to work, the carrier must first determine how much capacity to deploy and then price the service accordingly. Because transport capacity would be priced on volume, probably with discounts for high-volume customers, this leads to a commodity business in which the network operator sells transport capacity, not a service. For incumbent telephony carriers, this is a major challenge and a direction they are unlikely to take willingly.

Customer Premise Equipment Issues

At the customer premise, there should be the ability to provide service to existing telephones while providing the possibility of adding new futuristic products at a later date. The easiest way to do this is to provide some form of gateway functionality, as shown in Figure 6–3. In the case of both DSL modems and cable modems, two or three interfaces are provided. One serves to connect to the existing twisted-pair inside wiring to which normal telephones are attached, while a second provides an Ethernet LAN for the customer's computers. In the case of the cable modem, an additional interface may be provided for either analog or digital television services.

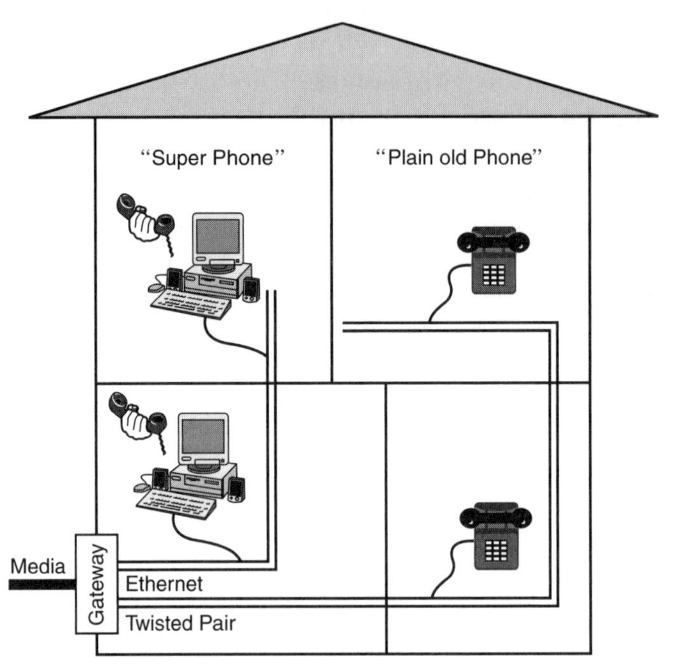

FIGURE 6–3 *Customer premise gateway.*

It is also possible to provide this gateway as a plug-in to an existing system, such as a home computer. This gateway allows the customer to receive telephone service on existing instruments, and it also allows new telephone instruments, such as SIP phones or PC telephony applications, to be served. Thus, these gateways allow the support of existing services and a path forward to new IP-based services. The gateway should be completely programmable through the network to allow future changes in its operation without replacing it or sending technicians; such programmability can reduce the cost of future upgrades.

In the case of some carriers, the gateway can be simplified by providing only the Ethernet interface. This would not allow the service to extend to existing telephones, but some carriers will not care about this. If their plan is to initially focus on the customer as a data service provider and then to add telephony to the portfolio of services offered, this could be a viable plan. The gateway equipment for such carriers would be simpler and have lower cost. But for carriers who require the service to work from existing telephones, a more complex gateway will be needed, with greater cost for both the initial equipment and for its ongoing operations.

Some critical decisions include whether the gateway is to be powered from the network, from local power or by batteries, where it is located within the customer premise, and how it is to be paid for. Each of these is a critical issue with a few options that complicate any decision.

Location

First, consider where the gateway illustrated in Figure 6–4 is to be located. Based on FCC rules for regulated carriers in the United States, the demarcation between network and customer lies at the wall of the premise. If the gateway is inside the premise, it belongs to the customer, but if it is outside, it belongs to the carrier. If a carrier wishes, it can lease or sell the equipment to the customer. However, the customer must be free to purchase equipment from another source. These are important distinctions, since they affect the outcome of service outage disputes as well as manufacturing requirements.

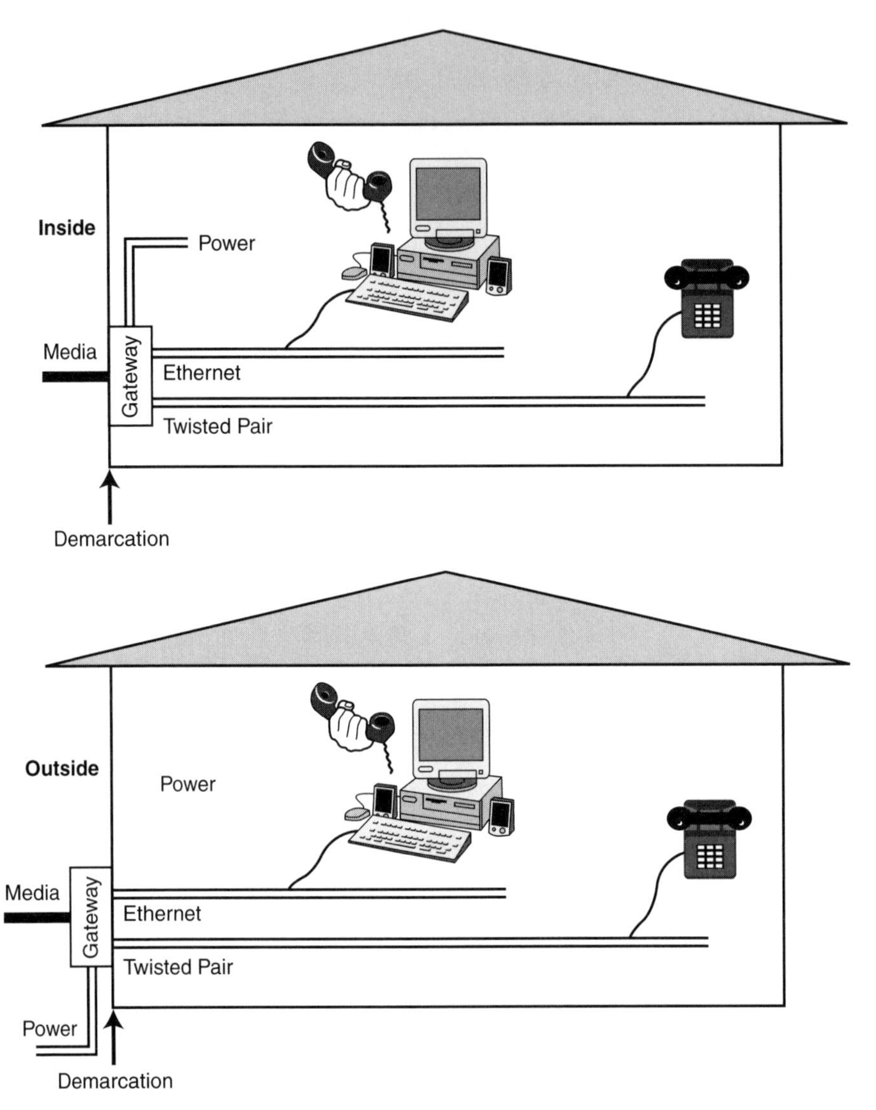

FIGURE 6–4 *Gateway location.*

If the equipment is outside, it must be powered from the network and must be hardened against weather and other environmental assaults. This will make the equipment more expensive. If powered by the network, it will have to be much simpler than the gateway depicted previously and probably would be limited to a very basic system that can

determine if a fault has occurred in the access network. If it is inside, alternate powering arrangements are possible, and it will be in a friendlier environment. These factors combine to determine some portion of the expense of this apparatus as well as who owns it and its operation and maintenance plan and costs.

Powering

Next, we must consider how the gateway is to be powered. If the equipment is to provide lifeline telephone service, the gateway and one or more instruments must be powered continuously and have high reliability. In traditional telephone service, the network provides the power for the telephone, since it is possible to do so. But it is not possible to power today's gateway systems, PCs, or SIP phones over the loop because of their high power consumption. In the future, this may change, but for the present, it is simply not possible to power even a DSL modem or a cable modem other than from local commercial power. It should be remembered that for many modern telephones, such as those including answering machines or a calling party display, commercial power is already used.

If commercial power is used, there should be a set of batteries contained in the gateway and terminal that can provide power for some period of time, perhaps a few hours, to enable communications in case of an emergency wherein power fails. Since the batteries degrade over time, there must be some means for testing and replacing them. This responsibility might lie with the customer or with the carrier, depending on who owns the system or on some agreement such as a maintenance contract.

Who Pays

When planning a new service, an important issue is determination of who pays for the customer premise equipment. Because this issue exists for every customer, it can have a very big impact on a business plan because of the large multiplying factor.

If the various architectures for the PSTN and the new telephony are compared, a few interesting possibilities become apparent, as depicted in Figure 6–5. In today's PSTN, the cost of circuit switching is dominated by the line card interface that serves each individual customer. As such, this cost is part of the capital outlay for the network. In the new telephony architectures, these interfaces are moved to the customers and become candidates for lease or purchase by the customer. This moves a large portion of switching cost to the customer and can significantly reduce the capital outlays by the service provider for such a network.

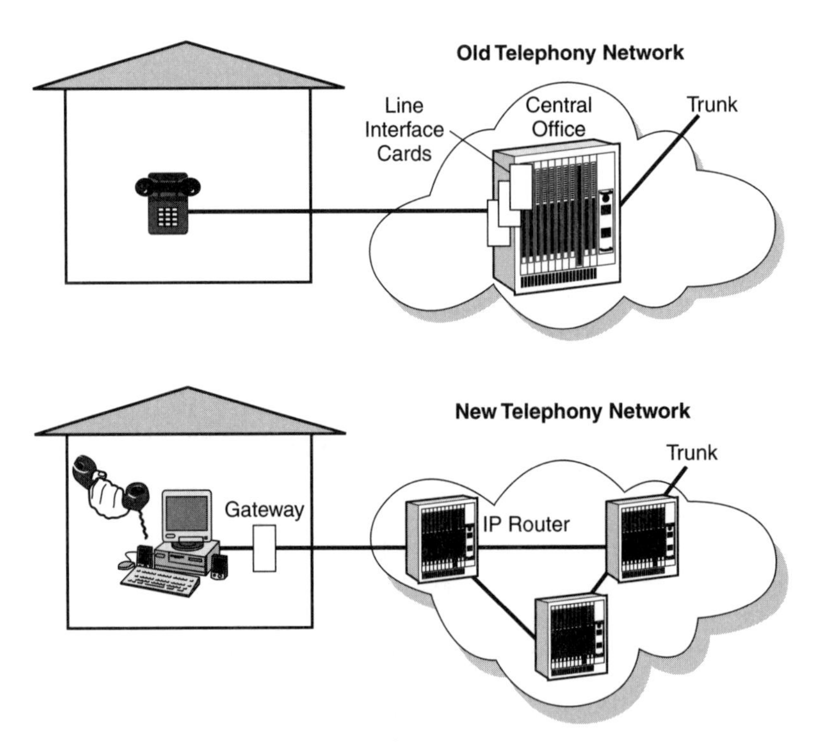

FIGURE 6–5 *Comparing architectures.*

If the carrier provides the equipment as part of the service, it must be factored into the business plan as a cost

that must be recovered. This will drive up the price of the service. If the customer purchases the equipment, it will not add cost to the business plan, but it will reduce the number of potential service buyers, since they will have to purchase the gateway. If the equipment is provided as a lease, it can show some modest return on cost. If the customer purchases the equipment but also has a maintenance contract with the carrier, it can have a positive effect on revenues.

It must be remembered that if the customer purchases and owns the equipment, the carrier will not have control over upgrades or changes to it. Since the customer premise equipment can have a major role in providing service, this is not something a carrier will do lightly. Since the ownership of this equipment can have a major effect on the business plan and can influence the future of the services offered, ownership is a critical item in planning a new offering.

So, the new telephony architecture has the potential to lower the capital outlay for a network provider. This is further amplified by the relatively low cost of IP routing systems that will replace the circuit switches. While this is generally a good result, it is still unknown how successful it will be. Early results with cable modem purchase/lease plans and similar offers for DSL services tend to show that the customer will accept such offers. Assuming that telephony is not the only service provided by the network, then it can be expected that customers will continue to accept lease/buy packages, resulting in lower capital costs for the carrier. Certain customers will not be inclined to pay these fees or to purchase expensive equipment. So, there is a tradeoff to be examined regarding market acceptance and capital outlay. In a competitive battle, this factor can create a major differentiation.

Access Network Issues

The access network reaches the customer through existing media such as cable TV coax, fiber optics, copper loops, or wireless radio schemes. The keyword here is *existing*. Many carriers have contemplated and even begun deployment of new access systems such as Fiber-to-the-Home (FTTH), Fiber-to-the-Curb (FTTC) and Fiber-in-the-Loop (FITL). The high cost of such an investment and the lengthy times needed to install such systems have limited their use to areas of new construction where no existing access arrangement has been deployed. The cost of replacing today's access network with entirely new media is prohibitively expensive and would require decades to accomplish. The existing media include:

- Copper loops reaching residential and business customers that can be evolved to DSL for digital transport.
- Cable television coaxial facilities that can support two-way digital transport using cable modems.
- Fiber optics that reach large business customer sites, office complexes, and large residential buildings such as high-rise condominiums.
- Wireless radio systems that are in place and can be upgraded to be IP-capable.

These are the preferred access solutions. In each case, the media can be supplemented with new technology that enables the digital transport of IP to reach the customers. In some cases, SONET transport or ATM over SONET might be used to carry IP in the access network. But the preferred long-term solution is IP directly over the physical access media, since this can lower the initial cost of equipment and simplify operations by eliminating overlapping operations functionality within the various layers.

As will be discussed in the next chapter, it is possible that a new telephony carrier will lease rather than build these access facilities. This is a major factor in planning a new service. New construction of access media is prohibitively expensive, making it unlikely that a new entrant will choose to do so. This will tend to give an advantage to the incumbent carrier who owns such facilities.

However, regulatory bodies have demanded that copper loop access be "unbundled," meaning that competitors are able to lease these facilities at comparable costs to those which the incumbent incurs. This mandate has existed in the United States since the Telecom Act of 1996, and there is considerable debate about the success of this measure. For the most part, incumbent carriers have been slow to make unbundled access available, and new entrants are quick to complain that the fees charged for leasing access are unrealistically high. This situation is depicted in Figure 6–6. Another related regulatory requirement is *colocation,* in which an incumbent carrier is required to make floor space available to a competing carrier for placing equipment near the customer's interface.

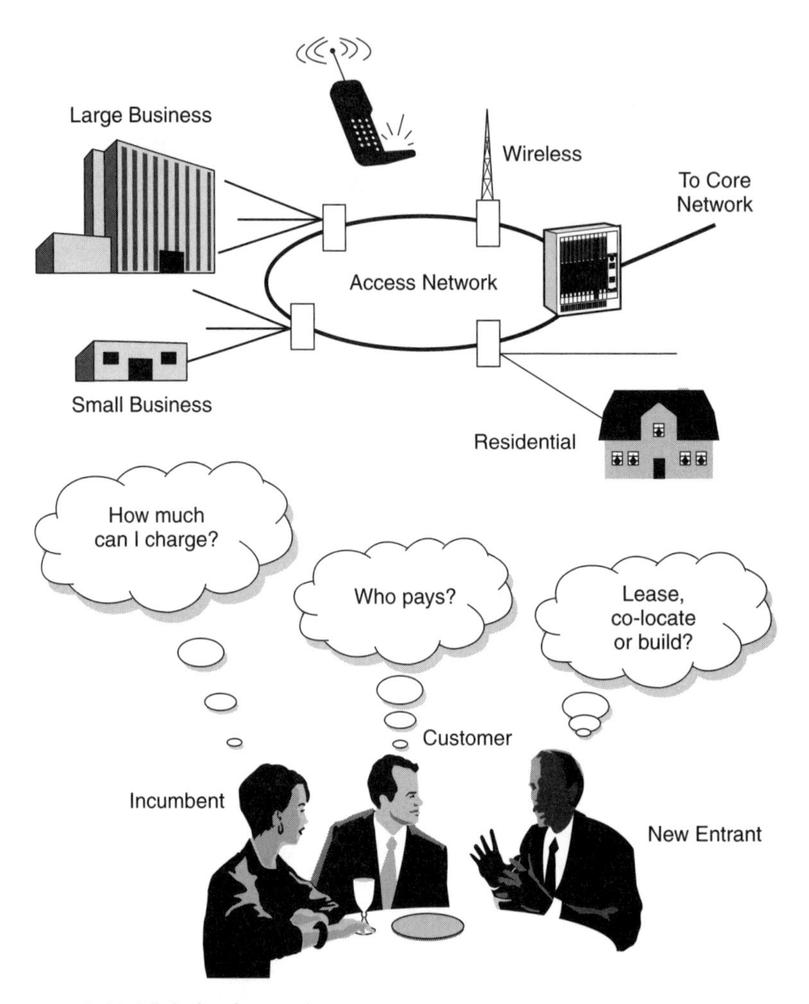

FIGURE 6–6 *Access issues.*

So long as incumbent carriers are fully integrated as a business, it is difficult for them to be cooperative. If the incumbent were separated into two businesses, one selling access connectivity on a wholesale basis and one selling services on a retail basis, a greater degree of cooperation might be possible. But this is not yet required of regulated carriers, and they are strongly resisting it.

It is less clear whether or not the cable television industry will be required to support unbundled access to cus-

tomers. In some regards, cable television carriers are required to provide access to content providers on a fair basis. But this is with regard to television channel programming. By and large, the cable television industry is unregulated and is free to adopt whatever business practices it wishes. Today, these carriers offer Internet access services, but this is often bundled with television services, and customers cannot select their Internet service provider. This is quite different than the situation for offering DSL service over unbundled telephone company loops. Litigation began in 2001 that may change this situation in the near future.

In any case, the availability of leased access arrangements and the cost of constructing an access network are critical to achieving a competitive landscape for local telephony and must be factored into the business planning of both incumbent carriers and new entrants.

Core Network Issues

In order to provide new services and greater functionality, the core network should be based on IP. A few service examples that illustrate this are multimedia conferencing, integration of Web browsing and telephony in a multi-user setting, co-editing of documents, and many other applications. IP is the choice for the network because the bulk of these applications are data-centric and they use IP. Furthermore, there is an army of programmers familiar with IP and its capabilities who can facilitate the creation of the required applications. So, the core network should be IP. This also means that the Internet can be the core network. Likewise, it means that any carrier with such a network can become a part of the Internet.

From an evolution perspective, an IP network can have many different forms. Ultimately, where the industry seems to be headed is IP with MPLS and DiffServ using optical switching techniques over fiber, as depicted in Figure 6–7. This allows packets to bypass routing steps while operating at tremendous speeds. At the present time, this solution is still being developed by systems manufacturers and is not yet deployed in practical large-scale networks.

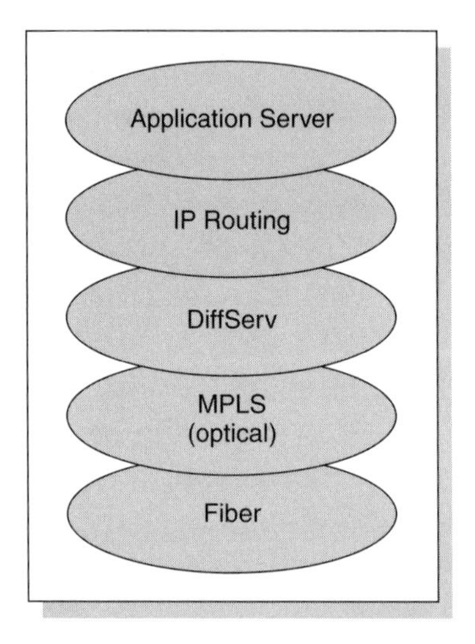

FIGURE 6–7 *Core network functions.*

In the interim, carriers must use IP routers over some other lower layer protocols. If IP over SONET is used, the only practical capability for meeting quality of service is to over-engineer the capacity of the network. As stated in earlier chapters, this is generally not an affordable means for providing good service. However, IP over ATM over SONET supports MPLS and DiffServ, and can be engineered and configured in today's networks to ensure quality of service, as discussed in Chapter 4. However, IP/ATM/SONET is not a good long-term architectural choice because there are large overlaps in operational capabilities that introduce inefficiencies in operating the network and excessive overheads that reduce the available capacity of the network. The added cost of ATM and SONET is undesirable but appears to be the only short-term method of providing quality of service at this time. Also, in some incumbent carrier networks, ATM equipment has been deployed for existing services such as Frame Relay, while SONET is used for regular telephony. This existing infrastructure, if available, can be utilized.

Thus, carriers face a serious architectural puzzle for their core network that depends on the timeframe in which they wish to evolve their network. If they can, they should wait for the emerging optical IP networks. If they cannot, they must deploy IP over ATM over SONET. Depending on other issues, such as the state of competition, the existing economy, and other corporate goals, this choice will be moved to either an earlier or later timeframe. Once this is known, the choice becomes apparent.

Less obvious is the choice regarding call control software. Of the three choices, H.323, MEGACO, and SIP, MEGACO seems the best solution for carriers who are choosing to re-create the existing telephony services at the customer premise gateway. This is because of the high degree of programmability that MEGACO has. However, in the longer term, it is likely that SIP will be more popular with new end systems and will work better with other Web-based services. In this case, the carrier's investment in a MEGACO call control solution could be wasted if the users eventually bypass it. So, again, the choice depends on when the network must be deployed and whether the goals are focused on emulating today's telephony or building new services.

Numbering and Addressing Issues

An important aspect of telephony is the E.164 ITU specification for numbering, since it provides the basis for routing calls to the desired party and for directories such as White Pages and Yellow Pages. The management of telephone numbers is also a means for controlling business, since only registered LECs can have numbers allocated to them. The telephone number is, of course, the mechanism for routing calls within the PSTN. For these and other reasons, E.164 and its domestic embodiment, the North American Numbering Plan, are unlikely to disappear.

Since the telephone network will continue to use E.164 numbers and the Internet will continue to use URI[2] and IP addresses, there is presently no easy means for directly establishing connections between two endpoints located on the two different networks. This is because a telephone user cannot "dial" a URI and the Internet does not route based on E.164 numbers. The only means possible today is to first establish a session between the user and a gateway connecting the two networks, and then request a connection to the destination address in the other network. For example, an Internet-based PC could run an application that collects a phone number from the user and then establishes a session with a gateway on the PSTN. Once this is done, the application could then transmit the phone number to the gateway that will then request the PSTN to connect it. Similar gateways for calls from the PSTN into the Internet could be provided, but this is more difficult, since the telephone user has no convenient way to enter a URI or an IP address.

However, Telephone Number Mapping (ENUM) is a proposed solution for at least part of this issue. As shown in Figure 6–8, ENUM uses the Domain Name System (DNS) to translate E.164 telephone numbers into URI. While ENUM can be used to initiate telephone calls, ENUM is also intended to serve as a global means for communicating with a user, not just for telephony purposes. In fact, it can provide an ordered list of such addresses and their protocols so an application can choose the media that is best suited for the intended communication. Today, if you wish to send email to a party and do not know the email address, there is no means for discovering it. If this party had registered his or her phone number and email address in ENUM, then it would be possible to first discover the phone number through the normal telephone company

2. Uniform Resource Indicator. Most readers will be more familiar with the term URL (Uniform Resource Locator), which carries the protocol, host, and object name. URI is a generalization of URL. See RFC-2396 for further details.

white pages and then query DNS for the email address associated with that phone number. This is a powerful capability that could be used by many different applications, not just telephony.

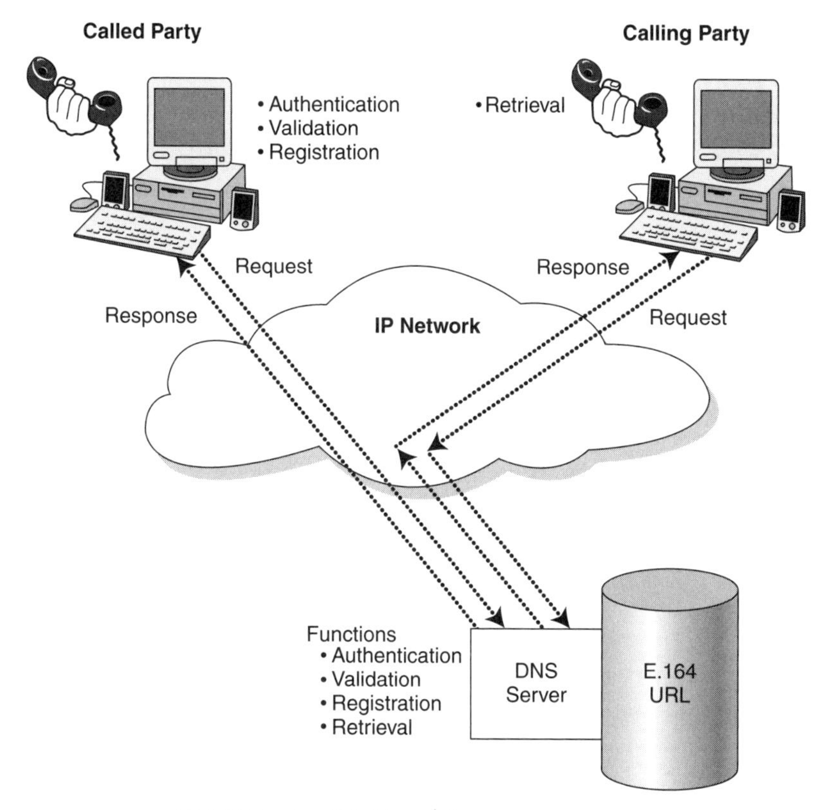

FIGURE 6–8 *ENUM architecture.*

ENUM works very simply. First, the user must register his or her E.164 number and set of URI addresses with the DNS. The information is stored in the order provided by the user. This is so later retrievals can know the user's preference for being contacted. Later, the user can update the information. Once this is done, any subsequent DNS query carrying that user's E.164 number will retrieve the set of URIs in the order that was provided. The retrieving application can then select the highest preference URI that is suitable for the application. A second DNS query can translate the URI into an IP address, and the application can then begin communicating with the user. During operation, DNS secures the data from tampering by its usual means, including server authentication, and distributes data to all valid DNS systems, which keeps the database synchronized and up to date.

ENUM does not issue E.164 telephone numbers, IP addresses, or URIs. Local telephone companies will continue to assign numbers to users. ENUM simply provides a facility for registering and linking E.164 numbers to URI. At the time of this writing, there is not yet an agreed upon mechanism for authentication of users who wish to register or for validation of their right to use a particular E.164 number and URI given. Until this is resolved, there is likely to be difficulty with ENUM because it will be vulnerable to number and identity theft by criminals and pranksters. For this reason, it is critical that ENUM establish procedures that meet the needs of users with regard to security and privacy.

Quality Issues

As any successful carrier knows, there is a proper level of service quality that must be met if the business is to be run profitably. It is admirable to provide excellent quality at all times for the users of the network, but this can have a cost that drives profits out of the business. For example, today's PSTN is not engineered to handle the volume of calls that occurs during a few peak hours of use on Mother's Day each year. The capacity needed to meet such a surge would be unaffordable and would be grossly underutilized during the rest of the year.

However, if customers do not normally experience an acceptable level of quality, they will first complain to the carrier, an action that will drive up costs for handling the complaints, and then switch carriers should the condition persist, an action that will drive down revenues. To avoid this death spiral, it is necessary to balance service quality against network and operations costs, as shown in Figure 6–9, so that customers are satisfied but an affordable level of expense for network investment and operations cost is maintained. Since the network infrastructure is a leading component of these costs and is a key cause of customer dissatisfaction, it must be considered carefully.

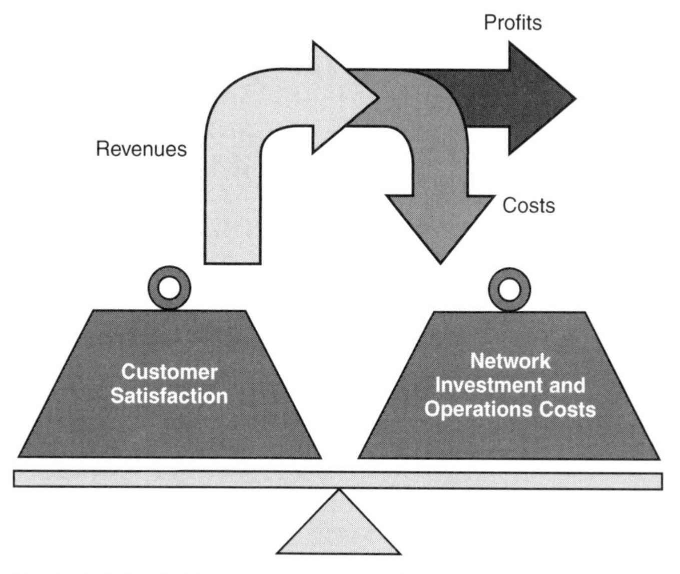

FIGURE 6–9 *Balancing service quality.*

Early versions of VoIP had significant speech quality issues that dissatisfied many users and caused some carriers to curtail initial VoIP deployments. Even today, the method for assuring quality is not completely established. Certainly, large incumbent carriers should approach VoIP carefully, since their brand is so closely associated with high quality. However, there is no known fundamental technical shortcoming in VoIP that will prevent a carrier from providing the same or even better quality than today's PSTN. The combination of MPLS and DiffServ over high-bandwidth optical connections appears adequate for ensuring quality. As an interim step, DiffServ and MPLS routing over virtual paths using ATM/SONET coupled with good capacity engineering seems to be a good solution for those carriers having ATM/SONET networks. This said, it remains to be seen how well large VoIP networks will perform, and there will no doubt be some scaling issues that arise as larger and larger networks are deployed.

Besides speech quality, there are other areas, mentioned in Chapter 2, that affect the customer's perception of service quality provided by the network. These include network availability, dial-tone delay, cut-through delay, call blocking, and disrupted calls. Of these, only dial-tone delay can be disregarded. Since the customer premise device provides dial tone, there should be no significant delay. But there can be problems in all the other areas. For VoIP solutions, special care must be given to reduce cut-through delay and avoid call disruption. This is difficult because changes in IP traffic volumes can have significant impact in the amount of time needed to complete a call due to retransmission of call establishment requests or can disrupt calls that have already been established and are in progress through packet loss. In general, most problems in IP networks originate from traffic overloads that cause packets to be discarded, forcing retransmission of packets. Retransmission can cause even higher levels of congestion due to the transmission of more packets, so it is critical to avoid moving into such a state.

Reliability

In the early 1990s, desktop computers were just not reliable enough to use as telephones. These systems had to be rebooted several times per day. Since reboots would interrupt telephone service, these systems were unsuitable for providing a reliable telephony service. Besides the end systems, servers within the network had similar problems. But today's systems are far more reliable. Certainly, those users wishing to operate VoIP from a desktop system will have to tolerate the occasional computer software failure and reboot, but it is reasonable to expect that computers will close the gap on reliability. Also, the use of dedicated systems such as SIP phones improves reliability. Because these systems are not subjected to the constant infusion of widely differing applications, they are less likely to encounter problems. Overall, the reliability of these end systems should continue to improve and eventually match that of the common telephone.

Any new telephony network will utilize servers and routers as crucial elements within it. In this capacity, reliability is quite critical, since failures can cost enormous sums of money as either lost revenues or increased costs. Although anecdotal, an article published in *Information Week* provides a perspective on how reliable servers and routers can be. It seems that at the University of North Carolina, a network server was lost for over four years. During that time, it operated faithfully and didn't miss a single packet during the entire time, but naturally, the university administrators wanted to locate it. Eventually, it was found inside a wall where it had been accidentally sealed in.

The use of standard, off-the-shelf servers and routers for providing packet forwarding and call control application within the telephony network is a new issue for carriers. In the past, the PSTN elements used for these functions, especially call processors, were specially designed units with multiple processors operating in locked step. If one unit failed, the alternate would continue. Some systems went so far as to provide four such units to achieve extremely high reliability. This was critical to the PSTN, since a failure here could leave tens of thousands of users stranded high and dry with either no dial tone or some other major failure in their service. But these systems use highly customized hardware and software that is very expensive and specialized.

In the current approach to VoIP, off-the-shelf, high-reliability routers and servers are intended to be used for processing calls and for routing the packets that make up the connection. In both cases, careful examination of the reliability and recovery times for processors in both operations and call control are needed. The use of conventional systems will drive cost down for the carriers, although the individual reliability of these systems is less than that of the PSTN equivalents. Table 6–2 shows some typical reliability and annual downtime values.

TABLE 6-2 *Reliability of Network Elements*

Network Element	Annual Downtime	Reliability (%)
Individual STP	2.6 minutes	99.9995
Circuit Switch	5.3 minutes	99.999
Core IP Router	17.5 hours	99.8
Core IP Switch	17.5 hours	99.8
Access Router	26.3 hours	99.7

To achieve the same overall network reliability figures as the PSTN, additional routers can be used and alternate paths for routing can be provided. By adding the correct number of additional elements and properly engineering their interconnection, a similar overall network reliability figure can be achieved for the VoIP service.[3] Possibly some relaxation of reliability requirements for the overall service could also be considered.

An issue related to reliability is the maturity of VoIP products. Since these are mostly recent developments, they have not yet been thoroughly tested, integrated, and made fully operational. Like any new product or concept, changes and modifications are still being made to make them successful. In some cases, products and services have been introduced before they were ready for deployment, leading to dissatisfied customers and complex manual operations steps. A carrier contemplating a deployment would be well advised to carefully plan their operation and to thoroughly test and integrate the network equipment

3. This is only the tip of a large iceberg. Calculation of end-to-end service reliability must also consider loop access reliability, end system reliability, and other critical factors.

with their operations platforms. Otherwise, a great deal of money can be wasted in fixing problems, resulting in either high capital costs for equipment replacement or high operating cost for technical support staff.

Operations Issues

Operations costs for the new network will set the stage for profitability by the carrier. In today's IP networks, there is a great deal of manual operations, especially in configuration of network elements and troubleshooting of problems. In the future, as these networks provide services to large numbers of users, the operations must become more automated and have greater flow-through of operations functions. It is important that manual intervention by technicians be eliminated in order to have low-cost operations and high profitability.

A complete operations solution for new telephony networks has yet to be provided by any supplier. There are solutions that have the correct structure for large carriers but are missing the IP focus. There are other solutions that perform excellent network and element management for small IP networks but do not provide a total business solution for a carrier or do not scale to large networks. This is a key gap in the needs of carriers wishing to deploy these networks.

In Chapter 3, Figure 3–16, an overall operations view for the PSTN based on having a Service Management Layer, a Network Management Layer, an Element Management Layer and an Element Layer was presented. A new telephony operations approach based on this general structure would embody many of these concepts and some of the systems shown. Certainly, there will still be customer contact systems and high-level business systems, as there are today. But these will need to manage the increased service portfolio being offered to customers and must adapt to new approaches to business. This will require very flexible, highly programmable software within these systems, something not easily obtained. At lower layers in the operations architecture, IP network element management is needed to keep the network operating smoothly. At all layers, there will be changes needed due to the greater scope of services and the use of an underlying packet network. Eventually, a simplified operations methodology will emerge that meets the needs of both customers and service providers.

This is a key issue for both new carriers and existing carriers because it will be impossible to achieve profitability in high-volume IP networks without automated operations. At the same time, waiting until developers create a full set of capabilities may not be possible if competitive forces are at play. Carriers who go ahead with highly manual operations risk their profits. Carriers who wait may not achieve any entry at all. And the cost of operations systems can be quite high. So, this issue has no easy resolution.

Regulatory Issues

Telephony has a long history of regulation but has been heavily deregulated in the last decade. Nevertheless, there are still various restrictions on some carriers and some control of rates and prices for services. Because much of regulatory practice is driven by politics, it is very hard to predict what steps the key regulatory bodies such as the FCC will take in coming years. For several decades, a key issue has been the introduction of competition within the telecom industry, focusing first on long distance and more recently on local service.

Regulators have stayed quite far from the Internet, and there have been strong arguments from various government offices and from the companies involved to allow open competition and normal business practice rather than regulatory mandates to establish the rules of the Internet. So far, regulators and government have not taken on a role, possibly because it is uncertain what direction the Internet will eventually go. However, there are a few issues that may only be solved by some form of government intervention and regulation. Regulations may be required to prevent lawlessness and to continue the presence of open competition.

Lawlessness

As everyone knows, the Internet is today's wild frontier. In any frontier, there is usually a high degree of lawlessness in its early days. The Internet is no exception, and everyone is aware of the many crimes perpetrated, some of which might not be possible otherwise. These include theft of identity, denial of service, theft or destruction of intellectual property, delivery of pornographic material, solicitation, invasion of privacy, and other criminal activities. If the Internet does not become more controllable in these areas, regulators will eventually be forced to step in and mandate some requirements.

An example is "spoofing," the practice of connecting to the network using one IP address during authentication procedures and then switching to a different one to preclude tracing by the network. Spoofing needs to be prevented, since it prevents discovery of a party committing an illegal act. This will require a change in the way carriers operate their networks and may require some technical changes in the protocols and equipment. If the Internet community of technologists and carriers does not act to prevent spoofing and other such schemes, regulators may force it on them.

Many technical requirements that are presently required of the PSTN may eventually be forced on the Internet. For example, wiretapping by law enforcement agencies is required of PSTN network systems. When telephony is widely implemented over IP networks, this will surely be a required capability. Also, requirements for Emergency 911 service would be needed, possibly with new extensions. Emergency override priorities for completing certain government agency communications in the presence of disasters and emergencies are yet another need.

These and other technical requirements may be mandated by regulators. Some of these will be easy to perform in an IP network, but others may require some modifications of the current systems.

Open Competition

As explained in Chapter 4, the Internet consists of a large group of ISPs that interconnect directly or through NAPs. This is to ensure that customers of these carriers have full access to all other Internet users. In general, it is desired by the carriers to perform this interconnection, since it extends the reach of their network and thereby the usefulness it represents to their customers. In fact, NAPs were created with just this in mind.

Today, however, most carriers interconnect directly, a condition known as *peering.* When interconnecting directly, carriers must reach an agreement on the terms and conditions. This includes such matters as traffic levels, routing policies, and fees to be charged. Reaching a peering agreement is the basis for interconnection. It is voluntary and no carrier is forced to peer with another carrier if it does not wish to do so.

Generally, this is in line with free market business practices, but it can become a tool to prevent competition in an open market. Today's Internet is dominated by a handful of large operators. A new entrant carrier may not be able to get any of these large carriers to peer directly with them. The new entrant will usually not have a large number of customers and can safely be ignored by the large carriers. If the new entrant goes to a smaller carrier and tries to interconnect through a "back door," it may find that the smaller carrier is also unwilling to help. In part, this is because the small carrier may have to renegotiate its peering agreements due to increases in traffic and other factors. If the new entrant cannot reach a peering agreement to carry its customers' traffic to the rest of the Internet, it will not be able to do business. Thus, peering can be used in an anti-competitive way.

Today, there are concerns that this kind of behavior has either already occurred or may happen soon in the Internet business. This could lead regulators to force large carriers to peer with any other carrier. This, in turn, would lead to a requirement for carrier registration. Today, this is required of local telephone companies; they are forced to connect with any requesting company that is a registered common carrier.

Once the regulators get started, there may be a flood of other regulations for the Internet to ensure fair and equitable business practices. It is impossible to know exactly what may or may not develop with the regulatory arm of government with regard to these issues. But when telephony over the Internet becomes commonplace, it seems most likely that some level of regulatory requirements will be enforced to ensure the ability of law enforcement agencies to do their jobs. Carriers should promote technology that helps prevent crime, assists law enforcement, and provides security and privacy to their users, or eventually some level of regulation to achieve these ends may prove necessary. Unless Internet carriers act to prevent lawlessness and continue to operate using fair, pro-competitive business practices, regulators may begin to establish requirements for them.

Conclusions

In summary, there are many options that carriers, both incumbents and new entrants, must consider. Table 6–3 shows but a few of these and their impacts. A lively debate can be had regarding these issues and many others, and this section has just scratched the surface of these issues. It is difficult to say what are the most important issues. Some affect market entry and profitability more than others. Also, the perception of the importance of these issues varies according to whether the situation of a new entrant carrier or an incumbent carrier is being considered. Nevertheless, these are clearly issues that can make or break the business of a carrier.

TABLE 6-3 *Issues, Options and Impacts for Carrier Consideration*

Issue	Options	Impacts
Services	Super phones or plain old phones?	Overall business goals, services, and technical direction
Billing	Bundled or a-la-carte?	Customer access/retention and marketing plans
Premise Equipment	Inside or outside?	Powering and cost of hardening the gateway; who pays for it
Access Network	Lease, co-locate, or build?	Overall investment costs, time-to-market, viability of the business
Core Network	New optical switching infrastructure or legacy ATM/SONET?	Timeframe for deployment or evolution, costs, service portfolio, and service quality
Numbering and Addressing	ENUM or other?	Ability to bridge Internet and PSTN services and provide directories
Quality	How much capacity to deploy?	Service quality, customer satisfaction
Reliability	Fully test and integrate before deployment, or after?	Time-to-market, customer satisfaction
Operations	Fully automated operations or manual control and maintenance?	Costs, time-to-market, customer satisfaction
Regulatory	Proactive adoption of likely requirements, or wait for mandates?	May preempt or delay undesirable regulatory initiatives

No doubt, any carrier actively involved in either the Internet business or the telephony business could add many more issues to this list and greater depth in the impact. But this serves as a useful introduction to the critical issues in deploying a new telephony service.

References

Berners-Lee, T., R. Fielding, and L. Masinter. "Uniform Resource Identifiers (URI): Generic Syntax," RFC-2396, Aug. 1998.

Do, T. "Future Optical Networks," Lazard Freres & Co., Feb. 2001.

Faltstrom, P. "E.164 and DNS," RFC-2916, Sept. 2000

Lowry, J. R., J. Kosowsky, and K. Bahl. "U.S. Communications Infrastructure at a Crossroads: Opportunities Amid the Gloom," McKinsey & Company, Aug. 2001.

Martin, A. *Enterprise Denied: Origins of the Decline of American Railroads, 1897–1917,* Columbia University Press, Jan. 1971.

Newman, D. "Trends in the Restructuring of the U.S. Telecommunications Industry," Presentation to the Second North American Telecommunications Worker's Conference, 1996.

Rendleman, J. "Server 54, Where Are You?," Apr. 9, 2001, *InformationWeek Daily.*

Schmidt, E., et. al. *The Internet's Coming of Age,* National Academy Press, 2001.

Si, C. and D. Sappington, "The Impact of State Incentive Regulation on the U.S. Telecommunications Industry," University of Florida, Department of Economics, Mar. 2001.

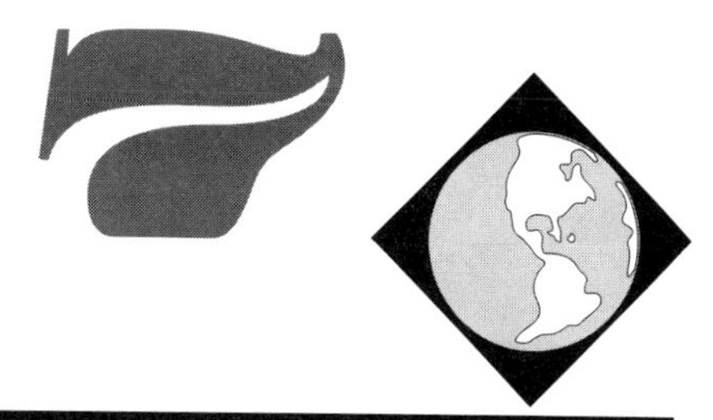

The Players and Their Games

Carriers today are faced with many challenges in their day-to-day business. It is easy for them to become so involved in resolving their current problems that they lose sight of what is going on around them. In his book, *The Innovator's Dilemma,* Christensen deals with these issues and their outcomes. In this chapter, some of Christensen's concepts are applied to the telecom industry. The first consideration is why telephony is a target for a disruptive technology. Next, the drivers that are influencing the direction of the industry are explained. Then, the players working in and around the industry—and how they may approach this challenge—are discussed. Among them are the Local Exchange Carriers (LECs), the Interexchange Carriers (IXCs), the Internet Service Providers (ISPs), the cable operators and some other leading corporations. The most likely approach for each of these groups to build a fully integrated packet data/voice network is presented. Then, the specific scenarios whereby one group or another might try to take over or evolve into the telephony business and the Internet are formulated. Could local carriers build new packet networks that carry voice as well as become a substitute for the Internet? Or might Internet carriers add capabilities that capture the voice market? Perhaps non-carriers could capture telephony as a service while utilizing the network assets of others. These and other scenarios, including partnerships between various entities, are proposed and examined. The circumstances that enable each scenario, the assumptions made about the scenario, and any barriers to its success are also discussed.

Why Take Over Telephony?

The short answer is money, and lots of it, around $226.9 billion for the U.S. market alone. As we all know, money brings out the best[1] in us, especially among highly competitive corporations. Another reason for taking over telephony is that there is no need for two networks. Ultimately, the Internet will surpass the telephone network in its ability to provide telephony service and will be a far better value proposition for end users, since it enables all kinds of services, not just telephony. But before rushing out to start a phone company, potential competitors should consider the scope and scale of the telephony business.

In the United States during 2000, there were 193.9 million local telephone lines in service. Of these, 127.8 million loops served 100.2 million residential households, while 66.1 million loops reached business customers. Note that 28.9 percent of residences have two or more phone lines. Local lines generated around 3,400 billion minutes of telephone use. Revenue for local loop-based telephone service grew slowly at around 3 percent per year but totaled $118.6 billion during 2000.

In the same year, long-distance telephone service accounted for about 451 billion minutes of intrastate toll calls, while interstate calls totaled 585 billion minutes of use. That's a total of 1,036 billion minutes of long-distance phone calls. Of this, residential callers made up about 42

1. Or the worst, depending on your perspective.

percent of toll calls, while business users were 58 percent. Revenue for all combined long-distance service was $108.3 billion.

That's a total telephony service market of $226.9 billion: Who wouldn't like to own even a small part of it? Naturally, being so large, competition has already begun.

The U.S. long-distance market has been competitive for many years. During 2000, around 70 companies competed for long distance revenues. During that year, AT&T held 48.4 percent of the market, WorldCom owned 22.2 percent, Sprint served 6.8 percent, and other carriers accounted for 22.6 percent. The former Bell Companies, which require special regulatory permission to provide long-distance, began providing service in the states of Connecticut, Kansas, Massachusetts, New York, Oklahoma, and Texas. They captured $8 billion of the long-distance market during 2000. Because 31 percent of long distance calls are intrastate, it is relatively easy for them to enter this part of the market.

In the local telephone service business during 2000, the large companies of SBC, Verizon, BellSouth, and Qwest earned about 70 percent of the revenues. Competition for local service, which started in 1996, resulted in CLECs serving 16.4 million homes, amounting to $6.5 billion in revenues during 1999. CLECs serve their customers using a mix of leased and owned loops with one-third of them being owned by the CLEC. Medium and large business customers represent about 60 percent of the market captured by CLECs. However, by the end of 2001, many of these CLECs were not able to continue operation and have gone out of business.

Broadband access using both DSL and cable TV coax steadily increased during 2000. At the end of that year, there were 3.1 million DSL users, of which 1.8 million were residential or small business customers. Hybrid Fiber Coax using cable TV systems had 3.6 million customers, of whom 3.3 million were residential or small business users. This means that cable modem access of residential and small business outnumbered DSL access by nearly two to one at the end of 2000. Estimates for 2001 close this gap a bit, with cable modems serving 6.4 million users and DSL serving 4.5 million users, but these numbers represent a very small penetration of the overall base of customers. When these access systems are widely deployed, customers will have the ability to choose from two or more local exchange companies.

Unfortunately, the investments required to become a major player in this business can be quite high. Ownership of a national network of switches and transmission systems is prohibitively expensive, usually costing many billions of dollars. Nevertheless, a significant number of companies successfully operate in this business without owning networks. One way of doing this is through leasing of facilities, such as access and fiber backbones, to avoid large capital outlays.

One downside in the telephony business is slow growth. For many years, growth in telephony has been around 3 percent, so incumbent carriers are looking for ways to expand their revenues. Internet services are such a way. New entrants to the telephony business can seek to capture existing markets in high margin areas such as business customers.

So, the local carriers want to capture long-distance revenues and become Internet juggernauts while maintaining their dominance in local services. At the same time, long-distance carriers want to maintain their market share in long distance and Internet backbone services while penetrating the local service market. Adding to the tumult, ISPs seek to grow their existing market through expanded services, such as e-commerce, while moving into both local and long-distance telephone services. And on the sidelines, a host of other companies, both large and small, look for opportunities to reach inside all of these businesses and take a share of the prize.

The Drivers of Change

In order to successfully plan and execute a strategy for capturing a significant portion of the telephony business, the key factors that can influence the carriers' options must be understood. Among these key factors are:

- Customers
- Economic climate
- Finance
- Regulatory environment
- Assets
  - Telephone
  - Access
  - Fiber backbones
  - Switching and routing
- Liabilities
- Inertia
- Responsiveness

These drivers are combinations of factors both internal and external to a company. Often, a company will have no control over some factors, but it can usually exert some influence on most of them. All of these drivers vary in time, some with a very low degree of predictability, so it can be difficult or impossible to forecast with any confidence what will happen in the future.

The business forces generated by these drivers can decide the fate of each and every company attempting to capture or retain some part of the telephone business. Each driver can influence individual companies in quite different ways. Sometimes, a driver that advantages one company or group of companies will have an adverse effect on the others. Or sometimes, it may influence them all the same way. Now each driver is discussed in some detail.

Customers

A valid consideration for carriers is that customers just want to keep making phone calls using their existing phones. Actually, this is a valid consideration in a certain context; however, the carrier who listens too closely to its customers can wind up in the bone yard. As Christensen argues in his book, *The Inventor's Dilemma,* companies that have the greatest market share in any business run the risk of being immobilized by their customers. Their services are certainly satisfying their customers; otherwise, they would not be the market leader. And the customers will almost surely tell the company that they like the service; after all, they're buying it. They will invariably ask for lower prices and incremental improvements. But they are unlikely to ask for something totally new, since they have no idea what that might be or how it might benefit them. In general, customers are skeptical about anything new until a benefit has been realized by some of them.

But when a competitor announces a new service using a "disruptive" technology, the customers may flock to it because of perceived or demonstrated advantages, or a lower price. The market leader that listens mostly to its customers can be blindsided by such a migration of customers and may not have the time or the will to respond. It is difficult to predict the actions of customers when new technologies are introduced. The various phases of introducing a new product and the issues associated with progressing from one phase to another are considered in *Crossing the Chasm* and *Inside the Tornado* by Geoffrey A. Moore.

Another critical issue to carefully consider is how many of the targeted customers are also customers of a competitor. For example, customers of an LEC are usually customers of a long-distance carrier. If both carriers offer the customer a new service, which company will have the greatest influence over the customer? Telecom customers in the United States often do business with several carriers, since they can choose different companies for their local, long-distance, Internet, and wireless services. Depending on the value proposition coming from one or the other of these carriers, the customer may choose to migrate all services to that carrier, leaving the others to watch the dust settle. Carriers must examine this issue carefully, since a company in any one of these businesses might invade the business space of the others at any time.

As is well known to marketing experts, retaining current customers is an easier proposition than getting entirely new ones. So, those carriers with a large customer base have an advantage over a new entrant with no embedded base of users. Since the incumbent will have a great deal of information regarding its customers, an analysis can be performed to determine many necessary parameters of a new offering, including price, performance, and features. Targeted introduction can be done to focus the efforts of early deployments and to minimize operations costs. These are tremendous advantages to a large incumbent. But the new entrant will have greater flexibility in its offerings and a new look and feel to its service. Also, remember that the new entrant may have customers in an entirely different line of business than telephony that might be successfully approached.

Economic Climate

When the economy is soaring and investment financing is readily available, carriers of all kinds can easily obtain capital to invest in their networks. This can be especially true for new carriers who promise rapid growth and high rates of return for investors due to innovative service plans. During the late 1990s, this was surely the case, and the telecom industry saw the launch of dozens of new businesses aimed at capturing the telephony marketplace. But when economic times are hard, investment capital evaporates. Since most new businesses normally go through a period in which their operating expenses outweigh their revenues, they depend heavily on investor funding to maintain their cash flow. Sadly, this may not be possible, and these companies can find themselves declaring bankruptcy or being acquired by a larger enterprise. Additionally, these companies may have high debt due to their initial capital needs.

The other thing that occurs during a downturn is a change in the outlook for obtaining customers. As the economy shrinks, both individuals and enterprises pull back from spending on anything other than basic necessities. This results in a smaller market for any new service or technology, leading to a glut of capability that drives down prices, revenues, and profits. The upshot of this is that the demand for anything new is diminished.

Starting in mid-year 2000, the U.S. economy began just such a downturn, and in less than 2 years, most of the most highly vaunted new carriers that launched in the late 1990's were either defunct or acquired. Besides these victims, a majority of the dotcom companies, whose e-commerce operation was a major driver for creating an improved Internet, also disappeared. Even the largest carriers instituted extensive layoffs and curtailed investments to preserve profitability. Until the U.S. economy begins an upturn, there is likely to be little or no investment capital available for starting new ventures in telecom and fewer customers clamoring for new or improved network services. Such is the nature of business.

Finance

New carriers must rely mostly on investors for financing, but large, established companies have other sources of capital for investing in their networks and services. Because they own collateral such as their existing network and have established credit ratings, they can borrow money from financial institutions. For example, the largest of these carriers have assets around $70 billion even after depreciation is applied. Naturally, they must borrow carefully to avoid upsetting their balance sheets by becoming overextended, but it is possible for these companies to continue building new services and new networks even during trying economic times. The financial "muscle" of the largest of these companies can be enormous. Depending on other drivers, such as the economy or regulatory rules, they may choose not to make such investments or to limit them to some minimum level necessary to maintain their existing business. But if they see good reasons for investing in a new network or a new service, they have the ability to do so.

One way in which large incumbents can invest is to purchase startup companies that have launched a successful concept. During hard economic times, many of these can be purchased at bargain basement prices. Since the start of the economic downturn of 2000, there has been a steady stream of acquisitions and mergers reported. Acquiring a resource is usually less expensive and faster than building it, especially if there is a fire sale. Why build it when you can buy it! This is sound logic for those companies with the ability to do so. In general, only the large companies have the financial strength to make such moves. Even these companies must be careful that their acquisition does not destroy the very resource they are hoping to obtain. In the case of physical assets, there is little danger of this, but much of the value of a startup lies in its culture and innovative ideas. An acquisition strategy that does not carefully consider how to retain the employee base and nurture the intellectual assets will not get the maximum benefit of the purchase.

Regulatory Environment

Many of the companies competing in the telecom industry labor under some degree of regulation. No matter how "enabled" an enterprise may be, if it is blocked by regulators, it cannot succeed. In the past, the telecom industry has had a high degree of regulation. Regulators controlled charging rates, determined the rates of return for carriers, approved capital investment budgets, and decided what businesses carriers could or could not enter. Features that seemed simple and obvious extensions to telephony were not allowed due to regulatory concerns about competition.

The regulatory environment is heavily—some would say entirely—influenced by politics. Regulations are intended to produce fair competition among the combatants and good services for the buying public, but there can always be a difference of opinion about how this should be done. As a result, when one political party displaces another in governance, the newly elected officials can make a significant change in the direction of regulatory practice.

The current direction for regulators now is deregulation. Little by little, the telecommunications industry is being allowed to operate as a free market with less and less regulation. The long-distance segment of telecom has long been open to competition, and carriers operating in this business are free from nearly all restrictions. There is special attention being given to creating competition in the local telephone segment. A particularly thorny issue for introducing competition is that the most ubiquitous means for accessing customers is the local copper loop. Because the loop is owned by a single local carrier, the FCC, in 1996, mandated that the loop and other network systems be unbundled so they can be leased to a competing carrier at a fair price.

There has been speculation by some FCC watchers that LECs might be split into two entities. One would own and operate local loops, and the other would be a fully deregulated company free to sell whatever services it wished. If this were done, the loop operating entity would be motivated to lease its loops to any carrier and would have no vested interest in helping one carrier over another. But thus far, the FCC has not shown any inclination to do this.

Among the LECs, especially SBC, Verizon, BellSouth, and Qwest, there is a strong desire to enter the long-distance market. These carriers can easily serve a high percentage of intrastate long-distance calls, because both endpoints of these calls lie inside their serving area. The potential revenues are quite large. During 1999, intrastate tolls were $33.6

billion, or about 30 percent of the entire U.S. long-distance market. In order for these companies to enter the long distance business, they must pass a 14-point checklist established by the FCC that measures the degree of competition for local service present within their serving area. This includes unbundling the loop and other parts of the local telephone network. Once these key criteria are met, the carrier can enter the long-distance market. These must be satisfied state-by-state. As of August 2001, only Connecticut, Kansas, Massachusetts, New York, Oklahoma, and Texas have granted permission for the incumbent LEC to provide long-distance services. During January 2002, Verizon gained approval from New Jersey regulators and is now filing for FCC permission.

Since its inception, the Internet has operated relatively free of regulation, but it is possible, as stated in the previous chapter, that regulators may step in to control various aspects. The key issues being discussed relate to lawlessness and continuing fair competition. It is impossible to say what, if anything, regulators may do. But if the Internet carriers do not find some way to bring some of these issues under control, regulators may decide to do it for them. The likely results would be regulations fostering fair practices for peering and transit agreements, and capabilities that enable law enforcement. At some point, the government may wish to establish greater control over the Internet, a step that could make an enormous difference to those companies operating in this business.

Assets

The companies that are competing for the new telephony have equipment, right-of-way, systems, processes, intellectual property and human resources that can be applied to achieve success. Generally speaking, the more assets that are available, the better their chances. However, care must be taken in identifying assets that are not reusable in the target architecture. Whatever is not an asset is most likely a liability.

Three critical physical assets for success in the new telephony are the company's ability to provide broadband access to its customers, its high-speed fiber backbone network, and its packet-switching capabilities. To the extent that any of these are not present, the company will have to build, acquire, or lease such facilities. The absence of one or more of these assets can be a difficult challenge to overcome, but it is possible for a successful entrant to own very little network equipment. By having reasonable leasing arrangements, the company can have great agility in entering the market. This, coupled with the right value proposition for customers, can build a successful enterprise. So, it is not necessary to own or build everything, especially physical network assets.

Telephone

Even though the customer owns this device, the telephone is a critical element worthy of consideration. The telephone has the advantage of being ubiquitous but is a poor instrument for any service other than voice telephony. Fortunately, the telephone is quite inexpensive and can easily be replaced by a customer should a better alternative be made available that is affordable. Nevertheless, any carrier who plans a new service and counts on customers acquiring a new instrument faces a hurdle to a successful deployment and profitable operation. There are ways of reducing this risk, such as bundling a new instrument in with the service, but these schemes will increase the cost of deployment. An alternative is to sell a new "super-phone" to the customer, but this will reduce the number of customers accepting the service due to the additional cost. One low-cost approach uses the customer's existing computer for the instrument and provides software that defines its telephony functions. Since about 60 percent of U.S. homes have a computer, this could reach a significant market.

As carriers face the future, this will be a very difficult choice. In the short term, any carrier wishing large-scale service penetration will want to accommodate the simple telephone. Yet the telephone is the most inhibiting factor to better and more sophisticated services. Any carrier deciding to offer a new telephony service faces a key decision as to whether or not it will support existing telephones, new super-phones, or both. Because the customer premise equipment can be the dominating cost of any deployment, this is not an easy decision. Small differences in cost from one approach to another can make a large difference in profitability.

Access

At present, high-bandwidth loop access is the key impediment to achieving improved networking for users. There are two means possible today: DSL modems over the existing copper loop of the local telephone company or cable modems over the coaxial distribution network of a cable operator. Both DSL and cable modem support similar bit rates for transmitting data.

As an asset, the local copper loop is of tremendous value to the LEC. It is ubiquitous, reaching virtually every U.S. home and business location. While it has limitations in speed, it can still serve as a moderately high-speed transmission media. The operations systems are in place, as are technicians and inventory for its repair. The LEC knows very well how to maintain the loop and has become highly proficient in its care. However, the presence of loading coils on longer loops precludes their use of DSL. This limits the number of customers to which DSL service can be offered. Also, deployed Digital Loop Carrier (DLC) systems cannot accommodate high-speed digital transmission such as DSL on the local loop. Until such time as they provide this capability, DLC systems would not be an asset in the new telephony architectures. However, this could easily change as DLC suppliers create new plug-ins for their equipment that support DSL.

Besides the existing local copper loop reaching customers, there is also the cable TV coaxial distribution network. These cable plants require upgrades to extend their bandwidth so additional digital channels can be added for either video entertainment or for data transport to customers. When this is done, it is also necessary to upgrade the network to allow the transport of data from the customer to the network so that two-way transmission can occur. The cable modem has proven to be quite popular and outsold DSL during 1999 and 2000.

Both DSL and cable modem deployments have a difficult obstacle to overcome: the installation of the modem at the customer's location and proper configuration of the customer's computer software. Presently, this requires a visit by technicians, who spend between 4 and 12 hours to install and configure the modem and its software. This is a very expensive proposition, and a version that can be installed by the customer is needed. Without this capability, neither access method can be rapidly deployed to tens of millions of customers on a profitable basis. The initial cost of deployment sinks the profitability of the service for many years. Both this cost as well as the cable network and loop network upgrades must be considered when developing a deployment plan.

During the second half of 2001, there was significant progress in marketing a "self-install" version of both cable and DSL modems, and field experience with this approach has been successful so far. No doubt, some customers will have problems due to marginal conditions in their copper loop or cable distribution system. But overall, the success rate for self-installation appears promising. This is a significant development in provisioning broadband access, a gating issue for offering new services.

Fiber Backbones

Fiber networks are a key asset that most existing carriers possess, especially Internet backbone service providers,

IXCs, and LECs. By modifying the electronics at just a few locations, usually only the endpoints of the fiber optic, the carrier can quickly convert the transport medium from today's circuit orientation to a packet-based medium. Since these fiber optic networks can operate at gigabit speeds, they are capable of reliably transporting enormous amounts of information at very low cost.

As an asset, SONET is reusable as carriers move to packet-based transport. This is due to its concatenated payload capability. However, to utilize this, field changes to some of the SONET systems are necessary. Those operating at extremely high speeds, usually confined to large backbones, will not require any change at all. These systems will not be involved in packet processing and will simply multiplex and route tributaries reaching these systems that are carrying packets. In some cases, it will only be necessary to change the provisioning of the system to use concatenated mode. However, in others, especially those systems operating at lower speeds at the bottom of the hierarchy, it will be necessary to change the interfaces currently provided for tributary terminations to a different interface capable of sending and receiving packets.

For the most part, these fiber backbones represent a true asset with little or no required upgrades. For many decades, there have been substantial improvements in the capacity of these systems, and this is likely to continue for the foreseeable future. Since the capacity in these networks is already sufficient or easily upgraded, a fiber backbone is a good asset that allows its owner to expand service.

Switching and Routing

Today's circuit-switching systems, such as local exchanges and tandem switches, leave much to be desired. They are expensive to purchase, operate, and maintain. They have a high degree of complexity, which makes training for technicians expensive and lengthy. This in turn demands premium pay for the more valuable technician. This complexity also leads to more sophisticated management systems and a greater chance of operations problems due to human or machine errors. Although there have been many schemes for increasing data rates in these switches, deployed systems do not support transport rates greater than 64 kbps. For this reason, they are of very limited use for data applications. These switches are, however, the basis for today's PSTN, including all the embedded services such as call forwarding, call waiting, toll-free service, and so on. Thus, they enable an enormous revenue stream for every PSTN carrier and cannot be discarded casually.

Like the local exchange, tandem switches are also a bottleneck for high-speed data. They only switch 64 kbps voice circuits and cannot easily be modified to provide higher speeds. Because of their intense call loads and their importance to the existing revenues for voice telephony, they too cannot easily be discarded.

IP routers will eventually replace circuit switches. This can be costly and slow for carriers with a large embedded base that must depreciate and retire these expensive circuit switches over many years. New carriers have an advantage, since they can deploy IP routers as their initial transport system and avoid the cost of retiring a large asset.

Parts of a carrier's SS7 network have the potential to be reusable in some of the new architectures of the new telephony. Assuming the continuation of telephone numbers, a certainty for the foreseeable future, many of the various Service Control Point (SCP) databases could be reused. Further, the SCP is a generalized high-speed, high-reliability processing system that might be used in any number of places. Signal Transfer Points (STPs), on the other hand, are candidates for replacement with a more data-centric product, such as IP routers. Depending on the desired characteristics of the new telephony service, not all of the STP functions might be retained. Certain functions associated with reliability and end addressing might better be performed differently or dropped altogether. Thus, as an asset, SS7 has both value and liability when moving forward.

In considering assets, IXCs face similar problems as LECs. Their circuit switches are the basis of their large existing telephony revenues and will need to be retired. However, the three largest IXCs also operate the three largest Internet backbone networks, so they have broadly deployed IP networks and have data offerings. These companies are well positioned with large IP networks that can be expanded to absorb their circuit-switched traffic.

Liabilities

Network equipment, operations systems, business processes, corporate culture, human resources, and debt can significantly deter competitiveness within a scenario's framework. These items may be deeply embedded in the current operation of the company. As previously described, the circuit-switching equipment that is the mainstay of operations for most telephony carriers must be retired on an accelerated schedule, resulting in major annual write-offs. This can be a very difficult step for even the largest of these companies.

In some mergers and acquisitions, the cost of integrating the operation of the acquired company can be staggering. This can occur due to replacement of systems and software for combining operations in order to create the new company. The training of staff to operate a new technology, incubation of a new culture, and changes to operations systems to manage the business can be very expensive.

Some companies incur huge liabilities due to legal actions taken against the company by competitors or the government. These can result from patent infringement, operations that limit competition, and business practices that are either questionable in nature or can be interpreted in ways that invite litigation. Sometimes, these legal costs can break a company or cause it to be restructured in ways that make it noncompetitive.

So, for companies to succeed in the new telephony, they must be careful not to incur liabilities that compromise their ability to compete. No one is immune to these problems. The largest of companies can take actions that land them in difficulties simply because of their size. Small companies who operate as entrepreneurs can later find that their methods come under fire when the stakes are higher and the company is succeeding. Liability can neutralize the best of plans.

Inertia

A company's intellectual mindset and commitment to its current products and the generation and delivery of these products can impede success of an otherwise successful contender. This domain includes the company's suppliers, its marketing channels, and its current customers, all of which can slow down the company's ability to adopt a new set of operations processes necessary to sell a new product. Large companies are especially susceptible to this problem.

Even if management truly wants to make changes, it can be very hard to implement them. The natural processes institutionalized at large companies tends to work against change. People are generally reluctant to change what they do at work. They prefer the method they know and understand to the one they do not. There is a huge investment that the company has made over its years of existence in a corporate culture that is the basis of its success. If that culture is allowed to dominate, the company simply cannot change its way of doing business.

Management must be very resourceful in order to effect change by placing the correct metrics and rewards in place to accomplish what they intend. Clear messages must be given to the staff of the company so that everyone can understand the new direction, its importance, and a road-

map for getting there. Otherwise, inertia will prevent rapid movement towards the new target.

Responsiveness

In any company, there are always entrepreneurial people around. These people have excellent technical and managerial skills for introducing new products and the ability to think creatively. They are able to propose clever ideas, methods, and procedures that could advantage the corporation. These people can make the company very responsive when entering a new market or encountering competition, provided the company can overcome the systemic suppression of innovation. The track record of a company in introducing new products through responsive subsidiaries or small groups is one indicator of its ability to transition to a new product.

A large company needs to locate such skill within itself and supplement it from the outside so as to build an effective team that can introduce the new product. Acquiring or merging with a company that has this skill is another path that can be taken. By working through this smaller group, the large company can begin moving in a new direction through an empowered and capable team. The team must be given whatever is needed to succeed, and they must use these resources to respond in the most effective manner to market needs with the new product. In the case of an acquisition or merger, the parent company must be careful not to stifle the very attribute it is seeking, for this can easily happen.

Overall Drivers

Table 7–1 summarizes the drivers in terms of the questions that can be asked when considering what chance of success a company or group of companies has in the new telephony.

TABLE 7-1 Drivers of the New Telephony

Driver	Questions to Consider
Customers	How many customers does the company have? How tightly bound are they? Are they customers of other competing groups? Will they adopt new features? Do they also require the old features? How much will they spend? Will new customers be needed?
Economic climate	Is the economy expanding or shrinking? Are customers able to afford new services? Will economic initiatives help or hinder the operation? Is investment capital readily available? Will this continue, and for how long?
Finance	Are interest rates attractive for loans? How should money required for new or upgraded apparatus be obtained? Are internal capital programs sufficient to accomplish the changes? Are these properly directed?
Regulatory environment	Are regulations protecting incumbents or encouraging competitors? If so, will this continue? Will regulators possibly introduce new barriers to business? Will costs be driven up to meet mandated requirements?
Assets	Is the equipment inventory useful in the new business? Are upgrades needed? How extensive are the required investments? Is the necessary intellectual property in place and protected?

TABLE 7-1 *Drivers of the New Telephony (cont.)*

Liabilities	How rapidly can obsolete equipment be retired, and at what cost? Does the staff have the necessary skills for the new product? Can they be trained, and at what cost? Are there potential legal problems that could result in high expenses?
Inertia	Can the company infuse change in its operations? What examples of this are there from the past? How long will it take to change the core business processes, and at what cost? What metrics and rewards will instill the desired changes in the corporate culture?
Responsiveness	Can the company rapidly introduce a new product? Are there enough entrepreneurs within the company? Should talent be sought through a merger or acquisition? Can a core team be assembled and enabled to move the product forward in the initial thrust? Can they then expand the new business model and its processes throughout the company?

These key drivers, as well as other factors, can influence the chance of success for any company launching or transitioning to a new telephony business.

Suppliers

While carriers and partners that can compete in telephony services are the main focus of this book, the role of suppliers cannot be forgotten. Every major supplier has made large investments in products to support this new direction, including investments in IP routers, soft switches for call control in a VoIP architecture, and optical switching equipment. Among these suppliers are large companies such as Alcatel, Cisco, Fujitsu, Lucent, NEC, and Nortel as well as newer ones, such as Ciena, Sonus, Telcordia, and Westwave. A comprehensive list of these companies would probably number close to 200.

Having made their investment in new products, these companies are naturally hoping to sell their wares and are busy convincing customers and investors that they have the right product at the right time. This is another battlefield of the new telephony, and there are already casualties among startups who simply did not have the staying power to keep pace with the larger manufacturers during tough economic times. Even the larger ones suffered during the economic downturn of 2000.

One influence of the suppliers' marketing activity comes in the form of product brochures, presentations, and white papers. These argue convincingly that the carrier of the future will use the supplier's product because it will make their services singularly attractive to customers and their operation untouchable by competitors. No doubt, such a message is met with a healthy dose of skepticism on the part of carriers, but there is truth to many of these claims. Either way, the carrier absorbs this information and becomes more knowledgeable about the choices that it and its competitors face. Often, the carrier becomes convinced that a new direction is being established.

Such is the case for the new telephony. It would be hard to name a carrier of any stature anywhere in the world today that has no plans or no interest in deploying a multiservice IP network. Much of this is due to the suppliers who have been busy pollinating the carrier community with information about VoIP and various service mixes that this could enable. The potential of increased revenue at lower cost is attractive to the carriers. And, while suppliers differ in some details, they are all moving towards a common target, the use of IP over optical networks with controlled quality of service for multiple services, including telephony. This has had an enormous influence on the carriers and has been the basis for many new startups who were funded by investors to take on the incumbent carriers and beat them at their own game, using the new technology and innovative business concepts.

Scenarios for the New Telephony

In this section, a set of six scenarios is described that, given the right set of driving forces, might come to fruition. To some degree, each scenario will succeed at one time or another, often with many of them moving forward simultaneously. But as forces that shape the business align in some direction and the players achieve some of their goals, one or two of the scenarios will have a greater likelihood of dominating. As stated earlier, key drivers for each group of players include their utilizable assets, the skills of their workforce, their customer base, their financial strength, the economic climate, and the regulatory environment. These drivers will shape the landscape for success by the players.

None of these scenarios are likely to succeed quickly; the most likely prospect is that it will take several years to tell which group of players is really capturing the business of telephony with a new business model. Although a specific list of competitive companies is listed for each scenario, this is not to imply that only these companies are among the players or that the companies listed belong only to that scenario. These companies are simply among the largest examples that fit each category and have the most open reporting of their financial results and strategic initiatives. There are a lot of companies poised to offer a new telephony service to their customers, and it is impossible to mention all of them in this book.

The scenarios and their primary players in the United States are:

- **Business as Usual** – Everyone
- **Telco Takeover** – Verizon, SBC, BellSouth, Qwest

- **Top Down** – AT&T, WorldCom, Sprint
- **Inside Out** – AOL Time Warner, Comcast, EarthLink
- **Perfect Together** – Microsoft, Net2Phone, Yahoo!
- **Dark Horse** – Utility industry and satellite operators

The listed companies represent a balanced perspective of what is happening across the telecommunications industry. These companies are major providers in their market segment. This is not to say that small companies have no chance at playing the new telephony game, but unless they have something significant, such as intellectual property or a particularly clever business scheme to offer through a partnership, not much impact will be evident. For the most part, this struggle is between giants with enormous resources, but small companies with the "right stuff" will find ways in which they can play a significant role that could tip the balance of the outcome.

In order to understand the scope and scale of these companies, their annual revenues[2] and a few other key indicators from their annual reports for 2000 are given. Investors should not use this information in any way for determining whether or not to invest in these companies. These figures do not provide a complete picture of the company as an investment. And, of course, past performance is no guarantee of future results.

Business as Usual

In this scenario, depicted in Figure 7–1, nothing happens to change the status quo. There continues to be a telephone network and an Internet. Other than some weak interactions between the two networks, such as Internet call waiting,[3] data and telephone networks are separate. The

2. All financials throughout this chapter are given in billions of U.S. dollars.
3. Here, a dial-up Internet customer receives a display at her computer when she has an incoming phone call. She can decide whether or not to interrupt her Internet session to take the call.

primary drivers for this scenario are the economic climate and the regulatory environment.

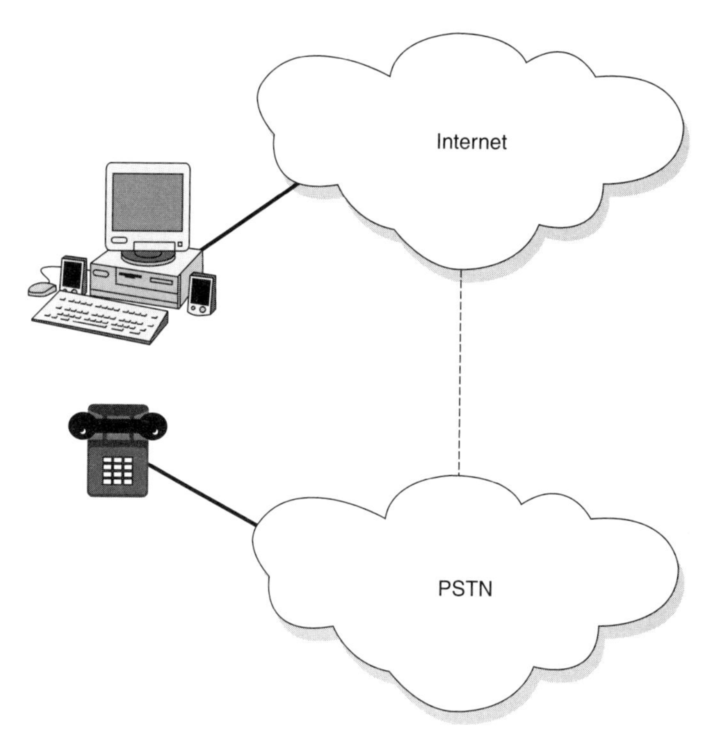

FIGURE 7–1 *Business-as-usual scenario.*

In hard economic times, such as the United States began experiencing in 2000, there is little or no investment in infrastructure. The larger companies with established customers simply tighten their belts to survive. But smaller companies attempting to begin a new business or creating network infrastructure fail due to lack of revenues and investment capital. During 2001, nearly all CLEC startups went out of business because they were operating on investment capital rather than service revenues. When the investors withdrew from further rounds of funding requests, these companies had insufficient service revenues to sustain them. Some merged and stayed in business, but most were acquired by larger carriers. By the end of 2001, all but the largest U.S. carriers had curtailed major investments in any new infrastructure due to cost control and a lack of serious competition.

When economic circumstances are good, competition will abound and existing carriers will improve their IP network infrastructure by adding the necessary systems to provide quality of service and call control for telephony. Those lacking an IP network infrastructure will deploy it. Investors will make capital available to those companies with the most innovative and competitive business concepts and service plans. Loans will be made to those with good credit ratings. Competition will ensue and force carriers to invest in their network and expand their service portfolio.

Although unlikely, this scenario could be reinforced if regulators begin to control the operation of the Internet in ways that make it less attractive to provide either telephony or a service bundle. This might include various restrictions or requirements that increase costs. At present, there is no such dark cloud on the horizon, but it is also equally clear that some additional level of regulation over the Internet will probably occur. The U.S. Congress has already enacted legislation relating to privacy and protection of minors. At the minimum, regulators will act to require carriers to preclude some of the problems associated with lawlessness.

The Telco Takeover

In this scenario, LECs, including Verizon, SBC, Bellsouth, Qwest, and others enter the long-distance business by adding IP packet networks. As shown in Figure 7–2, the LEC begins with its local circuit-switched voice network and adds an IP network for long-distance voice and data services. Later, it would convert its local networks to IP. This would occur over a long period of time, since these are expensive assets and cannot be retired rapidly. As these networks grow, the LEC's local exchange switches and customers could gradually be migrated to IP.

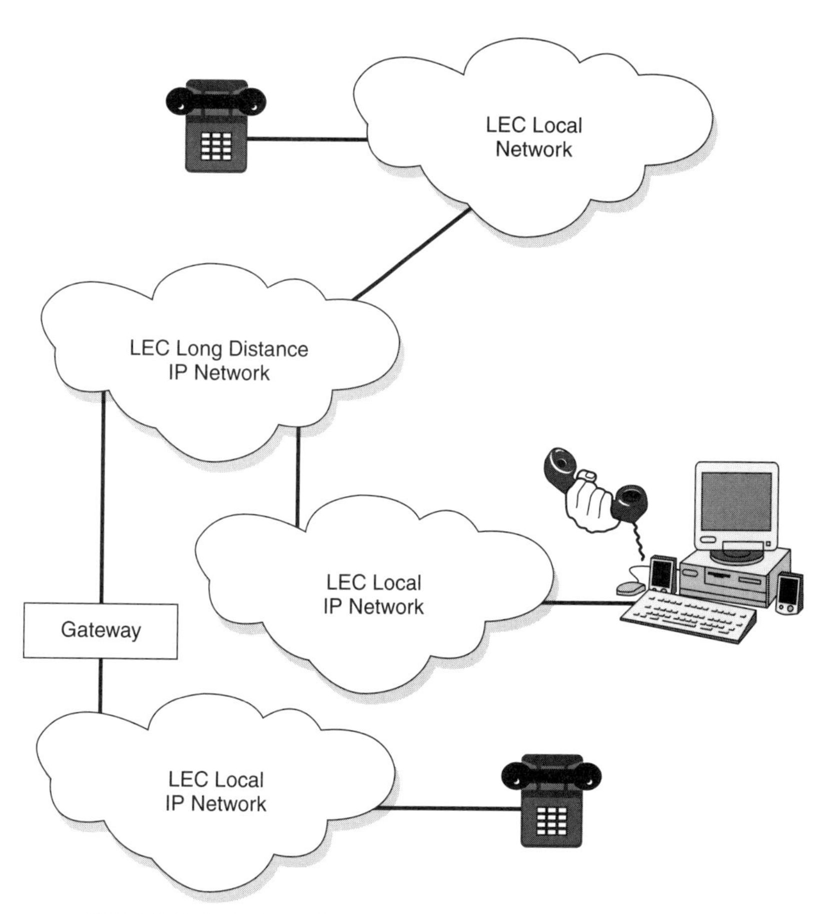

FIGURE 7–2 *Telco takeover scenario.*

This strategy would provide the LEC with a modern, high-quality IP network that expands to become a large part of the Internet. By retaining existing customers and gradually moving them to the new infrastructure, it could control the pace of change and minimize costs. By bundling branded value-added services, it could provide an attractive option for customers. Its brand is well known inside and outside its serving areas, an asset the LEC can use to its advantage.

The key indicators for these companies are shown in Table 7–2.

TABLE 7-2 Key Indicators for Some "Telco Takeover" Participants

	Verizon	SBC	BellSouth	Qwest
Revenue	$ 57.6	$ 51.4	$ 26.2	$ 16.6
Net Income	$ 11.8	$ 8.0	$ 3.5	$ (0.8)
Network Operating Cost	$ 34.1	$ 31.0	$ 17.2	$ 5.4
Network Assets	$ 73.5	$ 47.1	$ 51.0	$ 73.5
Capital Investment	$ 17.6	$ 13.1	$ 7.0	$ 7.0
Customers	33,000,000	N/A*	17,600,000	29,000,000
Broadband	975,000	767,000	215,000	N/A
Employees	260,000	220,090	103,918	71,000

* Not Available.

These companies are truly giants in the telecommunications industry, the "steamrollers of telecom." Their net income is larger than most competitors' revenues. They have large capital programs for upgrading their networks that can be used to introduce new technology. They have an enormous number of customers and extensive market information about their needs. However, the loyalty of these customers is not entirely certain. They are large wireless carriers as well.

In order to offer long-distance service, these carriers must meet a 14-point checklist established by the FCC and obtain local regulatory approval. They have already begun by applying for permission to introduce long-distance services in 11 states and have gained approval in six of those applications.

These carriers are entering the Internet business as well. Verizon has acquired part ownership of Genuity, the sixth largest ISP in the United States. Qwest operates an IP data network that provided its revenues prior to acquiring U.S.

West and is the fifth largest IP backbone provider in the United States. The others also have ISP subsidiaries but with modest market share. They have also begun deploying broadband access using DSL.

These companies have immense size and financial strength, allowing them to weather adverse economic conditions and to consider large acquisitions. Their size also works against them because they have high inertia with the current PSTN. However, they have also shown responsiveness by deploying wireless and data services in small subsidiaries that operate in a very entrepreneurial manner.

Issues they face include replacement of circuit switching (which is a very large asset base), changing the technical expertise of their staff to operate the new IP network, thinking differently about services for their customers, changes in their supplier chain, and other businesses issues. They must also supplement their operations support systems and processes as well as adapt them to IP packet switching. A big problem for this group is the regulatory environment that prevents them from taking rapid action in providing new services or making certain investments. Also, since the general regulatory trend in local services is to foster local competition, regulators are generally less likely to enable LECs to compete freely due to their greater size, financial strength, and market position. But LECs do possess the financial strength to evolve their networks, weather economic downturns, and acquire competitors should the regulatory environment allow them to do so.

Top Down

In this scenario, IXCs such as AT&T, WorldCom, and Sprint, who are already major players in the Internet and the long-distance business, begin to penetrate the local telephone business using leased or acquired customer access. Since they already have packet networks and an ISP subsidiary, they are well positioned to upgrade their existing IP networks to be telephony-capable. Once this is done, they can begin to route their long-distance traffic on the packet network. Then, by either leasing or acquiring access to the end user, they can start to capture local telephone service. These companies also have metropolitan fiber distribution networks in many cities to reach large business customers; these networks can be expanded to reach residential and small business users. As shown in Figure 7–3, these carriers can build on these assets to provide services. Most are already working to enter local services, and all have large wireless divisions. At the same time, they want to block local carriers from entering long distance for as long as possible to protect their market.

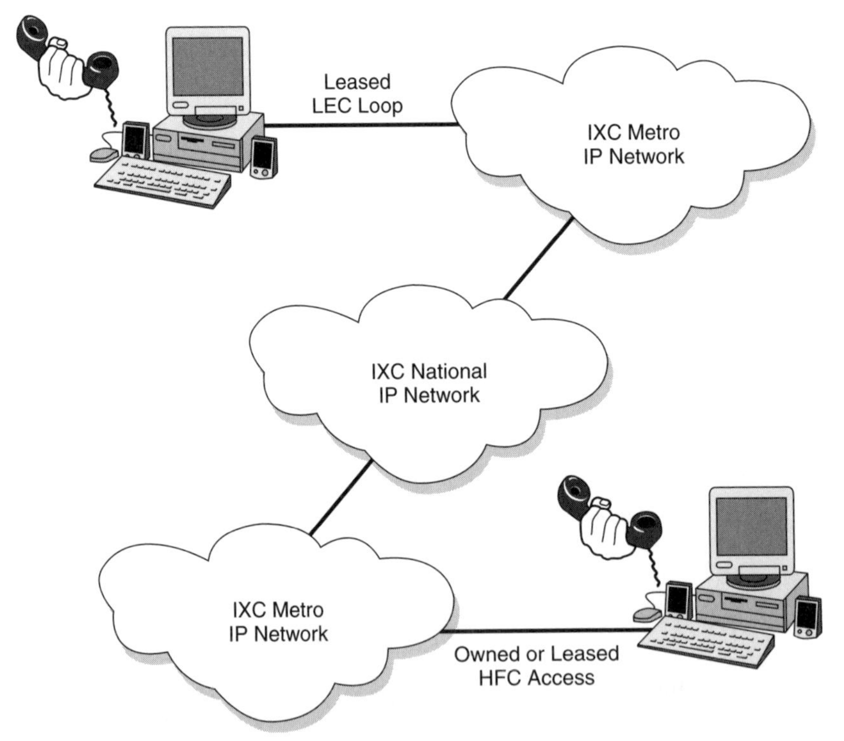

FIGURE 7–3 *Top down scenario.*

These companies are attempting these approaches. WorldCom is the largest Internet backbone provider in the

United States, followed closely by Sprint and AT&T. Key indicators for these companies are shown in Table 7–3.

TABLE 7-3 *Key Indicators for Some "Top Down" Participants*

	AT&T	WorldCom	Sprint
Revenue	$ 66.0	$ 51.4	$ 23.6
Net Income	$ 4.7	$ 4.1	$ 0.1
Network Operating Cost	$ 17.6	$ 15.5	$ 23.1
Network Assets	$ 51.2	N/A	N/A
Capital Investment	$ 15.5	$ 11.5	N/A
Customers	60,000,000	22,000,000	23,000,000
Broadband	1,100,000	22,000	23,000
Employees	165,000	83,000	84,100

These companies have excellent financial strength and resources. They also posses a large customer base; however, long-distance customers have demonstrated their willingness to switch carriers at a moment's notice, usually for a lower price. Bundling services, as described earlier, has reduced churn for these carriers. They have large TDM-switched networks that must be replaced by expanding their existing IP networks, but they should have the financial muscle to make this investment. Although they are large companies with good financials, the long-distance business has been reduced to a commodity with very low profits. This limits, to some extent, the ability of these companies to invest in upgrades and new technology. Also, an economic downturn can force them to sell critical assets, such as the sale by AT&T of its cable network to Comcast at the end of 2001. In some cases, a takeover of some of these carriers could be engineered by a competitor. The size of these companies makes it hard for them to do anything quickly, but once they are moving, they can be unstoppable. Their staff members are used to working in a highly competitive environment and are responsive and customer focused.

The key obstacle for these carriers is gaining local access to the customer. For large business customers, this problem has been solved using private lines and direct fiber. But for residential and small business sites, the carrier needs to either lease a loop from the LEC, gain access through a cable TV carrier, or deploy a wireless system. They already have an operations platform for their Internet offerings, but these must be adapted to telephony service. They must also retire their circuit-switching assets and increase the number of technical staff skilled in IP operation.

Inside Out

In this scenario, ISPs and cable operators such as AOL Time Warner, EarthLink, Comcast and others evolve into the telephony business by gaining broadband access to the customer through either cable modems or DSL and begin selling telephone service. This access might be either leased or acquired and owned by them. Gaining high-speed access simultaneously improves their current services to customers and allows them to add additional services such as telephony. They will continue to use existing Internet backbone providers for connectivity between their facilities in metropolitan areas, as shown in Figure 7–4. Calls that originate from one of their users could be completed by several means. If the call were directed to another of their customers, it could be routed through their backbone provider to their remote metro network, which would complete the call. If the called party is in a metro area they serve but is not one of their customers, it would be routed through the backbone provider to their metro network but then it would be handed off through a gateway to the incumbent LEC for call completion. In the event that the called party is not within any of their metro areas, it could be routed through a gateway to an IXC. In some cases, depending on rates negotiated with other carriers, any of these calls might be completed through an IXC network if it were cheaper to do so. These companies are being encouraged by regulators to compete with the LEC, especially those working through cable TV operators.

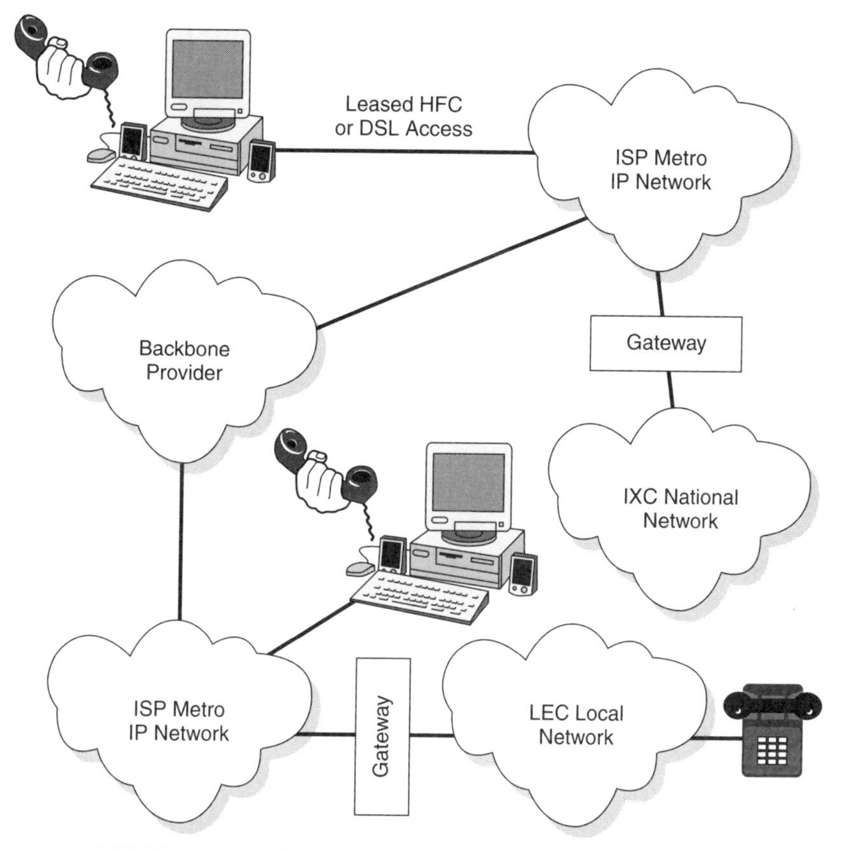

FIGURE 7–4 *Inside-out scenario.*

Some of the major players in this scenario are listed in Table 7–4.

TABLE 7-4 *Key Indicators for Some "Inside Out" Participants*

	AOL Time Warner	Earth Link	Comcast
Revenue	$ 7.8	$ 0.8	$ 8.2
Net Income	$ 1.2	$ (0.3)	$ 2.0
Network Operating Cost	$ 3.8	$ 0.9	$ 3.5
Network Assets	$ 1.0	$ 0.3	$ 6.8
Capital Investment	$ 0.5	N/A	$ 0.5
Customers	30,000,000	4,700,000	8,400,000
Broadband	1,700,000	406,000	400,000
Employees	56,500	N/A	N/A

These operators already have customer access points of presence in metro areas all across the United States. Most rely on other carriers for backbone capabilities. This arrangement gives them great flexibility. While all offer a dial-up arrangement, they are rapidly moving their customers to broadband access. The preferred broadband method for these companies is the cable modem. Deploying this broadband access is the primary issue facing these companies.

The cable industry passes 97.7 million households, of which 69.5 million are subscribers. Among the cable operators, the 10 largest in 2001 were AT&T Broadband, AOL Time Warner, Comcast Cable Communications, Charter Communications, Cox Communications, Adelphia Communications, Cablevision Systems Corporation, Insight Communications, Mediacom LLC, and CableOne. Of these, the first two claim a total of 27 million customers and the next three serve 26 million customers collectively. The remaining companies in the top 10 service about 12 million customers. At the end of 2001, AT&T announced the sale of its cable network to Comcast, which will make Comcast the largest U.S. cable operator.

These companies are all improving their cable network assets to provide digital television to their users simply to compete better with satellite television. As these upgrades are being deployed, they are also adding the necessary systems to enable cable modems for Internet service. Such upgrades are commonplace throughout the cable industry. In fact, the cable industry expended around $12.3 billion during 2000 on network upgrades to extend cable modem service to an estimated 81 million homes, of which approximately 6.4 million are subscribers. This allows these companies to provide an alternative access method for telephony.

Some of these companies do not have high financial strength, and many ISPs are small or medium sized businesses. During an economic downturn, this can result in failure. For example, Excite@Home, a leading ISP, announced the termination of its operation in December 2001. The modest size of most ISPs can limit the scope of their business plan. However, their size does give them excellent responsiveness and the ability to rapidly infuse new services. Since they do not have a large existing base of circuit-switched systems, these companies have no need to retire expensive systems and no "culture" attached to this method of operation. While they already operate IP networks, their operations systems will need improvement and expansion to handle telephony users. Their success will depend heavily on rates charged to them by the backbone provider and the leases, if required, for cable modem or DSL access.

Perfect Together

Partnerships between various companies such as Yahoo!, Microsoft, and Net2phone can also try to capture the telephony business using the approach shown in Figure 7–5. These companies rely on ISPs to reach customers and the PSTN to complete calls that terminate off their network. By providing software in the user's computer and interworking equipment that can bridge calls between the PSTN and the Internet, they are able to create a telephony service. In this scenario, companies such as Net2Phone provide the interworking function, while the other partners bring in the customers. The customer simply installs a small software module in his or her computer. This software will access systems through the Internet that cause the call to be routed to the interworking point nearest the call's destination, where it will be handed off to the PSTN. In this scenario, the network becomes a basic commodity, much as advocated by Isenberg.[4]

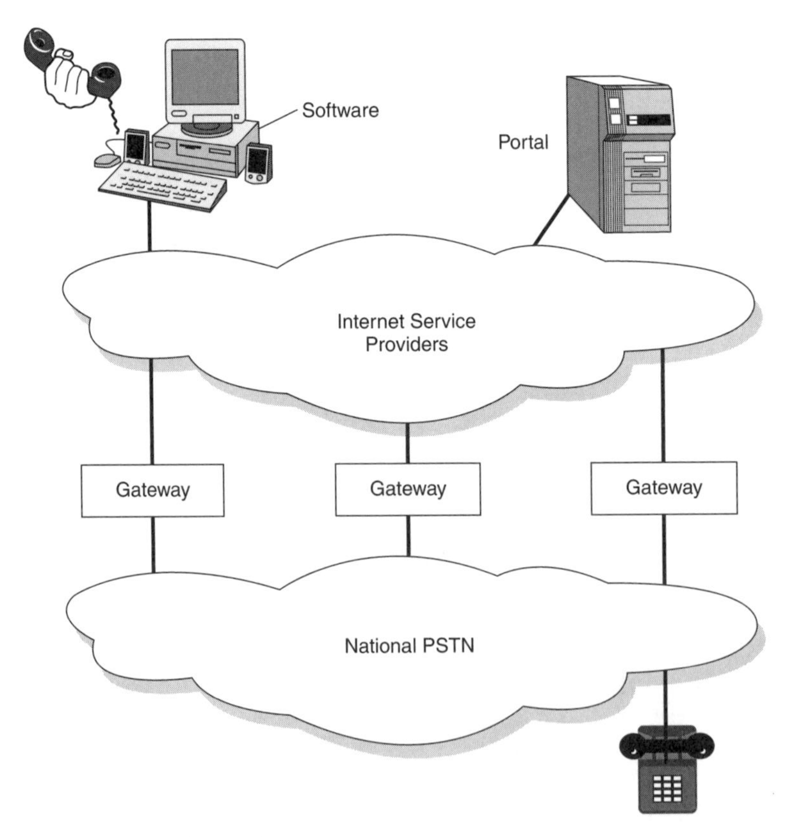

FIGURE 7–5 *Perfect Together scenario.*

4. See "The Dawn of the Stupid Network" in the references section.

TABLE 7-5 *Key Indicators for Some "Perfect Together" Participants*

	Microsoft	Yahoo!	Net2Phone
Revenue	$ 23.0	$ 1.1	$ 0.2
Net Income	$ 7.3	$ 0.071	$ (0.4)
Network Operating Cost	N/A	$ 0.2	$ 0.1
Network Assets	$ 2.3	N/A	$ 0.1
Capital Investment	$ 5.0	N/A	N/A
Customers	500,000,000	180,000,000	400,000
Broadband	N/A	N/A	N/A
Employees	50,000	3,259	400

Portal companies provide access for much of the content and information that users want. Some have network assets, but most prefer to lease capacity for both access and backbone transport, as shown in Table 7–5. This gives them a very controllable cost basis and the ability to select the lowest cost transport provider. In an environment with excess network capacity, such as now exists in the United States, this is a good scheme for operating at low cost. As they begin to acquire customers for telephony services, their networking demands will grow. By carefully managing contracts with carriers, they can capture customers with very low incremental cost. The portal could bill the customer for the software and its updates as well as minutes of use for the calls through a gateway. Possibly, traffic that stayed within the ISP's network would not have any additional charges.

The key roadblock for these companies is that telephony is not their core business, and most of these companies are focused on more critical aspects of providing content and other services over the Internet. Their key assets are their customer base and their flexibility. Many have strong financials and can weather economic downturns. For example, Yahoo! has $1.7 billion in cash and no debt. Microsoft operates a successful ISP network, MSN, with 7.7 million customers, second only to AOL Time Warner. Microsoft also has bundled a telephony application in its latest operating system release, XP, which allows the customer to select one of several interworking companies, including Net2Phone. It has been estimated that there were 6.2 billion minutes of VoIP in 2001 used internationally, and it is quite likely that as XP deploys, this will increase dramatically.

Dark Horses

Satellite television distribution companies and companies in the utility industry, mainly electric power companies, have assets that could be used in providing telephony services. Among utilities, these assets consist mostly of right-of-way corridors that reach end users and also run between major cities. Some of these companies are quite large and have an enormous base of customers who could be offered a telephony service. Figure 7–6 shows how these players might approach networking.

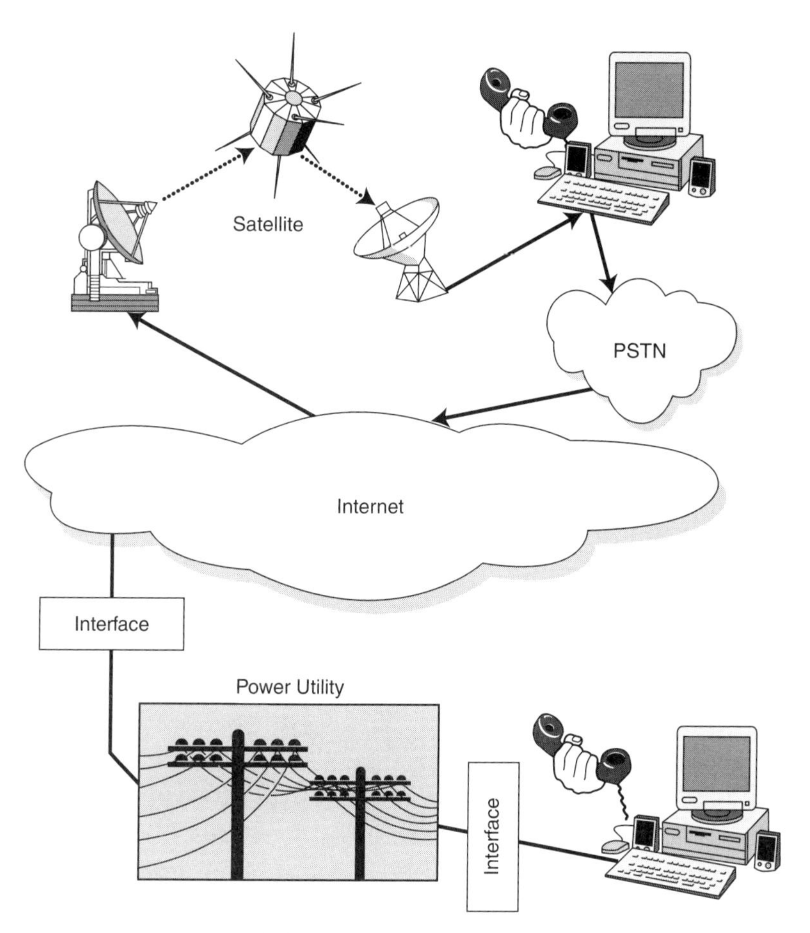

FIGURE 7–6 *Dark horses scenario.*

Unfortunately, to provide access, these assets need completely new unproven technology to enable telecommunications services that must operate in difficult environments. There have been various attempts to create such technologies, but none have been deployed. During 2001, Power Line Telecommunications Corporation introduced a system that obtains 18.8 Mbps over distances of 0.2 miles on overhead medium voltage power lines or 15 Mbps over distances of 1,000 feet on underground power lines. This system can serve 50 to 200 users. Indeed, if this system can be deployed and meets these specifications in field operation, it could become an alternate means for reaching the end user. Such a system could compete very well with DSL and cable modems but would have a very late start.

The power utilities may consider deploying such a system, but most are struggling today with the deregulation of their core business and the introduction of competition. So far, power utilities have not been a serious threat to the telephony industry, but this could change with time. Many utilities have looked closely at both telephony and Internet access businesses as a possible next step for their corporation. Some have deployed fiber optic in their right-of-way that can be used for backbone networking, and these facilities, once installed, have been leased to other operators. This could become a basis for entering the telecom market, especially for Internet backbone services.

Satellite television companies have deployed digital transmission, so there is a direct one-way digital link from the earth station through the satellite to the customer's set top. A set top could be provided to the customer that enables the reception of high-bandwidth Internet traffic. However, for upstream traffic from the customer to the network, some other media, such as a telephone line, must be used. Also, the downstream traffic to the customer must be shared among customers, so during peaks, performance can degrade, especially since so many users are sharing the channel. Unlike cable systems, which can be segmented to provide higher performance, the satellite operator has no easy means for doing this other than dedicating more channels to carry the traffic, an expensive proposition.

Summary

This chapter has provided an introduction to the issues of competition for the new telephony business. Among the key drivers for change are customers, economic climate, regulatory, finance, assets, liabilities, inertia, and responsiveness. The winds of time can affect these drivers and, through them, the outcome of the scenarios in which various companies are competing. The key issues that are faced include the economic outlook, gaining broadband access to the customer, retiring circuit-switching systems, adopting new operations support systems and processes, and changes in the regulatory environment.

There are six scenarios in which the new telephony may find itself. In the business-as-usual scenario, there is no change, so the PSTN and the Internet simply plod along. During 2001, this was the primary scenario and was driven by the economic climate. In the telco takeover scenario, LECs deploy IP networks for long-distance and data services that expand and become large segments of the Internet over which their customers get telephone service. In top down, IXCs succeed in capturing local services by getting customer access through DSL or cable TV networks. In some cases, these carriers may partner with a cable operator. Yet another scenario, inside out, has ISPs selling telephony as part of their service portfolio, using cable modem or DSL access. In perfect together, portal and content providers establish telephony services through partnerships with others and use interworking between the Internet and the PSTN. Lastly, the dark horses of the satellite and power utility industry might find ways to introduce telephony service using their assets.

For each scenario and its players, the various impacts of the driving forces can have profound effects on the final result. It will be interesting indeed to see what happens when the United States experiences an economic recovery and business as usual melts away to be replaced by a more dynamic scenario.

Which one will it be?

References

Anderson, K., et al. "Convergence 101: A Primer on Tomorrow's Telephone Network," J. P. Morgan Securities, Inc., Jan. 2001.

AOL Time Warner Annual Report(s) for 2000.

At Home Annual Report for 2000.

AT&T Annual Report for 2000.

BellSouth Annual Report for 2000.

Comcast Annual Report for 2000.

Earth Link Annual Report for 2000.

Federal Communications Commission, "Trends in Telephone Service," Aug. 2001.

Genuity Annual Report for 2000.

Isenberg, D. "The Dawn of the Stupid Network," *ACM Networker Magazine,* Feb./Mar. 1998.

Khosla, V. "The Terabit Tsunami," Kleiner Perkins Cufield & Byers, May 2000.

MCI Annual Report for 2000.

Microsoft Annual Report for 2000

Mohney, D. "Data Over Power Lines—A Step Closer," *ISPworld,* Aug. 2001.

Moore, G. A., *Crossing the Chasm: Marketing and Selling High-Tech Products to Mainstream Customers*, Rev. ed. Harper Information, Aug. 1999.

Moore, G. A., *Inside the Tornado: Marketing Strategies from Silicon Valley's Cutting Edge,* Harper Information, June 1999.

National Cable & Telecommunications Association (NCTA). "Cable Telephony: Offering Consumers Competitive Choice," July 2001.

Net2Phone Annual Report for 2000.

Qwest Annual Report for 2000.

SBC Annual Report for 2000.

Sprint Annual Report for 2000.

T. M. Denton Consultants, "Netheads versus Bellheads," Report U4525-9-0038 to the Federal Department of Industry of Canada, Mar. 1999.

Verizon Annual Report for 2000.

Yahoo! Annual Report for 2000.

The Future

One of my hobbies is astrophotography, a difficult and complex undertaking. In order to take photographs of the night sky, I must travel to remote locations and stay for several days during the new moon each month. My favorite dark sky site is an empty field in north central Pennsylvania. It is a very peaceful place with no connection to the outside world. No cell phones, no pagers, no newspapers, no TV, no cable modems, no DSL connections. This place has mostly trees, grass, deer, the occasional skunk, and a pack of coyotes that howl for me to leave. And a dark night sky. It's easy to concentrate here. At night, I am busy operating my equipment, taking hour-long photographs of deep sky objects, and enjoying the beauty of the night sky. But during the day, I can reflect on the events that occurred during my year of writing as well as on other matters and consider what these bode for the future. So, from a tent in the midst of an empty field, I formulated this closing chapter.

From my musings, four subjects emerged that are shaping the future and seem worthy of discussion. These are the events of September 11, the economy, the S-shaped curve, and new technologies.

September 11

The terrorist attacks of Tuesday, September 11, 2001, at the World Trade Center in New York City and at the Pentagon in Washington D.C. had a profound effect on the United States and the world. The human loss and suffering of that day are impossible to comprehend. All Americans were stunned by this horrific event. The subsequent anthrax attacks through the U.S. Postal System and some frightening but unsuccessful terrorist attacks further strengthened the resolve of Americans to defend the United States. In response, the United States began a campaign around the world against terrorists and the governments that support and harbor them. It is important to consider the effect these events had on the new telephony.

Immediately following the attack, telecommunications in lower New York City became inoperable. Not only were wire-line networks shut down, wireless services were also disrupted due to the loss of transmitters, receivers, antennas, and terrestrial links that connected them to the PSTN. That which was not destroyed was overloaded with service demand. One effect of this loss of telecommunications was that Wall Street, which was not directly impacted by the attack, could not operate for the remainder of the week. Work to restore telecommunications to the New York Stock Exchange went on around the clock for five days in order for the market to reopen. Considering the magnitude of the facilities destroyed, it was only through superhuman efforts that telecommunications were restored in only five days.

This attack will affect the business of telecommunications and the new telephony in many different ways for years to come. While many of the effects will not be known for some time, two seem evident at the time of this writing.

First, the attention of everyone immediately focused on security issues. Vast sums of money will be spent on airport security, postal safety, and other defensive measures at home. The cost of conducting the war against terror in Afghanistan and elsewhere will be high. Security became the U.S. national priority. The terrorists who attacked on September 11 may not have fully realized the disruption their cowardly act would have. The impact of their attack on telecommunications in New York and Washington was probably incidental from their perspective. But in the future, other more deliberate attacks may occur, and these could have far greater impact. This possibility has caused increased concern about electronic warfare. The telecom network is being subjected to considerable scrutiny, and operators are looking at ways to make their networks less vulnerable to terrorist attacks and more survivable should an attack occur. For the most part, this will result in spending to harden the existing PSTN and Internet facilities, but there may be some acceleration in deploying networks that are more data-capable. This will probably slow the pace at which carriers might move forward in the scenarios of the previous chapter. Introduction of a new telephony is not a high priority when human safety is threatened.

Second, consumers and businesses will become even more reliant on electronic media for commerce, entertainment, and communications. News during the months following the attacks bears this out. Americans significantly reduced their travel, as witnessed by the vast losses in the travel industry following the attacks. People stopped flying altogether or curtailed trips to locations they considered possible targets of terrorism, such as large amusement parks. Instead, they used telecommunications, including audio/video conferencing. During November 2001, sales of DVD players and discs rose by 25 percent. Just after the anthrax mailings, some newscasters suggested that the public should use electronic mail instead of traditional greeting cards during the 2001/2002 holiday season. Of course, these short-term trends do not necessarily indicate a long-term change in American culture. But if terrorism does not end quickly, as predicted by most, American dependence on electronic commerce and telecommunica-

tions may very well increase significantly. If this occurs, revenues for carriers will increase as users begin to make greater use of networking in their daily lives. This will reinforce the demand for introducing a secure and survivable new telephony network with fully integrated services for telecommunications of all types that would benefit businesses and consumers.

The Economy

The economic woes that began in mid-year 2000 took a significant toll on productivity and well being in the United States. Unemployment became very high. Corporations failed. Investors lost money. On a daily basis, corporate executives reported lower than expected earnings, causing further deterioration of the market and the economy. The events of September 11, 2001, had a clear impact on economic conditions, as witnessed by large drops in the stock market. However, by November 2001, those losses were recouped and the market had stabilized with a slight trend towards improvement. Most forecasts pointed to a recovery during 2002, possibly late in the year.

The business of telecommunications was affected dramatically by this economic downturn. Commercial businesses that were in trouble reduced their spending on telecommunications, and individuals who became unemployed reduced their services as well. Due to this, all carriers saw loss of revenues in both their business and residential markets. In response, they reduced their own staff and slashed spending in every way possible.

Competition was also affected. Many startup companies that were providing new services or manufacturing new equipment were forced to close their doors when investment capital became unavailable. The upshot of this was a reduction in competitive pressure on large companies. This was tragic in many ways, not the least of which was the loss of these entrepreneurs and their forward-thinking ideas for telecommunications.

No one can be certain when the market will improve. Consumer confidence is low, but Congress is working to create economic reform legislation. There is no doubt that a recovery will take place eventually, but it is not at all certain when it will occur or how the turnaround will be stimulated. Also in question is what business sector will lead the recovery. Until a recovery begins, "business as usual" will be the most likely scenario for the new telephony.

But when a recovery starts, telecommunications companies will share in the economic expansion. Customers in business and residential markets will begin to spend. Entrepreneurs will start up again, and competition will increase. Large companies will begin to spend more on capital programs, and one or more of the new telephony scenarios will come to the fore.

The S-Shaped Curve

Consider the famous S-shaped curve, shown in Figure 8–1. Conventional wisdom states that every new product begins at the bottom of this curve and moves up it, reaching full maturity at the top. Anyone launching a new product always places it at the initial starting point on the curve, and then, by observing current adoption rates and by estimating the total market for the product, predicts that it will reach various points on the curve in a certain number of months or years. This always seems to be impeccable logic when hearing from a party who truly believes in the new product. Figure 8–1 depicts this in its first curve, labeled Theory. The futurist always believes that the new product or concept will start up the curve very soon and that success is just around the corner.

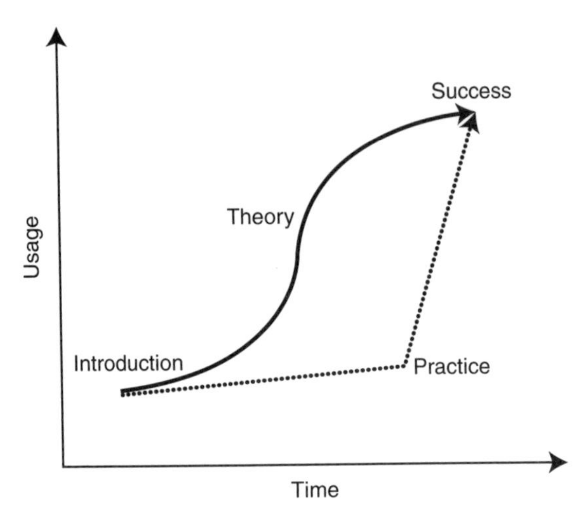

FIGURE 8–1 *The S-shaped curve.*

Rarely does one hear much about this curve when products are at a mid-level of maturity. There are a few reasons for this. For one, the product may not have been successful after all, and it has languished and died on the lower hinterlands of the curve. No one wants to point this out to an audience. Besides, the original presenter is now on her new job, promoting a new product! Our failures just seem to wither away. Furthermore, it always seems that products, even the successful ones, never move up the curve as soon as anyone predicts.

But once a product really does start up this curve, many of them move to the top at lightning speed. Examples of this include mobile phones and the compact disk. In just a few short years, these products sprang from the laboratory to the consumer in massive numbers, as depicted in the second curve of Figure 8–1, labeled Practice. No one was able to predict the speed with which these products penetrated the marketplace. Consider as well the rapid adoption of Internet Web browsers that mushroomed into overnight popularity.

As a consequence, little confidence can be placed in the S-shaped curve. Although there are plenty of exceptions,

the most interesting products seem to be adopted later than expected but at a faster rate. Our ability to predict whether or not this will happen is uncertain at best.

With regards to the new telephony, the adoption of VoIP is in a similar situation. There are those who measure minutes of use and forecast that we are on the initial slopes of the S-shaped curve. From this, they deduce that in just a few short years, VoIP will dominate telecommunications. But it will probably take much longer than a few years, although when adoption occurs, it may occur far faster than most would believe. Part of the rationale for this logic is that adoption of VoIP will be similar to the growth of browsers for the Internet. Until there was a critical mass of Web sites to browse, nobody needed a browser. But once that was achieved, everybody wanted one. So it will be with telephony. Until sufficient connectivity is obtained, adequate quality provided, and some advantage demonstrated, not many users will demand the new telephony. But once these obstacles are surmounted, the adoption will be very rapid.

New Technologies

This is perhaps the most unpredictable domain of all, because it depends on the innovation of the human mind. On this issue, about all that can be done is to look all across the spectrum of research in telecommunications in order to detect something new. And there is always something new. Perhaps a breakthrough in high-speed electronics might create a new direction for switching and routing. Or maybe a new concept in network architecture will make an existing optical networking technology more attractive. Possibly, a new approach to optical storage and retrieval will usher in the all-optical packet switch. When it comes to predicting what the human mind will conceive, our crystal balls are very opaque.

Today, the emphasis in telecommunications research is on optical networking. Because of the many perceived

advantages of optical processing, surely the all-optical network will continue to be the target of researchers everywhere, and in the long-term, this will be achieved. The most probable outcome in the near term is that research in IP routing over optical switching will produce deployable products that combine MPLS and DiffServ (or some variant) in an optical transport that operates beneath a fast, electronic, software-controlled IP routing processor. Such systems will provide very high capacity having controlled quality of service for packet switching with a high degree of flexibility and adaptability. This is exactly what is needed to advance the new telephony, and a tremendous effort is being made by manufacturers around the world to achieve just such a capability. At the end of 2001, there were prototypes and proof-of-concept demonstrations. Deployable products could not be far away.

Following this success, new operations systems and operations processes are needed to integrate this apparatus into a commercial network that can support new business models. The systems themselves will need to be thoroughly field tested, and the usual corrections made that accompany the introduction of any new technology. Lastly, innovation in business models, a subject that will not likely garner many headlines, may have the greatest effect of all.

Conclusions

So, what is the future of the new telephony? The economic downturn of 2000 and the events of September 11, 2001, caused a major disruption in what many would have considered a certain path forward only a year earlier. Certainly, when this book was begun, no one foresaw these events or their dire effect on the world and on telecommunications. But it is certain that the U.S. economy will rebound. As this occurs, the new telephony will begin to move forward

The Internet will surely absorb the services of the telephone network. It is inevitable. The only questions are,

how long it will take, and who will be the winners when it happens? The race depicted in Figure 8–2 has begun. Victory will belong to the swift, the innovative, and the powerful. The times definitely are a-changin'.

FIGURE 8–2 *The race is on for the new telephony. ("The Race" by Miko Walters. Used with permission.)*

It is my hope that this book has given its readers enough technical knowledge and business insight to watch what happens in the world of telecommunications and to interpret for themselves the actions of major competitors with better clarity. For those readers who are in a position to influence the direction these events are to take, I hope this book will serve as a milepost and that it places their efforts in a balanced, overall perspective.

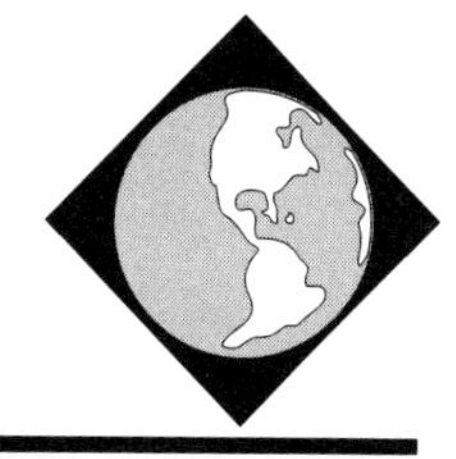

ACRONYMS

AAL	ATM adaptation layer
ACK	Acknowledgment
ADSL	Asymmetric digital subscriber loop
AF	Assured forwarding
A-law	A European standard for representing speech samples
ANSI	American National Standards Institute
AOL	America On Line (now AOL Time Warner)
ARP	Address resolution protocol
ARPA	Advanced Research Project Agency
ARPANet	A network project funded by ARPA
AS	Autonomous system
ASN	Abstract syntax notation

ATM	Asynchronous transfer mode
BGP	Border gateway protocol
BML	Business management layer
BP	Backbone provider
BS	Base station
BSC	Base station controller
CATV	Cable television
CCS	Common channel signaling
CDMA	Code division multiple access
CEO	Chief executive officer
CIDR	Classless interdomain routing
CLEC	Competitive local exchange carrier
CLP	Cell loss priority
CMTS	Cable modem termination system
CODEC	Coder decoder
COMET	Condition met
CPCS	Common part convergence sublayer
CPI	Common part identifier
CRC	Cyclic redundancy check
CSRC	Contributing source
DARPA	Defense Advanced Research Project Agency
DARPANet	The renamed ARPANet
DC	Direct current

DiffServ	Differentiated services
DLC	Digital loop carrier
DNHR	Dynamic non-hierarchical routing
DNS	Domain name service
DOCSIS	Data over cable service interface specification
DOS	Disk operating system
DSL	Digital subscriber loop
DSLAM	Digital subscriber loop access module
DTMF	Dual-tone multifrequency
DWDM	Dense wave division multiplexing
EC	Echo cancellation
EF	Expedited forwarding
email	Electronic mail
EML	Element management layer
ENUM	Telephone number mapping
Ethernet	A local area network standard
FCAPS	Fault, configuration, accounting, performance and security
FDM	Frequency division multiplexing
FDMA	Frequency division multiple access
FITL	Fiber-in-the-Loop
FTP	File transfer protocol
FTTC	Fiber-to-the-curb

FTTH	Fiber-to-the-home
G.711	An ITU standard for speech
G.723.1	An ITU standard for compressed speech
G.726	An ITU standard for compressed speech
G.729	An ITU standard for compressed speech
GFC	Generic flow control
GMPLS	Generalized multiprotocol label switching
H.248	An ITU specification of MEGACO
H.323	An ITU specification for call control of multimedia sessions
HEC	Header error check
HLR	Home location register
HTML	Hypertext markup language
HTTP	Hypertext transfer protocol
ICMP	Internet control message protocol
IDRP	Interdomain routing protocol
IETFI	Internet engineering task force
IP	Internet protocol
IPv4	Internet protocol version 4
IPv6	Internet protocol version 6
ISDN	Integrated services digital network
ISP	Internet service provider
ITU	International Telecommunications Union

IXC	Interexchange carrier
JPEG	Joint photographic experts group
LATA	Local access and transport area
LDP	Label distribution protocol
LEC	Local exchange carrier
LTM	Line termination module
LTU	Line termination unit
MAE	Metropolitan area exchange points
MCU	Multipoint control unit
MEGACO	Media gateway control protocol
MOS	Mean opinion score
MPLS	Multiprotocol label switching
MPλS	Multiprotocol lambda switching
MS	Mobile station
MSC	Mobile switching system
MSO	Master system operator
MTP	Message transfer part
NAP	Network access point
NCP	Network control protocol
NE	Network element
NML	Network management layer
NPA	Numbering plan area
NSF	National Science Foundation

NSF Net	A network project funded by the NSF
NTP	Network time protocol
NTU	Network termination unit
OAM	Operations, administration and management
OSPF	Open shortest path first
PIM	Personal information module
POP	Point of presence
POTS	Plain old telephone service
PPP	Point-to-point protocol
PSTN	Public switched telephone network
PTI	Payload type identifier
Q.931	An ITU signaling recommendation for ISDN call control
QoS	Quality of service
RF	Radio frequency
RFC	Request for comments
RIP	Routing information protocol
RMS	Root mean square
RR	Receiver report
RSVP	Resource reservation protocol
RTCP	Real-time transfer control protocol
RTP	Real-time transfer protocol
SDES	Source description

SDH	Synchronous digital hierarchy
SIP	Session initiation protocol
SLA	Service level agreement
SML	Service management layer
SMS	Signaling management system
SMS	Short message service
SMTP	Simple mail transfer protocol
SNMP	Simple network management protocol
SONET	Synchronous optical network
SR	Sender report
SS7	Signaling system #7
SSP	Switched service Point
STP	Signal transfer point
STS	Synchronous transfer signal
T-1	A physical layer transmission standard
TCP	Transmission control protocol
TDM	Time division multiplexing
TDMA	Time division multiple access
TTL	Time to live
TTU	Trunk termination unit
UDP	User datagram protocol
μ-law	A U.S. standard for representing speech samples
URI	Uniform resource identifier

URL	Uniform resource locator
URN	Uniform resource name
U.S.	United States
VCI	Virtual circuit identifier
VLR	Visited location register
VoIP	Voice over internet protocol
VPI	Virtual path identifier
WAP	Wireless application protocol
WDM	Wave division multiplexing
WDP	Wireless datagram protocol
WSP	Wireless session protocol
WWW	World wide web

INDEX

Symbols

Numerics

A

D

E

F

N

O

P

S

W

Y

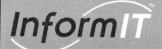

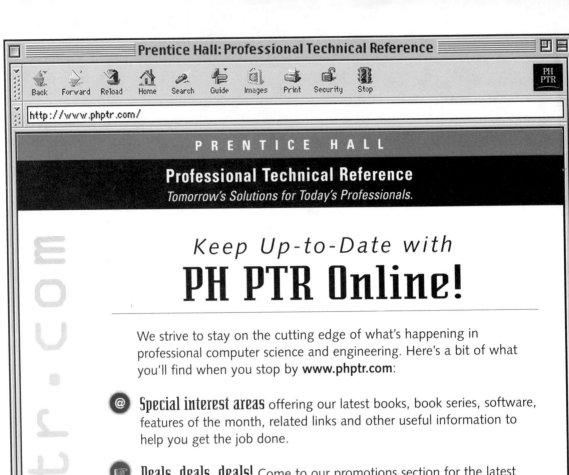